Teaching
Academic Subjects
To
Diverse Learners

Teaching
Academic Subjects
To
Diverse Learners

Edited by
Mary M. Kennedy

Teachers College, Columbia University
New York and London

Published by Teachers College Press, 1234 Amsterdam Avenue, New York, NY 10027

Library of Congress Cataloging-in-Publication Data

Teaching academic subjects to diverse learners / edited by Mary M. Kennedy.
     p.   cm.
   Includes bibliographical references and index.
   ISBN 0-8077-3089-0 (alk. paper)
   1. Teaching. 2. Cognition in children. 3. Intercultural education.   I. Kennedy, Mary M.
LB1025.3.T43   1991
371.1'02—dc20   91-3814

ISBN 0-8077-3089-0

Printed on acid-free paper.

Manufactured in the United States of America

98 97 96 95 94 93 92 91   8 7 6 5 4 3 2 1

Contents

Preface

The history of teaching is replete with complaints about teachers' lack of knowledge—either their lack of understanding of children or their lack of understanding of their subjects—and with easy prescriptions of what teachers should know. It used to be assumed that a baccalaureate degree would ensure sufficient subject matter knowledge, for instance. Now, virtually all teachers have a baccalaureate degree, and we are still not satisfied with their understanding of subject matter.

When the credential itself is under attack, we can no longer assume that it will serve as a proxy for the knowledge we care about, and teachers' credentials are clearly under attack today. But we will not go far toward improving the credibility of a teaching credential until we define the nature of knowledge that teachers should have. Anyone who wants to improve the curriculum of teacher education must first define what teachers need to know. Anyone who wants to assess teachers prior to giving credentials or master teacher status must first define what novice or master teachers need to know.

This is not to say that we lack proposals for answering this question. There are many. Blue ribbon commissions have taken positions on the issue, politicians have taken stands on it, and professional associations have made statements on it. But these official proclamations are often unsatisfying, for two reasons. First, many prescriptions are offered at a relatively high level of abstraction. It is easy to say, for instance, that teachers should know their subject matter but much harder to say what subject matter knowledge consists of. It is easy to say that teachers should know something about how students learn, or about culturally different kinds of students; it is much harder to say what exactly they need to know about these students.

The second reason these prescriptions are unsatisfying is that many participants perceive the discussion as a debate between two opposing views—knowledge of subject matter *versus* knowledge of students. This is not productive, for teaching entails teaching *something* to *someone*. In United States public schools in particular, it entails teaching academic subjects to diverse learners. To teach subject matter to diverse learners, teachers must necessarily know both the subject and the audience. Rather than debating which knowledge is more important, then, it would be more productive to debate what is most important to know about each domain. What aspects of the subject are most pertinent to teaching, for instance, and what aspects of students are most important to understand for the purpose of teaching?

This book is intended to address these difficult issues. It was originated with the premise that teachers must understand both subject matter and students, that teaching is necessarily an act that requires serious attention to both. But it began, too, with the assumption that defining the knowledge that is really needed *for teaching* is no simple task. What one needs to know about subjects in order to teach them may be quite different from what one needs to know to use these subjects in other walks of life, for instance. Similarly, what one needs to know about children in order to teach them may be quite different from what one needs to know to interact with them in other ways. This difficulty is further compounded in disciplines where, when asked, members of the same discipline define their subject differently.

My goal is to further conversations about the special character of teachers' knowledge by explicating areas of agreement and disagreement—not with respect to the relative importance of subject matter or students in the teaching trans- action, but instead with respect to what is most important *within* each of these domains. The arguments presented here do not define an ideal teacher education curriculum, an ideal assessment instrument, or an ideal policy for certifying teachers. Instead, they raise questions about the important assumptions that underlie all decisions about curricula, assessments, and policies: What is the knowledge that matters most in teaching? What knowledge should the curriculum impart; what knowledge should the assessment measure; what knowledge should our policies reward and encourage?

To this end, I tried to identify major differences in views within each field and invited people who best represent those views to prepare chapters for this book. The topics I asked people to address include four school sub- jects—mathematics, science, history, and writing—and two kinds of student characteristics—on the one hand, what they know and how they learn, and on the other, their cultural backgrounds and how those affect learning.

Acknowledgments

Since I am not expert in any of the areas under investigation in this book, I have relied heavily on the advice and consultation of others in defining the issues and the points of view expressed in this volume. I would like at this time to thank each of these people. They are Charles Anderson (science), Deborah Ball (mathematics), Mary Gomez (writing), Suzanne Wilson (history), Robert Floden (student knowledge and learning), and G. Williamson McDiarmid (student cultural backgrounds).

I also owe a special gratitude to Anna Edridge, whose unusual knowledge of word processing and desk-top publishing enabled us to print the manuscript for this book in several different formats and, eventually, to produce the camera-ready copy needed for publication.

In addition to my own acknowledgments, several authors wish to acknowledge those who offered them assistance.

Suzanne Wilson wishes to acknowledge an earlier collaboration with Gary Sykes. The ideas, and many of the words, in her conclusion are borrowed from work she has done with Gary Sykes on the certification of history teachers.

James Banks wishes to thank Cherry A. McGee Banks and Walter C. Parker for helpful comments on an earlier draft of this paper.

Preparation of George Hillocks' chapter was supported by funds from the Benton Center for Curriculum and Instruction at The University of Chicago.

Parts of John Gage's chapter will appear in a larger, more formal work entitled "A General Theory of the Enthymeme for Advanced Composition" to be published in *On Teaching Advanced Composition* (Boynton/Cook), edited by Katherine M. Adams.

Preparation of Carl Grant's chapter was supported by the Wisconsin Center for Educational Research, School of Education, University of Wisconsin-Madison.

G. Williamson McDiarmid gratefully acknowledges the comments and suggestions of David K. Cohen, Mary Kennedy, Robert Floden, and Suzanne Wilson.

Teaching
Academic Subjects
To
Diverse Learners

Part I

TEACHING ACADEMIC SUBJECTS. . .

Teaching Science

When policy makers think about science education, they often think about the number of science courses they should require of high school students. Yet there is ample evidence that students are not learning much even when they take science courses. American high school students, even those who are college-bound, perform worse on science tasks than comparable students in numerous other countries.

So discussions about what teachers need to know to teach science necessarily center on what is wrong with current science teaching, and how science teaching can or should be changed. Our two authors in this area, Charles Anderson and Anton Lawson, agree that science consists of a lot more than memorizing facts, and that too much science education is limited to this kind of learning. And both agree that at least a part of learning science entails altering one's own a priori misconceptions about physical and biological phenomena. To understand the solar system, for instance, one must be persuaded to put aside the intuitively appealing idea that the sun revolves around the earth. Both authors are interested in the psychological processes involved in what they call *conceptual change*. The idea that learning requires conceptual change reinforces our theme of *teaching something to someone*, for teaching science means knowing both the scientific idea to be taught and knowing the faulty way(s) in which this idea might be misconstrued, or may already have been misconstrued, by learners.

But although our two authors share similar goals for science teaching, they offer different methods for teaching science. For Anderson, the central task of the science teacher is to give students a deep understanding of concepts developed by scientists and to help students adopt, as a social norm, the kind of reasoning and argumentation that contribute to learning about natural phenomena. For Lawson, on the other hand, the central task of science education is to acquaint students with the particular methods and reasoning patterns used by scientists, so that students learn to reason and evaluate evidence as scientists do. Anderson's ideal teacher tries to alter social norms; Lawson's tries to promote students' ability to apply the scientific method.

3

1

Policy Implications of Research on Science Teaching and Teachers' Knowledge

CHARLES W. ANDERSON

The central fact with which any discussion of science teachers' knowledge must contend is the failure of our present system of science education. This failure is not of recent origin, nor is it absolute, but recent evidence from a variety of sources has documented the nature and extent of our failure more thoroughly than ever before. For example, when Yager and Yager (1985) tested students' ability to select correct definitions for terms from the biological and physical sciences, they found evidence that seventh graders did better than third graders, but there was no improvement at all between seventh and eleventh grades, despite the fact that most students take several science courses in between. In the most recent studies of science achievement by the International Association for the Evaluation of Educational Achievement (1988), American high school seniors were dead last among 13 ranked countries in their assessed biological knowledge; they ranked eleventh in chemistry, ninth in physics. Jon Miller (1988) found that only 48% of American adults knew both (a) that the earth revolves around the sun, rather than the other way around, and (b) that it takes a year to do so, rather than a month or a day.

This pattern of failure is not a surprise to anyone who has spent much time observing science classrooms. A lot of science teaching is dull and meaningless stuff—an amalgam of boring lectures, cookbook "experiments," and worksheets or written work. Textbooks are for the most part poorly written and overloaded with technical vocabulary. Even what we normally call "good" science teaching generally fails to engage students deeply enough to help them achieve a meaningful understanding of science (see Anderson & Smith, 1987). These observations lead to an obvious question: Why do teachers keep teaching this way? Don't they *know* any better?

THE KNOWLEDGE NEEDED TO TEACH SCIENCE WELL

Although the pattern of failure described above is widespread, it is not universal. Some teachers are successful in engaging their students in meaningful science learning. Let us consider a brief episode from the teaching of one such teacher. This teacher, whom I will call Ms. Copeland, taught a seventh-grade ecology class in a suburban school district that served mostly working- and middle-class families (see Hollon & Anderson, 1987). The vignette below comes from a unit on photosynthesis. The main point of the unit can be simply stated: Plants use light to make their own food through a process known as photosynthesis. However easy this may seem, many middle school students (and adults) find this idea and its implications difficult and confusing (see Anderson & Roth, 1989).

MS. COPELAND'S TEACHING

The first day of Ms. Copeland's unit focused not on food for plants, but on a topic more familiar to the students: food for people. The students discussed whether each of a variety of substances could be considered a kind of food. Most substances they agreed about easily. For example, they had no trouble agreeing that meat and potatoes were food. They also agreed that even though babies sometimes eat dirt, dirt was not food for people. Water, though, was a problem. The students knew that they needed water to survive, yet they would starve to death if they only drank water. Was water a food or wasn't it? Initially, the students were unable to reach consensus about this question.

Ms. Copeland suggested a resolution to the problem based on the scientific definition of food offered in the textbook.

> FOOD refers only to materials that *contain energy* for living things. All living things must use food to grow and keep all their parts working properly. (Roth & Anderson, 1987, p. 16)

Given this definition of food, most students agreed that water was not food. Staci, however, continued to argue vehemently that water *was* a kind of food. The issue had not been fully resolved when the first lesson of the unit ended.

Ms. Copeland began the second lesson of the photosynthesis unit with a short review of the previous day's lesson concerning the nature of food for plants and the definition of food as energy-containing matter. Staci, who had argued the day before that water was food, commented,

Now I'm convinced. The people I polled say you need food and water to survive. . . . I asked my dad and he said food has to have calories so I believe that.

After discussing the role of water, Ms. Copeland posed several questions about how plants obtain food. By now, most of the students had become silent and appeared puzzled by the questions. Ms. Copeland explained that items "like plant food and food sticks make it *sound* like a plant reaches out and munches food."

At this point, Ms. Copeland told the students to write down their thoughts about how plants get food and how food moves in a plant. She then asked the students to talk about how food moves around inside plants. Several students described food entering through the roots of the plant, from carbon dioxide in the air and from water in the soil. On the blackboard she wrote, "How Plants Get Food," and listed students' responses. The list included "water from the soil," "carbon dioxide from the air," "soil," "sunlight," "rain," "other plants," "roots and leaves," and "themselves."

It is notable that the list contains several substances, including water, that the class had just decided were not food. To many students, though, this still did not seem unreasonable. The previous day's discussion had been about food for *people*; this was food for *plants*. Ms. Copeland, however, did not let them off the hook so easily. As they discussed items on the list, she continued to bring up the scientific definition of food from the day before.

> TEACHER: Look at the list up there. If they get it from the soil, is it like there's little "Big Macs" in there?
> STUDENT 1: It's minerals and nutrients . . .
> TEACHER: Do minerals supply energy?
> STUDENT 2: Yeah . . . things like potato peels in the soil give it minerals.
> TEACHER: Do plants *make* the food or are minerals the food? Do minerals supply energy?
> STUDENT 3: Sometimes . . .
> TEACHER: Does that mean "just on some days"? Anybody think more on that one?
> STUDENT 4: If they supply energy, they'd be food, right? But wouldn't that be the same as saying water is food?
> TEACHER: How many calories in minerals? Is food for plants the same as food for people? If that were true, all you'd have to do is give them minerals . . .

After discussing each item on the list, Ms. Copeland asked if any of the items were really food for plants. A few individuals insisted that some items were food, while others made comments like, "I'm confused . . . where are we?" One student volunteered, "All that stuff just *helps* the plant make its food." Ms. Copeland repeated the statement, emphasizing the words "help" and "make," then repeated the original question about the plants:

> TEACHER: Where do they get their food?
> STUDENT: (*several call out*) They make it!

At this point most of Ms. Copeland's students were on their way to developing a basic minimal understanding of what it means to say that plants make their own food. The unit, however, continued for another week as the students considered an array of related questions: *How* did the plants make their own food? If all those other substances listed on the board were not food for plants, then what *were* they? How did plants use them? Why did plants die in the dark? How was it possible for seeds to sprout and start growing underground, where there was no light? How do humans and other animals depend on photosynthesis?

Ms. Copeland's students figured out the answers to some of the above questions themselves; others were answered initially by Ms. Copeland or by the text. Several questions provoked lively discussions as students worked out for themselves whether the answers made sense and how they were connected with the answers to other, related questions. The students wrote about their ideas and participated in laboratory activities as well as talking and reading. In one activity, for example, the students used iodine to test for the presence of starch in various parts of plants, including seeds (such as beans), stems, leaves, and roots (such as potatoes). They then wrote explanations of how the plants had made, transported, and stored the food that they had detected. Although Ms. Copeland treated student ideas with respect, she expected her students, in the end, to produce answers that reflected canonical scientific understanding.

EASY ANSWERS TO HARD QUESTIONS

What is there to see in the vignette above? What does it tell us about Ms. Copeland and her knowledge of teaching? I believe that most education professionals—teachers, professors, or administrators—would find aspects of Ms. Copeland's performance that they considered praiseworthy, at least in comparison with the text-dominated teaching that prevails in most science classrooms. Explanations of what is good about her teaching, however, would be many and varied.

Many of those explanations are associated with "catch phrases" that purport to capture the essence of what Ms. Copeland knew or what she was doing. She was engaged in "student-centered" teaching or "inquiry" teaching, she was "teaching process as well as content," she was "using wait time," and so on. The problem with these analyses is not that they are wrong; in fact, they often capture something important about the nature of good teaching. At the same time, however, these catch phrases and instant analyses all tend to encourage the belief that there is some relatively straightforward "key idea" that explains Ms. Copeland's teaching—some small set of prescriptions that would enable other teachers to teach like Ms. Copeland if they would only follow the prescriptions. In spite of the differences between them, these analyses all ultimately convey the impression that good teaching is like, say, safe driving: A relatively simple pattern of behavior based on skills and attitudes that teachers could master if they were willing to do so.

Simple characterizations of good teaching may sometimes be useful, but they become troublesome when they are used as a basis for policy. Administrators see little reason why teachers should continue teaching in dull and ineffective ways when more interesting and effective methods are available, so they search for sanctions or incentives that will convince teachers to abandon their hidebound ways, or they try to develop workshops that will train teachers in the skills that are lacking. Teachers, in contrast, tend to attribute their failure to teach like Ms. Copeland to factors beyond their control. They must cover so much content that they don't have time for discussions of the students' ideas, for instance, or Ms. Copeland's style of teaching is really more appropriate for students who are older, or younger, or richer, or poorer, than the ones that they are teaching.

The flaw in the reasoning on both sides of these debates lies in the implicit assumption that Ms. Copeland simply "decided" to engage her students in the discussion quoted above, or that she was exercising some generalizable and easily mastered "teaching skills." In fact, what she was doing was more complicated than that. Neither is it true that Ms. Copeland simply possessed some inexplicable talent or personality trait that enabled her to do things that other teachers could not. In fact, Ms. Copeland's "talent" consisted primarily (though not exclusively) of skill and knowledge that she had developed through years of hard work. Ms. Copeland's achievement was more like building a well-designed house than like learning to drive safely. It was a complex, multifaceted endeavor that relied on an extensive and well-organized body of knowledge.

The complexity of teachers' work and knowledge often goes unrecognized because, unlike houses, the "structures" that teachers build are largely invisible. Nevertheless, they are real and important. The above episode, for example, could not just happen spontaneously. To understand how and why it happened in Ms. Copeland's classroom, we must see that Ms. Copeland and her students acted as they did because they understood this particular discussion to be part of a much larger *pattern of practice* that extended across the school year. Ms. Copeland's pattern of practice included the social norms and expectations that prevailed in her classroom, the kinds of work that her students did and her ways of evaluating it, the judgments that she made about what science content to teach and how to teach it, her ways of treating individual students who encountered problems, and many other facets.

The following sections are devoted to explicating the nature of Ms. Copeland's pattern of practice and discussing the knowledge that made it possible. First, I will discuss the social and pedagogical knowledge that Ms. Copeland used to create and maintain the patterns of social interaction in her classroom. Then I will discuss the nature of the *knowledge of science* and the *knowledge of students* that Ms. Copeland used and communicated in her teaching.

SOCIAL AND PEDAGOGICAL KNOWLEDGE

As a teacher, Ms. Copeland functioned as the leader of a "learning community" that operated within her classroom. The participants in this community, Ms. Copeland and her students, had developed shared understandings of their roles and responsibilities, the ways that they should speak and act, the kinds of work that they would do, and so forth. This section focuses on three aspects of life in Ms. Copeland's classroom community: (a) social norms and expectations that Ms. Copeland established in her classroom, (b) the kinds of academic work in which she engaged her students, and (c) the teaching strategies that she used. The section concludes with a discussion of the knowledge that she needed to create and maintain these particular aspects of her pattern of practice.

Social Norms and Expectations

The first thing that a casual visitor to Ms. Copeland's room might have noticed is that the class seemed enthusiastic, but not completely orderly. Sometimes students called out answers or questions without raising their hands; sometimes more than one student talked at a time. At this level, an observer's evaluation might be based on the relative importance that he or she attached to enthusiasm and order. There is more to see than enthusiasm and order, though. The vignette also provides evidence of other, more subtle norms and expectations that are probably more important in terms of their effects on students' understanding of science.

Consider Staci's behavior, for example. It was interesting and somewhat unusual for a seventh-grade girl. She held on to her opinion against the opposition of her teacher and most of her classmates, continued to discuss the question with other people outside of class, and conceded in the end that she had been wrong all along. This is not typical behavior for 12-year-old girls, who are more likely to avoid intellectual arguments and confrontations with their teachers or their classmates, to talk about anything but science outside of science class, and to avoid at all costs being wrong when everyone else is right. So why did Staci continue talking outside of class about a scientific question? Why did she not seem embarrassed or concerned when she admitted that she had been wrong? It could be, of course, that Staci was simply unusually assertive and interested in science. There is nothing in the episode, however, to indicate that anyone considered Staci's behavior atypical, and other observations of Ms. Copeland's teaching seem to indicate that several other students besides Staci were also unusually assertive and interested in science. Although Staci's behavior would be unusual in other classrooms, it was not in Ms. Copeland's.

In fact, Staci's behavior was part of a normal and expected pattern in Ms. Copeland's classroom. Ms. Copeland had succeeded in creating a social environment where *sense-making* behavior was highly valued, and face-saving behavior was not. Most students believed that science was supposed to be coherent and sensible, for them personally as well as for others, and that they had a right to argue and ask questions if it was not. In Ms. Copeland's class these questions and arguments were perceived as worthwhile and enjoyable, and it was recognized that a cogent defense of an incorrect position might contribute more to the individual and collective sense making of the class than simply knowing the right answer. Correct answers were important, but so were good questions and good arguments, especially good arguments that helped clarify the reasoning behind the correct answers.

Academic Tasks

Walter Doyle (1986) argues that teachers inform students about their curriculum—their goals and expectations for student learning—primarily through their accountability systems. To know a teacher's *real* curriculum, Doyle argues, we should look not at formal statements of goals and objectives but at the work that students are engaged in and the ways that the work is evaluated.

What sorts of work were Ms. Copeland's students engaged in and what did that reveal about her curriculum? At a superficial level, the academic work in her class seems pretty ordinary: Class discussions, worksheets, laboratory activities, and so forth. At a deeper level, though, there were important differences between her students' work and the work of students in other science classrooms. Her students rarely copied facts and definitions or answered questions about laboratory procedures. Instead, there was a heavy emphasis in their work on *using* scientific knowledge, particularly to explain how and why things happen in the natural world. Which direction does food normally travel in the stem of a plant? Why do green plants die in the dark? What will happen to a raindrop that soaks into the soil around a large bean plant?

By way of comparison, consider the academic work associated with the chapters on photosynthesis in typical life science textbooks:

The method of making food by storing light and energy is called _____.
(McLaren, Stasik, & Levering, 1981, p. 55)

Plants usually get their food
   a. by absorbing it from the soil directly
   b. from fertilizers that are found in organic material
   c. from other plants and animals
   d. by absorbing minerals and water and then making food
(Oxenhorn, 1981, p. 74)

What conditions are necessary in order for a leaf to carry on photosynthesis?
(Kilburn & Howell, 1981, p. 390)

Thus teachers who wish to teach for understanding must learn to reject or modify the academic tasks supplied to them in most textbooks and other teaching materials. These "teaching aids" support a kind of teaching that leads to rote memorization of facts and definitions, not teaching that helps students deepen their understanding of the natural world.

Teaching Strategies

Textbook developers have good reasons for providing academic work that consists primarily of relatively easy but useless questions. The most important of these reasons is consumer demand: Many teachers want textbooks with these sorts of questions and would reject academic tasks like those used by Ms. Copeland as too difficult for their students. In a sense, they are right; without the help of sophisticated and demanding teaching strategies, most students cannot learn to answer questions like those Ms. Copeland asked. Such teaching strategies are neither new nor unknown. In fact, many people who have no training in professional education routinely use strategies more sophisticated and effective than those employed by most science teachers. Examples from out-of-school contexts include masters of a craft working with apprentices (Collins, Brown, & Newman, 1989) and mothers teaching their toddlers how to speak (Greenfield, 1984).

Collins, Brown, and Newman (1989) point out that such successful everyday learning situations have a number of common features. They occur within the context of a "culture of expert practice" where the learners are strongly motivated to master those skills or tasks that will help them become full-fledged members of that culture. Teachers and learners together generally work their way through a succession of activities in which responsibility for doing the task gradually passes from the teacher to the learner. Collins, Brown, and Newman summarize this sequence as *modeling* (the teacher does the task while the learner observes), *coaching* (the learner does the task with support and guidance from the teacher), and *fading* (the learner gradually assumes full control).

As Collins, Brown, and Newman (1989) point out, making teaching strategies like these work in a public school setting is fraught with difficulty. It is much easier to establish a "culture of expert practice" in an environment where "experts" outnumber learners than in a school setting, where learners are a large majority. Students often are not strongly motivated to learn in public school settings. In contrast to the visible activities of children learning to speak or apprentices learning a craft, students in a science classroom are learning patterns of thought and reasoning that are often silent and invisible. Thus Ms. Copeland's achievement was considerable. She created a social environment where students were intrinsically motivated to learn science and where they were willing to express their thoughts. When students "made their thoughts visible" to the class, Ms. Copeland could help them see the strengths and weaknesses in their thinking and engage in the modeling, coaching, and fading of canonical scientific reasoning.

Ms. Copeland's Social and Pedagogical Knowledge

This section has been devoted to describing what Ms. Copeland *did* as she taught her unit on photosynthesis. The pattern of Ms. Copeland's practice included the social environment that she created in her classroom, the academic work that she engaged her students in, her teaching strategies, and much more. To describe this pattern of practice, however, is not to say what Ms. Copeland *knew* that made it possible for her to create and maintain it.

Describing Ms. Copeland's social and pedagogical knowledge is difficult in part because it was personal and context-bound in at least two senses. First, her knowledge was tied to her particular teaching situation. The extent of her knowledge is evidenced by her success in developing a rich and effective pattern of practice with those particular students, in that particular course, using the particular teaching materials and other resources available to her at that time. It is hard to say to what extent Ms. Copeland knew how to develop this pattern of practice in a more general sense.

Ms. Copeland's social and pedagogical knowledge was also personal and context-bound in that it was largely tacit knowledge; she lacked a language or a set of categories to describe and explain what she knew. The language of simplistic solutions that prevails in workshops and methods courses is inadequate to describe what Ms. Copeland knew and did. So is the language of the "teaching suggestions" in the teacher's editions of textbooks. We don't really know very much about how Ms. Copeland developed the tacit knowledge that she used to lead her classroom community, develop academic tasks, and decide on teaching strategies. We believe that, like most teachers, she had no choice but to develop this knowledge largely through reflection on her own teaching experience.

Although this method of developing knowledge seems to have worked reasonably well for Ms. Copeland, there are two important reasons for believing that it is not working very well for the profession as a whole. The first is obvious: Without effective forms of support many teachers fail to develop patterns of practice as sophisticated or as effective as Ms. Copeland's. The second is more subtle: The absence of an adequate language for organizing and expressing their knowledge of practice condemns each generation of science teachers to rediscovering the knowledge of their predecessors through personal experience, rather than building on the knowledge of previous successful science teachers.

KNOWLEDGE OF SCIENCE

As a teacher Ms. Copeland was poised between two subcultures: an adult subculture of scientists and their work and a very different subculture of the 12-year-old children in her classroom. Her job was to transform the children, to make them somehow more like scientists than they were before they came to her. This left Ms. Copeland with a great many choices about what to teach, for her children were unlike scientists in a great many ways. It also left her with an immense problem, because the scientific subculture in its adult form is distant and inaccessible to most students. Scientists have access to a vast and complex body of knowledge that they communicate to each other in an arcane jargon full of technical terms. They work in ways that require a great deal of knowledge and technical skill, and often immense patience and perseverance, trying to answer questions that are often themselves incomprehensible to children.

Thus in order to transform her students Ms. Copeland had to transform science. She had to create a body of scientific knowledge and a version of the scientific subculture that were accessible to her students. In transforming science Ms. Copeland had to deal, at least implicitly, with some difficult and philosophically profound questions: What is science and what are its component parts? Out of the entire scientific enterprise and its products, what is important for seventh graders to learn now and what can wait until later? What is comprehensible to 12-year-olds and what is beyond their reach?

It is possible, of course, to teach science without thinking about these questions. Teachers have access to a variety of materials that provide, or purport to provide, ready-made answers; foremost among these are textbooks and curriculum guides. Unfortunately, there are many reasons to question the adequacy of the textbooks' representation of the scientific enterprise, including the statistics on students' learning. Science as represented in most textbooks seems to be pretty dull and disconnected, certainly not something that most children would want to find out about in their spare time. Even more troubling, the culture of most classrooms where those textbooks are used has little in common with the culture of adult science. Most adult scientists, for example, spend relatively little time copying facts and definitions out of books, yet that is the primary activity of students in many science classes. For many children, exposure to science textbooks and to the culture of science classrooms results not in understanding but in alienation from science.

Ms. Copeland's classroom and some other classrooms demonstrate that this alienation is not inevitable. It is possible to construct learning environments that represent the culture of science in a rich, full, and interesting way. Ms. Copeland succeeded in helping her students to see how science incorporates a useful and coherent body of knowledge, and she constructed a classroom environment that conveyed something of the nature of science as a social enterprise. Each of these characteristics of her teaching is discussed below.

Scientific Knowledge as Useful

Textbooks typically depict scientific knowledge as consisting of "content"—an array of facts, definitions, formulas, and so forth—and "process skills" that scientists use when they are discovering new content. Both parts of this depiction are troublesome. There is strong reason to doubt whether science process skills exist at all, at least as the generalizable and content-free skills often depicted in the science education literature (Kuhn, Amsel, & O'Loughlin, 1988; Millar & Driver, 1987). As for content, the typical textbook depiction of science makes it hard to understand what makes all those facts and definitions worth knowing. The textbooks are full of answers, but they generally fail to inform their readers about the questions scientists were asking when they invented those answers.

What is missing, in other words, from the textbooks' depiction of science content is a sense of why scientists seek their knowledge and what they do with their knowledge once they have it. Scientific knowledge provides us not just with statements about the nature of the world, but with a wide array of conceptual and technological *tools*. People who use these tools—the language, theories, and instruments of science—are capable of describing, explaining, making predictions about, and controlling the world with a precision, power, and depth of understanding that would otherwise be impossible. For example, the idea that plants use light to make their own food can be treated as a simple statement of fact; this is what most textbooks (and most science teachers) do. Used as a tool, however, this same idea can help explain many things about green plants: why they have leaves, why their leaves turn toward the sun, why they die without light, why animals depend on them, and so forth. Furthermore, the tools of science provide those who master them with access to the community of scientists and to the knowledge and power that community possesses. There is no clear line of demarcation between "scientific" and "unscientific" description, explanation, prediction, and control. People engage in these activities scientifically to the extent that they use the conceptual and technological tools of science to increase the power and precision of their performance.

These thoughts suggest a view of the science curriculum in which students develop a progressively deeper understanding of science by engaging in activities that use scientific knowledge as a tool. Children entered Ms. Copeland's class already describing, explaining, predicting, and trying to control the world around them, though often in ways that lacked power and precision. Ms. Copeland gave her students opportunities to increase the power and precision with which they engaged in these important activities, rather than limiting them to less significant activities such as recalling facts.

In contrast, many other science teachers teach students about the conceptual tools of science without teaching them how to *use* those tools. In these classrooms, students are generally exposed to large numbers of facts and vocabulary words, tested for recall, and moved on to the next topic (e.g., Eaton, Anderson, & Smith, 1984; Hollon & Anderson, 1987). The facts and vocabulary words are considered to be understood when students can associate them with other facts, definitions, or vocabulary words. They are rarely used for the purposes of describing, explaining, predicting, or controlling the real world. This instructional pattern is sometimes justified, implicitly or explicitly, by the assertion that students need to learn "basic facts" before moving on to "higher order thinking." Teachers argue that although they can expose students to these facts and concepts early on, students will develop meaningful understandings of these ideas only later, when they are capable of abstract thinking.

This reasoning is an empty rationalization. Children begin to engage in activities labeled as higher-order thinking—description, explanation, prediction, and control of the world around them—*before* they learn to memorize facts and reproduce them on demand. Students who are made to memorize and reproduce facts are practicing an activity that has little in common with meaningful uses of scientific knowledge and that does little to prepare them to use scientific knowledge meaningfully.

A common instructional pattern in the classrooms of skilled and experienced science teachers is one in which the *teacher* uses scientific knowledge meaningfully during lectures and discussions, but not the students. The students witness the teacher's performance and often participate in it in a limited way, providing important words or bits of information as requested by the teacher. However, their independent academic work still consists primarily of producing small bits of information on demand. Consider, for example, the way one such teacher, whom we will call Mr. Barnes, taught the same lesson on photosynthesis as Ms. Copeland. Like Ms. Copeland, he made a list on the board of students' ideas about where plants get their food. The discussion then proceeded as follows:

TEACHER: Let's go back to what we talked about yesterday. We said, we gave a definition for food. What was the definition of food?

STUDENT: Energy? Anything you can eat that is energy?

TEACHER: All right. In talking about food for ourselves, we say it's the things that we eat but it's to obtain energy for life processes. (*Writes on board: Food: Materials that contain energy to help living live and grow.*) That's close . . . on page 2 they gave a definition (*he reads it aloud*) . . . So that's pretty close to a scientific definition of food.

STUDENT: You left "things" out.

TEACHER: Yes. We could say "organisms." If a plant is a living thing. . . . Is a plant a living thing?

STUDENT: (*several nod yes*)

TEACHER: Sure, we all understand that plants are living things. If a plant is a thing, then it has to use some food for energy. What they want you to struggle with is where do they get food from. All too often we're brainwashed—the stuff we get from the store is labeled "plant food." That does help plants grow but does it contain energy?

STUDENT: (*very quietly*) No.

TEACHER: It's hard to visualize whether it does contain energy. It does seem to help plants grow. But it's like vitamins. . . . We came to this conclusion yesterday, didn't we? That vitamins don't give us energy but do help us live and grow. It's the same situation with plant food, the stuff we buy at the store. It's improperly labeled. They're fertilizers that help the plant grow but they don't contain energy. (*Pointing to "minerals" on the students' list on the board*) Minerals from the soil are fertilizer types of stuff but there's not really energy in minerals you get from the soil. (*Pointing to "air" on the list on the board*) The air does contain things that plants use but they really don't contain energy. Yesterday we saw a filmstrip. Anybody remember where all the energy that plants were using came from?

The same general pattern prevailed in most of Mr. Barnes' classes. He told his students much more about plants and photosynthesis than Ms. Copeland. Furthermore what he told them was generally accurate, well organized, and modeled the usefulness of scientific knowledge. Nevertheless, Ms. Copeland's students did better on a posttest assessing their understanding of photosynthesis.

These results are in keeping with a general pattern (Anderson & Roth, 1989): In order to master new scientific knowledge, most students need to *use* that knowledge themselves to make sense of the world around them. By helping her students to do this, Ms. Copeland conveyed to them a powerful and effective message about the particular scientific ideas that they were studying and about the nature of science in general.

Science as Coherent

It is notable in the vignette of Ms. Copeland's teaching that the primary language of discussion is the language of the students, not the specialized language of science. The class discussed "food," "calories," and "potato peels" rather than "organic compounds," "chemical potential energy," and "carbohydrates." In doing this she seemed to sacrifice much of the power and precision of scientific language. She made this sacrifice, however, in order to represent science faithfully in another, more important way.

Ms. Copeland's willingness to use her students' words when talking about science was one of several ways in which she made them aware that scientific knowledge is strongly connected with their personal knowledge of the world. She helped her students see science not as a list of strange and obscure facts but as a coherent conceptual system that was linked to the students' commonsense understandings. Students should expect the two types of knowledge to fit together into a single integrated understanding of the world.

Ultimately, the coherence of scientific knowledge can be fully expressed only in the specialized language, both verbal and mathematical, of science. Ms. Copeland recognized this and devoted much of her time to helping students understand new words, such as photosynthesis and scientific usages of familiar words, such as food or energy. Unlike Mr. Barnes, though, who tended to use a lot of scientific terms to maximize the coherence of his own presentations, Ms. Copeland used fewer scientific terms and sought to maximize the coherence of her students' understanding.

Science as a Social Enterprise

Recent work in the history and philosophy of science (Kuhn, 1970; Mayr, 1982; Toulmin, 1961, 1972) depicts scientists as engaged in a collective attempt to understand the natural world. They constantly search for new and more powerful ways to understand and control the world. Scientists who believe that they have developed some new knowledge communicate that knowledge to the community of their peers, and the knowledge is considered valid only after it has been reviewed and accepted by that community. No individual scientist knows all that is known about a topic; the growing body of scientific knowledge is the product, and the possession, of the entire scientific community.

In her classroom Ms. Copeland created an environment where students felt that, like scientists, they were engaged in a process of collective sense making. Their high level of involvement can be explained by the fact that within her classroom the students, not the teacher or the textbook, were the ultimate arbiters of new knowledge. New ideas from any source—the teacher, the textbook, or the students themselves—were subjected to "peer review" by the students. Most students undoubtedly realized that the ideas in the textbook would "win out" in the end, but they also understood that that was not really the point. They were enthusiastic in accepting their right, and their obligation, to demand that any new idea make sense to them, be useful to them, and be integrated into the growing body of their own scientific knowledge. Ms. Copeland recognized and rewarded the contributions of students who, like Staci, could mount sustained and reasonable defenses of incorrect points of view. She did so because arguments like Staci's were valuable to the sense-making enterprise of the students as individuals and of the classroom community as a whole.

The idea that in learning science students should "act like scientists" is not new. It was the basis for the development of "discovery" or "inquiry-oriented" science programs during the 1960s. The failure of those programs (Roth, 1984; Smith & Anderson, 1984) can, I believe, be attributed in part to two related factors. First, the inquiry programs concentrated on imitating the procedures that individual scientists follow in their laboratories rather than on the collective sense-making functions of scientific communities. Second, students in inquiry programs were often given few opportunities to use their scientific knowledge or to connect it with their own personal beliefs about the world. Thus while the hands-on activities of inquiry programs imitated the form of scientific research, I believe that Ms. Copeland's class activities came closer to representing its underlying substance.

Ms. Copeland's Knowledge of Science

Ms. Copeland chose to present science to her students in a way that emphasized some aspects of the scientific subculture, especially its individual and collective sense-making functions, while deemphasizing traditional content and process goals. Some educators, especially those who are highly scientifically literate like Mr. Barnes, may regard this as basically a value judgment, a choice among alternative reasonable goals. However, there is a growing body of empirical evidence (reviewed in Anderson & Smith, 1987) that this is not the case. Ms. Copeland's students did not just learn *different* knowledge, they learned *more*. Most students simply cannot make sense of and remember science as it is typically taught. Thus it is incumbent upon the education community to help more teachers learn how to present science as Ms. Copeland did.

Clearly, Ms. Copeland could not have taught as she did without knowing quite a bit about science. What she knew, however, was not the same as the "science" included in most science textbooks. Neither was it the same as (or a subset of) the science taught in most university science courses. University science courses are designed to provide an insider's view of science: to help induct new members into the scientific subculture, to prepare college students to communicate with scientists in their language and work with scientists on their terms.

Ms. Copeland, however, was not communicating and working with scientists; she was communicating and working with children. Rather than acting as a member of the scientific subculture, she worked as a mediator between the subculture of science and the very different subculture of children. Thus the nature of their work demands that Ms. Copeland and other science teachers develop an outsider's as well as an insider's view of science. They must decide what is essential to the scientific enterprise and what is peripheral, which aspects of scientific thought and language are accessible to the children they teach and which are not, how scientific thinking is like their students' thinking and how it is different.

Like her knowledge of practice, that portion of Ms. Copeland's knowledge of science that went beyond what is taught in science courses was largely a personal construction, knowledge developed in response to the problems that she experienced while trying to teach middle school science. The curriculum materials that were supposed to support her in this aspect of her work provided little useful guidance; they tended to focus on the superficial form of the scientific enterprise rather than its underlying substance: the collective search for coherent and useful knowledge of the natural world. Most universities offer courses that address these issues, but they tend to be hidden away in subdisciplines such as the history and philosophy of science, which are not usually viewed as relevant to the training of teachers. Ms. Copeland was able to overcome these difficulties and construct in her classroom a rich and meaningful representation of the scientific enterprise. Most teachers, unfortunately, are not.

KNOWLEDGE OF STUDENTS

The essence of Ms. Copeland's job was transforming students—or more accurately, helping them to transform themselves—into people who were more scientifically literate than they had been before they came to her. She could not do this job well without knowing quite a bit about her students and how they understood the world. This knowledge included both an understanding of how her students thought about specific science topics and an understanding of how her students' learning of science was influenced by more general social, cultural, and economic factors.

Students' Knowledge of Specific Scientific Topics

In order to understand science meaningfully, students must connect canonical scientific knowledge with their own personal knowledge of the world. Students who fail to do so end up viewing science as a collection of facts, definitions, and formulas that are about topics too distant from their own lives to have any personal meaning or significance. Too often, this is exactly the kind of learning that occurs in science classrooms. It is often hard to see how scientific knowledge connects with students' personal beliefs about the world. Most of Ms. Copeland's students, for example, knew little or nothing about photosynthesis before she began teaching them about the topic.

This does not mean, however, that the students had no relevant prior knowledge. In fact, the vignette from Ms. Copeland's teaching shows that the students had lots of ideas about food, about plants, and about food for plants (see also Anderson & Roth, 1989). Some of these ideas were useful and scientifically correct: The association between food and energy (or calories), for example. Other ideas were incompatible with canonical scientific knowledge, such as the students' tendency to associate food and eating. Middle school students know that food is what you eat. They reason, therefore, that food for plants is what plants "eat": water and soil minerals (or "plant food").

The students' beliefs about plants' structure and function showed a similar mixture of scientifically acceptable and unacceptable beliefs. Most middle school students, for example, understand that plants are living organisms. Thus they naturally try to understand how plants work by analogy with more familiar organisms, such as animals. In their attempts to make plants comprehensible, they reason that plants must engage in functions similar to those of animals, including eating and digestion.

Thus to understand photosynthesis, students must go through a complex process of conceptual change. They must abandon their assumptions about the metabolic similarities between plants and humans and restructure their thinking about the nature of food. Without this involved process of restructuring and integration of personal knowledge with scientific knowledge, students cannot be successful in using knowledge about photosynthesis to make reasonable predictions and explanations of real-world phenomena. In order to help her students transform their thinking, Ms. Copeland had to guide them through the conceptual change process.

Social and Cultural Influences

From the time of its origins in the seventeenth century through the mid-nineteenth century, modern science was virtually the exclusive province of upper-class, western European white males, mostly men of independent means who could practice science without outside financial support. Naturally, these men tended to make science in their own image, depending on the patterns of thought and language and the assumptions about the relationship between humans and nature that were most comfortable and familiar to them.

There can be no doubt that these men succeeded in constructing a body of knowledge that has significance for all humans. People of all cultures have accepted the validity and importance of Western science and have set about trying to master it. In contrast, Western views of history, or religion, or political philosophy have gained far less universal acceptance. At the same time, though, modern science retains some of the marks of its origins, and this is a problem for teachers of socially and culturally diverse groups of students. For example, Keller (1985) points out that modern science still tends to rely on metaphors and modes of thought that are associated with masculinity in our society. Many scientists continue to be interested in finding ways of controlling nature and of discovering the laws to which "she" is subject. Warmth, empathy, and love are regarded as dangerous emotions, as threats to the skepticism and cool objectivity that are necessary for the development of reliable scientific knowledge. Thus many girls get the subtle message that to be feminine and to be scientific are mutually exclusive alternatives.

Differences in language and culture can also affect the ease with which students master scientific reasoning and knowledge. Some of these difficulties may be quite specific. For example, Orr (1987) argues that students who speak black English vernacular often use function words such as prepositions and conjunctions in nonstandard ways, and that these nonstandard usages influence the way that students understand, and are understood, when they are dealing with quantitative problems expressed in standard English.

Other culture-related difficulties are more general in nature. For example, there is a large and complex literature on the effects of culture and literacy on patterns of reasoning (see Egan, 1987; Olson, 1986; Scribner & Cole, 1983). This research indicates that the patterns of our reasoning are influenced by the culture in which we are raised. Egan, for example, uses historical and anthropological evidence to contrast "literacy" and "orality" as alternate ways of knowing, each embedded in a rich cultural context. He notes, for example, the explanatory challenge posed by the Homeric epics. How could Homer (who apparently was illiterate) have constructed such a complex and extensive work of art? How could he even remember a sequence of works more than 28,000 lines long? Recent archeological evidence indicates that many of the events described in the *Iliad* actually occurred. How did an illiterate society keep this memory intact for half a millennium?

Egan responds that the Homeric epics, and similar myths in other oral cultures, were far more than just stories; they were the "libraries" of oral societies, the repositories of the accumulated knowledge of those cultures. The framework of the epics' story lines and a variety of technical devices, including rhyme, meter, and an array of repeated phrases, made it possible for illiterate poets not to remember a fixed text, but to "stitch together" their poems as they sang. In this way, the members of oral cultures could routinely perform what seem to us extraordinary feats of memory and preserve the accumulated knowledge of their cultures.

The knowledge accumulated by oral cultures took a form, however, quite different from knowledge as we think of it today. There were no clear divisions between fact and fiction, between myth and reality, between stories and theories.

These sorts of distinctions, as well as innovations such as syllogistic reasoning, were made possible by the development of writing as an alternate form of memory and our resultant freedom to manipulate and analyze texts and ideas. Egan makes this point by quoting a passage from Levi-Bruhl on the oral peoples that the latter studied:

> This extraordinary development of memory, and a memory which faithfully reproduces the minutest details of sense-impressions in the correct order of their appearance, is shown moreover by the wealth of vocabulary and the grammatical complexity of the languages. Now the very men who speak these languages and possess this power of memory are (in Australia or northern Brazil, for instance) incapable of counting beyond two and three. The slightest mental effort involving abstract reasoning, however rudimentary it may be, is so distasteful to them that they immediately declare themselves tired and give it up. (Levi-Bruhl, 1910/1985, p. 115)

Egan argues that orality did not disappear with the advent of literacy; modern cultures are complex mixtures of oral and literate traditions. Western science is, of course, the product of a highly literate class within a literate cultural tradition, so it depends strongly on literate rather than oral modes of thinking. Thus in scientific contexts, myth, metaphor, and story telling are devalued, while literate modes of thought involving clear distinctions and syllogistic reasoning are highly valued. This can be a problem for students whose own cultural traditions have strong oral roots.

The purpose of this argument is to suggest that science has deep-seated characteristics that tend to make it more easily accessible to men than to women, and to people who were raised in highly literate environments. Thus, at present, our schools succeed in teaching science to those students whose cultural roots are most compatible with the culture of science. We have an obligation, though, to nurture the scientific understanding of students whose social and cultural backgrounds are less easily compatible with the values and habits of thought characteristic of the scientific subculture.

Ms. Copeland's Knowledge of Students

Both Ms. Copeland's teaching and our interviews with her revealed that she knew a lot about her students and their thinking. She was able, for example, to predict in considerable detail how they would respond to questions about the nature of food and the functioning of plants, even before she began teaching the unit. Like her knowledge of practice, though, her knowledge of students was mostly personal and context-bound. She had developed this knowledge through her reflection on experience, with little help from teacher's guides, university courses, or inservice teacher education programs.

This was true even though the past decade has seen a revolution in our research-based understanding of students and their scientific thinking (e.g., Novak, 1987; Osborne & Freyberg, 1985), as well as research like that cited above concerning the effects of culture on knowledge and reasoning. The products of this research, though, are still mostly hidden away in the research literature and in graduate courses; they have so far had little influence on the developers of teaching materials or on the education of prospective or inservice teachers.

IMPLICATIONS FOR POLICY

This chapter focuses on the question, What do teachers need to know in order to teach science well? Earlier I compared science teaching with building a house, suggesting that both were complex, multifaceted achievements requiring an extensive and well-organized body of knowledge. The main part of this chapter has been devoted to explaining the nature of this achievement for one good science teacher and to discussing the knowledge that made her achievement possible. The point of this discussion is that successful teaching requires a lot of knowledge about social arrangements in classrooms, about pedagogy, about science, and about students. I would now like to return to the house-building analogy in order to make a second point: Although achievements like building houses and teaching science always require a lot of knowledge, the exact nature of the knowledge required depends on the context in which people work and the tools that they use.

Consider two extended case studies of house building: Laura Ingalls Wilder's description of how her father built a log cabin in *Little House on the Prairie* and Tracy Kidder's (1985) account of the building of a house in modern New England. The building of both houses required knowledge and skill. Here is an excerpt from Wilder's (1935/1971) account of how her father made the floor of their cabin:

> One day the last log was split, and next morning Pa began to lay the floor. He dragged the logs into the house and laid them one by one, flat side up. With his spade he scraped the ground underneath, and fitted the round side of the log firmly down into it. With his ax he trimmed away the edge of bark and cut the wood straight, so that each log fitted against the next, with hardly a crack between them.
>
> Then he took the head of the ax in his hand, and with little, careful blows he smoothed the wood. He squinted along the log to see that the surface was straight and true. He took off last little bits, here and there. Finally he ran his hand over the smoothness, and nodded. "Not a splinter!" he said. "That'll be all right for little bare feet to run over."
>
> He left that log fitted into its place, and dragged in another. (pp. 128-129)

By way of comparison, the following passage describes how Jim Locke planned the support structure for the floor of the Souwaine house.

> He has to decide where to put a lot of sticks, so that the fewest possible are used and the least amount of cutting is required. Plywood comes in four-foot-by-eight-foot sheets. He has to make sure that the floor joists are spaced in such a way that two edges of every sheet of plywood come to rest on something solid. He also has to determine exactly the boundaries of each room because some will be floored with oak, some with tile, some with carpeting, and each of those surfaces calls for a different quality and thickness of plywood. The trickiest part, though, is the girders, the beams they'll make to hold up the floor joists. Bill wants a sunken floor in the living room. At one edge of that room a very heavy hearth occurs. In essence there's a place where floors of three different levels will meet. Jim stacks one set of girders onto another, and goes on. One section of floor is a little too wide for those joists. Or he could use two-by-twelves of spruce. Or he could use Douglas fir two-by-tens. Which is cheaper? Which takes less time to install? Jim has settled on Douglas fir. It comes from the Pacific Northwest. His supplier has to order it specially, and Jim hopes that it will arrive on time. (Kidder, 1985, pp. 85-86)

As Resnick (1987) suggests, the knowledge that Charles Ingalls needed in his head and his hands is now built into the tools and materials that are routinely available to modern house builders. This does not mean that house building is now simple. Rather, by developing tools, materials, and support systems that were not available to Charles Ingalls, we have made it possible for modern house builders to construct houses that are far more complex, and far more comfortable, than the Ingalls' little log cabin. In the process, we have changed the nature of house builders' work and the knowledge that it requires.

Thus there can be no single answer to the question of what teachers need to know to teach science well. It will always depend on the nature of the contexts in which they work and the tools and materials available for them to use. I have suggested in this chapter that Ms. Copeland's work was more like Charles Ingalls' house building than like the house building process described in Kidder's book. In building her pattern of practice, Ms. Copeland was faced with a constant struggle to compensate for the deficiencies of the materials that she was using and the training that she had been given. It is still necessary for teachers like Ms. Copeland to devote much of their knowledge, time, and energy to doing this; I am not sure that the solution to our problems in science education lies mainly in trying to train other teachers to do the same.

The challenge that we face is not simply one of finding talented teachers or of improving science teachers' skills or attitudes. We must find ways of helping thousands of science teachers build patterns of practice that are more sophisticated and more effective than those that prevail today. Among the many science teachers that my colleagues and I have observed in our research and teacher education work, Ms. Copeland stands out as a rare (though not unique) exception. Most of the teachers we have seen have been sincere, hard-working people who developed patterns of practice that were far less functional than Ms. Copeland's. In the main, they succeeded in keeping their students well organized and busy and in helping their students memorize some facts and definitions, but they failed to help their students make sense of those facts (Anderson & Roth, 1989; Anderson & Smith, 1987; Hollon, Anderson, & Roth, in press).

The situation is not a "crisis"; it is simply the way things are. It is not primarily the fault of science teachers any more than it was Charles Ingalls' fault that his house lacked running water. Like builders' work, teachers' work is shaped by the knowledge that they possess, the context in which they work, and the available tools and materials. The knowledge, contexts, tools, and materials of science teachers' work currently support the maintenance of order and the memorization of facts. Many science teachers try to do more, to teach for understanding. To do more, however, is currently a very complex and difficult task. Only a few exceptional individuals are truly successful.

Teaching science for understanding is so difficult because it requires a pattern of practice based on knowledge that most teachers do not have, including social and pedagogical knowledge, knowledge of science, and knowledge of students. There may never be more than a few teachers who, like Ms. Copeland, manage to successfully develop and use that knowledge on their own. They should not *have* to do it on their own, though. Jim Locke could build a better floor than Charles Ingalls because the knowledge of many people, some of them long since dead, was built into the tools and materials that Locke used, and because he was supported by many people—architects, plumbers, electricians, and so forth—who had knowledge that he lacked.

Many other crafts and professions have also developed successful mechanisms for preserving and sharing important knowledge: farming, medicine, and engineering, for example. In contrast, we in the education profession have not been particularly successful at preserving and sharing knowledge. Teachers like Ms. Copeland must develop much of their knowledge through personal experience, and they must learn how to modify or ignore inadequate tools and materials. There is often not even a language that they can use to express what they have learned and share it with other teachers.

Changing this system for the better will be a long and difficult process, a process spanning generations rather than years, a process composed of thousands of small improvements in the knowledge and practice of individual science teachers. Policy makers cannot make this process happen, but they can encourage the development of better knowledge and more sophisticated patterns of practice. Ways in which policy makers can encourage the development and use of a better knowledge base include the following:

1. *Improving teaching materials.* Most current teaching materials are inadequate; they are tools that are not well suited to teaching for

understanding and that fail to incorporate important knowledge. It is possible, though time-consuming and expensive, to develop teaching materials that give teachers access to important knowledge and support effective patterns of practice (e.g., Anderson & Roth, 1989; Driver, 1987; Linn & Songer, 1988). It will be difficult and risky for commercial publishers to develop materials like these. They are likely to attempt to do so only in response to strong market pressures. Policy makers can begin to supply the necessary pressure by letting publishers know that they are paying attention to ways in which teaching materials incorporate worthwhile knowledge and support good practice.

2. *Teacher education.* The bulk of this chapter has been devoted to describing the social and pedagogical knowledge, knowledge of science, and knowledge of students that good science teaching demands, but that is currently missing from most preservice and inservice teacher education programs. We do not need more (or less) of the kinds of courses that we have now; we need courses that provide teachers with different kinds of knowledge. I believe we now know enough to make significant steps toward developing such programs, and we have experienced some success in our teacher education work (see Hollon, Anderson, & Roth, in press; Roth, Rosaen, & Lanier, 1988).

3. *Assessment and accountability.* It appears that, for better or worse, large-scale systems of teacher and student assessment are here to stay. It is important to recognize their limitations; teachers cannot be forced to engage in patterns of practice for which they lack the knowledge, the tools, or the time. It is possible, though, for systems of student assessment to encourage teaching for understanding and for systems of teacher assessment to encourage the development of sophisticated and effective patterns of practice. Some promising development work on such systems is underway (e.g., Anderson, 1988; Fredrickson, 1984; McDiarmid & Ball, 1988; Sykes, 1989). Policy makers can be aware of this work and use it.

4. *Time.* It takes time to teach well: Time to plan, time to respond to student work, time to develop new knowledge. The teaching loads that currently prevail in our schools deny teachers that time and thus work against the improvement of science teaching.

The changes suggested above are not "practical" in that they entail fundamental and sometimes expensive changes in our science education system. Decisions about what is practical, though, need to be made with consideration of their long-term effects. The statistics at the beginning of this chapter indicate that millions of students are currently wasting their time, learning virtually nothing of value in their science classes. What could be less practical than the years of quick fixes that have helped create this situation? The experience of other professions indicates that many small improvements can have a large cumulative effect over time. This happens, however, only if those small improvements are guided by some sense of shared purpose or direction. A determination to help science teachers gain access to and use new knowledge to develop more effective patterns of practice could help provide our profession with such a sense of shared purpose.

REFERENCES

Anderson, C. W. (1988, October). *Assessing student understanding of biological concepts.* Paper presented at the national invitational conference, High School Biology Today and Tomorrow, Washington, DC.

Anderson, C. W., & Roth, K. J. (1989). Teaching for meaningful and self-regulated learning of science. In J. Brophy (Ed.), *Advances in research on teaching: Vol. 1. Teaching for meaningful understanding and self-regulated learning* (pp. 265-311). Greenwich, CT: JAI Press.

Anderson, C. W., & Smith, E. L. (1987). Teaching science. In V. Richardson-Koehler (Ed.), *Educators' handbook: A research perspective* (pp. 84-111). New York: Longman.

Collins, A., Brown, J. S., & Newman, S. E. (1989). Cognitive apprenticeship: Teaching the crafts of reading, writing, and mathematics. In L. B. Resnick (Ed.), *Knowing, learning, and instruction: Essays in honor of Robert Glaser* (pp. 453-494). Hillsdale, NJ: Erlbaum.

Doyle, W. (1986). Content representation in teachers' definitions of academic work. *Journal of Curriculum Studies, 18*, 365-379.

Driver, R. (1987). Promoting conceptual change in classroom settings: The experience of the children's learning in a science project. In J. Novak (Ed.), *Proceedings of the second international seminar: Misconceptions and educational strategies in science and mathematics* (Vol. 2, pp. 97-107). New York: Cornell University Press.

Eaton, J. F., Anderson, C. W., & Smith, E. L. (1984). Students' misconceptions interfere with science learning: Case studies of fifth-grade students. *Elementary School Journal, 84*, 365-379.

Egan, K. (1987). Literacy and the oral foundations of education. *Harvard Educational Review, 57*, 445-472.

Fredrickson, N. (1984). The real test bias: Influences of testing on teaching and learning. *American Psychologist, 39*, 193-202.

Greenfield, P. M. (1984). A theory of the teacher in the learning activities of everyday life. In B. Rogoff & J. Lave (Eds.), *Everyday cognition: Its development in social context* (pp. 117-138). Cambridge, MA: Harvard University Press.

Hollon, R. E., & Anderson, C. W. (1987, April). *Teachers' beliefs about students' learning processes in science: Self-reinforcing belief systems.* Paper presented at the annual meeting of the American Educational Research Association, Washington, DC.

Hollon, R. E., Anderson, C. W., & Roth, K. J. (in press). Science teachers' conceptions of teaching and learning. In J. Brophy (Ed.), *Advances in research on teaching: Vol. 2. Teachers' subject matter knowledge.* Greenwich, CT: JAI Press.

International Association for the Evaluation of Educational Achievement. (1988). *Science achievement in seventeen countries: A preliminary report.* Elmsford, NY: Pergamon.

Keller, E. F. (1985). *Reflections on gender and science.* New Haven, CT: Yale University Press.

Kidder, T. (1985). *House.* Boston: Houghton Mifflin.

Kilburn, R. E., & Howell, P. S. (1981). *Exploring life science.* Boston: Allyn & Bacon.

Kuhn, D., Amsel, E., & O'Loughlin, M. (1988). *The development of scientific thinking skills.* San Diego: Academic Press.

Kuhn, T. (1970). *The structure of scientific revolutions* (2nd ed.). Chicago: University of Chicago Press.

Levi-Bruhl, L. (1985). *How natives think.* (L. A. Clare, Trans.). Princeton, NJ: Princeton University Press. (Original work published 1910)

Linn, M. C., & Songer, N. B. (1988, April). *Cognitive research and instruction: Incorporating technology into the science curriculum.* Paper presented at the annual meeting of the American Educational Research Association, New Orleans.

Mayr, E. (1982). *The growth of biological thought.* Cambridge, MA: Belknap.

McDiarmid, G. W., & Ball, D. L. (1988). *"Many moons": Understanding teacher learning from a teacher education perspective* (Issue Paper 88-5). East Lansing: Michigan State University, National Center for Research on Teacher Education.

McLaren, J. E., Stasik, J. H., & Levering, D. F. (1981). *Spaceship earth: Life science.* Boston: Houghton Mifflin.

Millar, R., & Driver, R. (1987). Beyond processes. *Studies in Science Education, 14,* 33-62.

Miller, J. D. (1988, October). *The development of student interest in science.* Paper presented at the national invitational conference, High School Biology Today and Tomorrow, Washington, DC.

Novak, J. D. (1987). *Proceedings of the second international seminar on misconceptions and educational strategies in science and mathematics.* Ithaca, NY: Cornell University Press.

Olson, D. R. (1986). Intelligence and literacy: The relationships between intelligence and the technologies of representation and communication. In R. J. Sternberg & R. K. Wagner (Eds.), *Practical intelligence: Nature and origins of competence in the everyday world* (pp. 338-360). New York: Cambridge University Press.

Orr, E. W. (1987). *Twice as less.* New York: Norton.

Osborne, R. J., & Freyberg, P. (1985). *Learning in science: The implications of children's science.* Portsmouth, NH: Heinemann.

Oxenhorn, J. M. (1981). *Exploring the living world.* New York: Globe Publishing.

Resnick, L. B. (1987). Learning in school and out. *Educational Researcher, 16*(9), 13-20.

Roth, K. J. (1984). Using classroom observations to improve science teaching and curriculum materials. In C. W. Anderson (Ed.), *Observing science classrooms: Perspectives from research and practice* (1984 yearbook of the Association for the Education of Teachers in Science, pp. 77-102). Columbus, OH: ERIC/SMEAC.

Roth, K. J., & Anderson, C. W. (1987). *The power plant: Teacher's guide to photosynthesis.* (Occasional Paper No. 112). East Lansing: Michigan State University, Institute for Research on Teaching.

Roth, K. J., Rosaen, C. L., & Lanier, P. E. (1988). *Mentor Teacher Project: Program assessment report*. East Lansing: Michigan State University, Institute for Research on Teaching.

Scribner, S., & Cole, M. (1983). *The psychology of literacy*. Cambridge, MA: Harvard University Press.

Smith, E. L., & Anderson, C. W. (1984). Plants as producers: A case study of elementary school science teaching. *Journal of Research in Science Teaching, 21*, 685-698.

Sykes, G. (1989). National certification for teachers: A dialog. *NEA Today, 7*(8), 6-12.

Toulmin, S. (1961). *Foresight and understanding: An enquiry into the aims of science*. Bloomington: Indiana University Press.

Toulmin, S. (1972). *Human understanding*. Princeton, NJ: Princeton University Press.

Wilder, L. I. (1971). *Little house on the prairie*. New York: Harper & Row. (Original work published 1935)

Yager, R. E., & Yager, S. O. (1985). The effect of schooling upon understanding of selected science terms. *Journal of Research in Science Teaching, 22*(4), 359-364.

2

What Teachers Need to Know to Teach Science Effectively

ANTON E. LAWSON

I find myself in substantial agreement with Charles Anderson. However, before proceeding with my answer to the question, "What do teachers need to know to teach science effectively?" I feel compelled to disagree with two of his points.

Anderson states that there is strong reason to doubt whether science process skills exist at all." But the issue is not whether science process skills exist. Rather, key issues center around the explication of their precise nature, their articulation with specific subject matter, and their means of acquisition. Considerably more will be said about this later, including a list of seven basic science process skills and numerous subskills.

In addition, Anderson's claim that the inquiry-oriented programs of the 1960s were failures is, at best, misleading. The only failure that can reasonably be attributed to these programs is that most teachers do not use them, and that some who do, do not use them correctly (e.g., Hurd, Bybee, Kahle, & Yeager, 1980). When these programs are used correctly, they are overwhelmingly successful. Shymansky (1984), for example, reported the results of an analysis of over 300 research studies in which traditional programs versus the inquiry-oriented science curricula of the 1960s and 1970s were compared. Results of the analysis showed that the inquiry-oriented curricula were superior across *all* measures of performance. The positive effect for the Biological Sciences Curriculum Study (BSCS) high school biology program was most impressive. The average BSCS student outscored 84% of traditional course students on attitude measures, 81% on process skills, 77% on analytic skills, and 72% on concept achievement.

Further, Lawson, Abraham, and Renner (1989) recently reviewed nearly 100 studies of science programs such as the Science Curriculum Improvement

Study (SCIS) K-6 elementary school program. The SCIS program was developed with National Science Foundation support during the 1960s and 1970s and utilizes the inquiry-oriented learning cycle method of teaching. This review clearly reveals the success of the SCIS program and the learning cycle method. Students using the program and/or this teaching method have a more positive attitude toward science, better understand the nature of science, have successfully acquired important science concepts, and their science process skills (i.e., general thinking skills) are enhanced so much that performance in other subjects, such as mathematics, social studies, and reading, is also enhanced. This is hardly a failure.

The only failure that I can see in all of this is that policy makers in this country have not pushed hard enough to have these excellent programs adopted or, when they have been adopted, policy makers have not worked with teachers to ensure that the programs are used as they were intended to be used. Getting back to Anderson's claim that these programs were a failure, it should be pointed out that he supported this contention with reference to a study by Smith and Anderson (1984) that found a failure of one lesson in one classroom, not a general failure of these programs. Specifically, over half the students in one fifth-grade SCIS class, after working through the relevant lessons, failed to realize that plants make their own food when exposed to sunlight. As I have argued previously (Lawson, 1988), this was not a failure of the SCIS lessons (I have taught them successfully many times), but rather a failure of the teacher to allow the experiments to run to their completion.

Perhaps the teacher cut the experiments short because she was under pressure to cover too many topics. If so, this is most unfortunate because rapid coverage of many topics results in superficial learning and misunderstanding, not the necessary deep processing Anderson shows us in Ms. Copeland's class. The implication is that policy makers need to see to it that schools adopt good inquiry-oriented programs such as SCIS or Elementary Science Study (ESS) and insist that teachers devote ample time to teaching them correctly. Funding inservice workshops to this end is a wise investment.

In a very real sense, I have just answered the central question of this chapter: What do teachers need to know to teach science effectively? They need to know how to read and follow directions so they can do what the teacher's guides for these programs tell them to do. Regrettably these excellent inquiry-oriented programs do not exist at all grade levels, and the question does, in fact, deserve an answer that not only tells teachers what science programs to teach, but also explains *why* they should teach those programs and explains how to design their own programs if necessary. Therefore, allow me to propose a second, more detailed answer to the question, is contained in answers to the following six subquestions:

1. What is science?
2. Why teach science?
3. What is the nature of scientific knowledge?
4. How do scientists acquire conceptual knowledge?
5. How can students develop scientific procedural knowledge?
6. What teaching methods best facilitate scientific knowledge acquisition?

WHAT IS SCIENCE?

On the first day of each semester, I ask the new students in my Methods of Teaching Biology course to mark each of the following sentences True or False.

1. Science is a process of discovery of the nature of things via observation.
2. Truth is attainable via proof through repeated observation.
3. An hypothesis is an educated guess of what will be observed under certain conditions.
4. A conclusion is a statement of what was observed (#3).

This semester, 73% of the students marked sentence 1 True. The other sentences, respectively, were marked True by 43%, 70%, and 53% of the students. These percentages are typical of those from prior semesters and indicate that the majority of my students hold some serious misconceptions about the nature of science. This is alarming for two reasons. First, these students are seniors or graduates who have majored in science. Second, many of them will become science teachers in the near future. Fortunately, by the end of the course most of the students appear to have acquired a better understanding of science and correctly mark all four sentences False. That better understanding is reflected by statements such as

1. Science is a process of discovery of the nature of things via the creative generation of alternative hypotheses (via analogical reasoning) and their testing. Observation may provoke questions and it provides data to allow the testing of hypotheses, but it does not lead to the discovery of the nature of things.
2. Ultimate proof and truth are not attainable using science. Rather, science merely allows us to present reasoned arguments and evidence for or against particular explanations for observed phenomena.
3. An hypothesis is a tentative explanation. A prediction is "an educated guess" of what is deduced to be observed under certain conditions provided the hypothesis is "true."
4. A conclusion is not a statement of what was observed, but is a statement of the relative "truth or falsity" of any particular hypothesis based on the relationship between its predicted consequences and the actual results of

some experimental and/or correlational test and the relationship between the hypothesis and the other conceptual systems that one holds.

Teachers need to understand the nature of the scientific process to teach science effectively.

WHY TEACH SCIENCE?

Misconception: The job of the teacher is to transmit scientific facts to students.

Alternative Conception: The job of the teacher is to foster creative and critical thinking skills.

In 1961 the Educational Policies Commission of the United States drafted a document entitled *The Central Purpose of American Education* (Educational Policies Commission, 1961). In that document the commission identified the central objective of education in America as *freedom of the mind*. Their belief was that no person is born free and thus schools must foster skills required for this essential freedom. A free mind is one that can think and choose. According to the Educational Policies Commission, there are rational powers that, if acquired, constitute the free mind. These powers allow one to reason; to apply available evidence to ideas, attitudes, and actions; and to pursue better whatever goals he or she may have.

In 1966 the Educational Policies Commission, recognizing the key role that science education could play in the development of the ability to think, published a second document entitled *Education and the Spirit of Science* (Educational Policies Commission, 1966), in which they emphasized science not so much as a body of accumulated knowledge but as a way of thinking, a spirit of rational inquiry driven by a belief in its efficiency and by a restless curiosity to know and understand. They also emphasized that this mode of thought, this spirit, related to questions that people may think are totally nonscientific—religious, aesthetic, humanistic, and literary questions. Thus the spirit of science infuses many forms of scholarship besides science itself.

Although it was recognized that no scientist may fully exemplify the spirit of science and that scientific work may not be totally objective, it is clear that the following key values underlie science as an enterprise:

1. Longing to know and to understand
2. Questioning of all things
3. Search for data and their meaning
4. Demand for verification
5. Respect for logic

6. Consideration of premises
7. Consideration of consequences

This list, by its nature, insists that students not be indoctrinated to think or act in a certain way. Rather, it insists that they acquire the ability to make up their own minds, to develop freedom of the mind, and to make their own decisions based on reason and evidence. In this sense, the values of science are the most complete expression of one of the deepest human values—the belief in human dignity. Consequently these values are part and parcel of any true science and, more basically, of rational thought, and they apply not only in science, but in every area of one's life. The Educational Policies Commission, then, is advocating science education not only for the production of more scientists, but for the development of individuals whose approach to life is that of persons who think creatively and critically (cf. Resnick, 1987). Thus, the central goal of science teaching at virtually any level is to foster this type of thought. To teach science effectively, teachers need to know this.

WHAT IS THE NATURE OF SCIENTIFIC KNOWLEDGE?

Cognitive science distinguishes two fundamental types of knowledge—declarative and procedural. The distinction is essentially between *knowing that* (e.g., I know that animals inhale oxygen and expel carbon dioxide) and *knowing how* (I know how to perform a controlled experiment). Anderson (1980) defines declarative knowledge and procedural knowledge in the following way: "Declarative knowledge comprises the facts that we know; procedural knowledge comprises the skills we know how to perform" (p. 222).

The Nature of Declarative Knowledge

The declarative aspects of science include a series of concepts of various degrees of complexity, abstractness, and importance. These are generally seen as the primary units of instruction. A concept has been formed whenever two or more distinguishable objects, events, or situations have been grouped or classified together and set apart from other objects, events, or situations on the basis of some common feature, form, or properties of both (after Bourne, 1966, p. 2). A concept can be considered to be a unit of thought that exists in a person's mind.

Concepts do not stand alone. Rather, they form meaningful systems, often with hierarchical structures of subordinate and superordinate concepts (cf. Ausubel, 1963; Bruner, 1963; Gagné, 1970; Lawson, 1958; Novak, Gowin, & Johansen, 1983). An example of such a conceptual system is the ecosystem from ecological theory. It includes concepts such as trees, sunlight, frogs, producers, consumers, food webs, community, environmental factors, and ecosystem itself. The basic units of trees, frogs, sunlight, and so on are at the bottom, and the concept of ecosystem is at the top. All the other concepts are integrated under the term *ecosystem.*

There are, I believe, at least three major ways in which meaning can be derived. Hence, there are three major types of concepts.

- Concepts by *apprehension*, where the meaning is derived directly from the internal or external environment, for example, hot-cold, dull-sharp, green, red, blue, hunger, thirst;
- *Descriptive* concepts, where the meaning is derived from postulation and tested through direct interaction with the "world out there," such as table, chair, on top of, next to, before, playing, running, eating;
- *Theoretical* concepts, where the meaning is derived from postulation but is tested only indirectly through the deduced consequences of the postulated entities, for instance, genes, atoms, electrons, ghosts.

Conceptual *systems* are of two types, descriptive and theoretical. A descriptive conceptual system is composed of concepts by apprehension and description only. A theoretical system is composed of concepts by apprehension, description, and theory. Examples of descriptive conceptual systems are human anatomy, early Greek cosmology, taxonomies, and games such as chess, football, and baseball. Each of these systems consists of concepts about perceivable objects and the interactions of these objects.

Examples of theoretical conceptual systems are atomic-molecular theory, Mendelian genetics, Darwin's theory of evolution through natural selection, and so on. In atomic-molecular theory, the atoms and molecules were imagined to exist and to have certain properties and behaviors, none of which could be observed. However, by assigning certain properties to atoms, observable chemical changes could be explained. In the same manner, Mendel imagined genes to exist in pairs, separated at the time of gamete formation, combined when egg and sperm united, and determining the course of development of the embryo. By assuming the gene to exist and to have certain properties and behavior, Mendel could explain the observable results from crosses of plants and animals.

The Nature of Procedural Knowledge

Knowledge about procedures used to generate declarative knowledge is called procedural knowledge. Reasoning patterns (cognitive strategies) such as combinatorial reasoning (the generation of combinations of alternative hypotheses), the control of variables (experimenting in a way that varies only one independent variable), and correlational reasoning (comparing ratios of confirming with disconfirming events) are components of procedural knowledge.

Because of the central importance of procedural knowledge in science and in creative and critical thinking in general, psychologists and educators alike have attempted to identify its components with as much precision as possible. One of the early attempts to do so contained eight central skills and several subskills (Burmester, 1952). Some of these skills are creative, while others are critical. Still others involve both creative and critical aspects of scientific thinking.

Skilled performance includes knowing what to do, when to do it, and how to do it. In other words, being skilled at something involves knowing a set of procedures, knowing when to apply those procedures, and being proficient at executing those procedures. Table 2.1 lists seven general skills and their subskills.

TABLE 2.1 General Creative and Critical Thinking Skills

1.00 Skill in accurately describing nature.
     1.10 Skill in describing objects in terms of observable characteristics.
     1.20 Skill in seriating objects in terms of observable characteristics.
     1.30 Skill in classifying objects in terms of observable characteristics.
     1.40 Skill in describing, seriating, classifying, and measuring objects in terms of variables such as amount, length, area, weight, volume, and density.
     1.50 Skill in identifying variable and constant characteristics of groups of objects.
         1.51 Skill in identifying continuous and discontinuous variable characteristics and naming specific values of those characteristics.
         1.52 Skill in measuring, recording, and graphing the frequency of occurrence of certain values of characteristics in a sample of objects.
         1.53 Skill in determining the average, median, and modal values of the frequency distribution in 1.52 above.
     1.60 Skill in recognizing the difference between a sample and a population and identifying ways of obtaining a random (unbiased) sample.
         1.61 Skill in making predictions concerning the probability of occurrence of specific population characteristics based on the frequency of occurrence of those characteristics in a random sample.

(continues)

Table 2.1 continued

2.00 Skill in sensing and stating causal questions about nature.

    2.10 Skill in recognizing a causal question from observation of nature or in the context of a paragraph or an article.

    2.20 Skill in distinguishing between an observation and a question.

    2.30 Skill in recognizing a question even when it is stated in expository form rather than in interrogatory form.

    2.40 Skill in distinguishing a question from a possible answer to a question (hypothesis) even when the hypothesis is presented in interrogatory form.

    2.50 Skill in distinguishing between descriptive and causal questions.

3.00 Skill in recognizing, generating, and stating alternative hypotheses (causal explanations) and theories.

    3.10 Skill in distinguishing an hypothesis from a question.

    3.20 Skill in differentiating between a statement that describes an observation or generalizes from the observation and a statement that is an hypothesis (causal explanation) for the observation.

    3.30 Skill in recognizing the tentativeness of an hypothesis or theory.

    3.40 Skill in distinguishing between a tentative explanation for a phenomenon (hypothesis) and a term used merely to label the phenomenon.

    3.50 Skill in systematically generating all possible combinations of generated hypotheses.

4.00 Skill in generating and stating logical predictions based on the assumed truth of hypotheses and imagined experimental conditions.

    4.10 Skill in differentiating between hypotheses and predictions.

5.00 Skill in planning and conducting controlled experiments to test alternative hypotheses.

    5.10 Skill in selecting reasonable alternative hypotheses to test.

    5.20 Skill in differentiating between an uncontrolled observation and an experiment involving controls.

    5.30 Skill in recognizing that only one independent factor in an experiment should be variable.

        5.31 Skill in recognizing the independent variable factor and the dependent variable factor(s).

        5.32 Skill in recognizing the factors being held constant in the partial controls.

    5.40 Skill in recognizing experimental and technical problems inherent in experimental designs.

    5.50 Skill in criticizing faulty experiments when:

(continues)

Table 2.1 continued

5.51 The experimental design was such that it could not yield an answer to the question.

5.52 The experiment was not designed to test the specific hypotheses stated.

5.53 The method of collecting the data was unreliable.

5.54 The data were not accurate.

5.55 The data were insufficient in number.

5.56 Proper controls were not included.

6.00 Skill in collecting, organizing, and analyzing relevant experimental and correlational data.

6.10 Skill in recognizing the existence of errors in measurement.

6.20 Skill in recognizing when the precision of measurement given is warranted by the nature of the question.

6.30 Skill in organizing and analyzing data.

6.31 Skill in constructing tables and frequency graphs.

6.32 Skill in measuring, recording, and graphing the values of two variables on a single graph.

6.33 Skill in constructing a contingency table of discontinuous variables.

6.40 Skill in seeing elements in common to several items of data.

6.50 Skill in recognizing prevailing tendencies and trends in data and to extrapolate and interpolate from them.

6.60 Skill in applying quantitative notions of probability, proportion, percent, and correlation to natural phenomena; recognizing when variables are related additively or multiplicatively; and setting up simple quantitative equations describing these relationships.

6.61 Skill in recognizing direct, inverse, or no relationship between variables.

6.62 Skill in recognizing that when two things vary together, the relationship may be coincidental, not causal.

6.63 Skill in recognizing additional evidence needed to establish cause and effect (see 6.62 above).

7.00 Skill in drawing and applying reasonable conclusions.

7.10 Skill in evaluating relevancy of data and drawing conclusions through a comparison of actual results with predicted results.

7.11 Skill in differentiating between direct and indirect evidence.

7.12 Skill in recognizing data that are unrelated to the hypotheses.

7.13 Skill in recognizing data that support an hypothesis.

7.14 Skill in recognizing data that do not support an hypothesis.

7.15 Skill in combining both supportive and contradicting evidence from a variety of sources to weigh the likely truth or falsity of hypotheses.

(continues)

Table 2.1 continued

    7.16 Skill in postponing judgment if no evidence or insufficient evidence exists.

    7.17 Skill in recognizing the tentativeness inherent in all scientific conclusions.

7.20 Skill in applying conclusions to new situations.

    7.21 Skill in refraining from applying conclusions to new situations that are not closely analogous to the experimental situation.

    7.22 Skill in being aware of the tentativeness of conclusions about new situations even when there is a close parallel between the two situations.

    7.23 Skill in recognizing the assumptions that must be made in applying a conclusion to a new situation.

These skills function in concert as thinking human beings learn about the world. They are learning tools essential for success and even for survival. Hence, a teacher who helps students improve their use of these creative and critical thinking skills has helped them become more intelligent and assisted them in learning how to learn. To teach science effectively, teachers need to understand the distinction between declarative and procedural knowledge, to have acquired knowledge of many scientific theories, and to have developed skill in using scientific procedures.

HOW DO SCIENTISTS ACQUIRE CONCEPTUAL KNOWLEDGE?

The Constructive Process

To acquire a sense of how the formation of descriptive concepts takes place, consider the drawings in Figure 2.1. The first row of Figure 2.1 contains five creatures called Mellinarks (Elementary Science Study, 1974). None of the creatures in the second row are Mellinarks. From this information try to decide which of the creatures in the third row are Mellinarks.

Deciding which of the creatures in row three are Mellinarks is a problem of descriptive concept formation. If you correctly identified the first, second, and sixth figures as Mellinarks, you have formed a concept for the term *Mellinark*. How did you do it? Outdated theories of abstraction (Locke, 1690/1924; Hume, 1739/1896) would claim that you *induced* a set of specific

Mellinarks

All of these are Mellinarks.

None of these is a Mellinark .

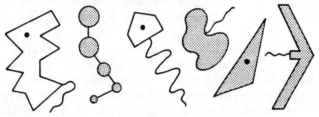

Which of these are Mellinarks ?

FIGURE 2.1: **Imaginary creatures called Mellinarks (from Elementary Science Study, 1974).**

characteristics and generalized it to other instances. Modern theories, on the other hand, emphasize the importance of hypothesis generation and the predictive nature of concept formation (e.g., Bolton, 1977; Holland, Holyoak, Nisbett, & Thagard, 1986; Mayer, 1983).

Let us consider a solution employing hypothesis generation and testing. A glance at row one reveals several features of the Mellinarks. They have tails. They contain one large dot and several smaller dots. They have an enclosed cell-like membrane that may have curved or straight sides. Which of these features are crucial? The nature of the membrane (curved or straight) can be eliminated immediately as both membrane types exist in row one. The importance of the other three features can be tested through a series of hypotheses; that is, Mellinarks could have

1. One large dot only
2. Several small dots only
3. One tail only
4. One large dot and several small dots
5. One large dot and one tail
6. Several small dots and one tail
7. One large dot and several small dots and one tail

Hypothesis 1 would lead one to predict that all the creatures in row one and none of the creatures in row two would contain one large dot. Since this is not the case, the prediction is disconfirmed and the hypothesis is also disconfirmed. The same pattern of hypothetico-deductive reasoning leads one to disconfirm hypotheses 2 through 6 as well, leaving hypothesis 7, that Mellinarks are defined by the presence of all three features. Thus only the first, second, and sixth creatures in row three are Mellinarks. Concept formation, seen in this light, is not viewed as a purely abstract process but rests on the ability to generate and test hypotheses. In this sense one's conceptual knowledge depends on one's procedural knowledge. As one gains skill in using these hypothetico-deductive procedures, concept formation becomes easier. More will be said about this later when we discuss the development of procedural knowledge.

The Role of Chunking in Higher-Order Concept Formation

The human mind at any one moment is able to handle only a limited amount of information. Miller (1956) introduced the term *chunk* to refer to the discrete units of information that could be held in working memory and transformed or integrated. He suggested that the maximum number of these discrete chunks was approximately seven.

Clearly, however, we all form concepts that contain far more information than seven units. The term *ecosystem*, as mentioned, subsumes a far greater number of discrete units or chunks than seven. Further, ecosystem itself is a concept; thus it probably occupies only one chunk in conscious memory. This implies that a mental process must occur in which previously unrelated parts—that is, chunks of information—are assembled into higher-order chunks (Simon, 1974).

Higher-order concept formation (chunking) reduces the load on mental capacity and simultaneously opens up additional mental capacity that can then be occupied by additional concepts. This in turn allows one to form still more complex and inclusive concepts (i.e., concepts that subsume greater numbers of subordinate concepts). To turn back to our initial example, once we know what a Mellinark is we no longer have to refer to Mellinarks as "creatures within an enclosed membrane that may be curved or straight, with one large dot and several smaller dots inside and one tail." Use of the term *Mellinark* to subsume all of this information greatly facilitates thinking and communication when all communicating parties have acquired the concept (see Ausubel, 1963, and Ausubel, Novak, & Hanesian, 1968, for details of the subsumption process).

How Theoretical Concepts Are Formed

The preceding discussion of descriptive concept formation leaves two important issues unresolved. How does concept formation take place when the defining attributes are not directly perceptible, that is, when the concept in question is a theoretical one? And what takes place when the theoretical concept to be acquired contradicts a previously acquired concept? Let us consider the process of conceptual change first. How are inappropriate theoretical concepts modified or discarded in favor of more appropriate theoretical concepts?

Conceptual change. To get a handle on this problem, Gruber and Barrett (1974) analyzed Darwin's thinking during the period 1831 to 1838 when he underwent a conceptual change from a creationist theory of the world to that of an evolutionist. Fortunately for Gruber and Barrett and for us, Darwin left, in copious diaries, a record of much of his thinking. Figure 2.2 highlights the major changes in his theoretical conceptual system during this time.

Darwin's theory in 1831 has been described by Gruber and Barrett (1974) as one in which the creator made an organic world (*O*) and a physical world (*P*). In this view, the organic world was perfectly adapted to the physical world (see part a of Figure 2.2). This view of the world served Darwin well and his thoughts and behavior were consistent with this view. Although Charles Darwin was a creationist in 1831, he was aware of evolutionary views. Nevertheless, on that day in 1831, when he boarded the H.M.S. Beagle as the ship's naturalist, Darwin was seeking an adventure—not a theory of evolution.

During the first two years of the voyage on the *Beagle*, Darwin read Charles Lyell's two-volume work, *Principles of Geology*, and found in it some persuasive ideas about the modification of the physical environment through time. At each new place Darwin visited, he found examples and important extensions of Lyell's ideas. Darwin was becoming increasingly convinced that the physical world was not static—that it changed through time. This new conception of the physical world stood in opposition to his earlier beliefs and created a serious contradiction. If the organic world and the physical world are perfectly adapted, and the physical world changes, then the organic world must also change. This, of course, is the logical extension of the argument. Its conclusion, however, was the opposite of Darwin's original theory that organisms did not evolve.

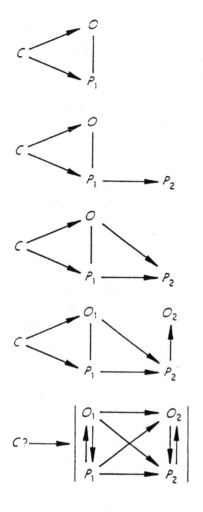

a. 1832 and before: The creator (C) made an organic world (O) and a physical world (P): O was perfectly adapted to P. Mental equilibrium exists.

b. 1832-1834: The physical world undergoes continuous change, governed by natural forces as summarized in Lyell's *Principles of Geology*. A logical contradiction is implied which induces a state of disequilibrium.

c. 1835: Activities of organisms contribute to changes in the physical world (e.g., coral reefs). Disequilibrium persists.

d. 1836-1837: Changes in the physical world imply changes in the organic world if adaptation is to be maintained; the direct action of the physical environment "induces" organic adaptations. Equilibrium is partially restored.

e. 1838 and after: The physical and organic worlds continuously interact and induce reciprocal changes to maintain adaptations. The role of the creator is unclear. He may have set the system into existence yet stands outside. Mental equilibrium is restored at a higher more complex plane.

FIGURE 2.2: Charles Darwin's changing world view from 1832 to 1838 as an example of mental equilibration (after Gruber & Barrett, 1974).

This contradiction of views put Darwin into what Piaget has called a state of mental *disequilibrium*, because Darwin did not immediately accept the logic of this situation and conclude that organisms must also change. In fact, it was not until 1837, after his return to England, that he converted to the idea of evolution of species (Green, 1958). It seems unlikely that it would have required this amount of time for Darwin to assimilate the logic of the situation, but the fact is that in the 2,000 pages of geological and biological notes made during the voyage, there is very little discussion of the evolution of organisms. What little there is opposes the idea.

Precisely how and why Darwin changed his view is, of course, not known. Figure 2.2, however, appears to be a fairly accurate summary of his changing world view. Smith and Millman (1987) have also carefully examined Darwin's notebook and have characterized Darwin's mind as in a state of "exploratory thinking," meaning that rather than accepting any particular theory, Darwin was considering various views (alternative hypotheses) to explain the situation as he saw it. If we assume that the weight of accumulating evidence forced a rejection of creationism, then this exploratory thinking was aimed primarily at explaining evolution. Part e of Figure 2.2 thus represents the partial restoration of mental equilibrium because it eliminates the contradiction implied in part b.

Piaget refers to the process of moving from a mental state of equilibrium to disequilibrium and back to equilibrium as *equilibration,* an initial answer to the question, "How does conceptual change occur?" The necessary conditions for equilibration appear to be: (1) data that are inconsistent with prior ways of thinking, (2) the presence of alternative conceptions/hypotheses (the hypothesis of evolution), and (3) sufficient time, motivation, and thinking skills to compare the alternative hypotheses and their predicted consequences with the evidence (cf. Anderson & Smith, 1986; Hewson & Hewson, 1984; Lawson & Thompson, 1988; Posner, Strike, Hewson, & Gertzog, 1982).

The use of analogy. Once Darwin had accepted the alternative hypothesis that organisms evolve, the question, "How?" immediately arose. According to the record (e.g., Green, 1958; Gruber & Barrett, 1974; Smith & Millman, 1987), Darwin's search for a theory to explain the evolution of organisms involved a number of initially unsuccessful trials and a good deal of groping until September 1838, when a key event occurred. Darwin read Thomas Malthus' (1798) *An Essay on the Principle of Population.* Darwin wrote, "I came to the conclusion that selection was the principle of change from the study of domesticated productions; and then reading Malthus, I saw at once how to apply this principle" (Green, 1958, pp. 257-258). Darwin saw in Malthus' writing a key idea that he could borrow and use to explain evolution. That key idea was that artificial selection of domesticated plants and animals was *analogous* to what presumably occurs in nature and could account for a change or evolution of species. As Gruber and Barrett (1974) point out, Darwin had read Malthus before but it was not until this reading that he became conscious of the import of the artificial selection process. But once it had been assimilated,

Darwin turned to the task of marshalling the evidence favoring his theory of descent with modification.

The example of Darwin's use of artificial selection suggests that analogy plays a central role in theoretical concept formation. The pattern that allowed Darwin to make sense of his data was analogous to the pattern inherent in the process of artificial selection. Hanson (1958) refers to this process of borrowing old ideas and applying them to new situations as *abduction*. Others have referred to the process as analogical reasoning (Karplus, 1979; Lawson & Lawson, 1979) or analogical transfer (Holland, Holyoak, Nisbett, & Thagard, 1986).

Thus, one answer to the question of how theoretical concepts are formed is that they are formed by applying a previously acquired pattern from the world of observable objects and events to explain unobservable events. The scientist must discover the analogy for him- or herself, but the student in the classroom can be assisted by the teacher.

The General Pattern of Concept Formation and Conceptual Change

Upon reflection we can identify a general pattern that exists in both processes of concept formation and conceptual change. What we are considering in both cases is not really two different processes but two ends of the same continuum. As Piaget reminds us, every act of assimilation to a cognitive structure is accompanied by some accommodation of that structure. No two experiences are ever identical, and therefore pure assimilation is not possible. Likewise, pure accommodation presumably does not take place because that would imply that a cognitive reorganization has taken place without any input from the environment. Thus, at the concept formation end of the continuum, we have the dominance of assimilation over accommodation, and at the conceptual change end of the continuum, we have the dominance of accommodation, over assimilation.

The general pattern is shown in Figure 2.3. Box A represents the question prompted by some experience (e.g., what is a Mellinark? How did the diversity of species arise?). Box B represents alternative hypotheses taken either from the perceptible features of the problem situations (induction) or from analogical reasoning (abduction) to other situations. The use of analogical reasoning is an important component of creative thinking, for the subconscious mind can play an important role in generating novel ideas.

To test alternative hypotheses some experimental and/or correlational situation must be imagined that allows the deduction of the ideas' logical consequences (Box C). The logical consequences (predictions) are then compared with the actual results of the test, which are represented by Box D. If the predicted results and the actual results are essentially the same, then

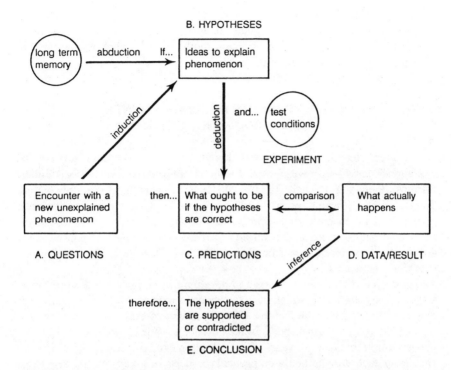

FIGURE 2.3: The basic pattern of hypothetico-deductive thinking.

support for the hypothesis has been obtained. If not, the hypothesis has been weakened and others should be generated and tested until a reasonable agreement is obtained. Note how the words *if . . . then . . .* and *therefore* in Figure 2.3 tie the elements of the hypothetico-deductive process together into a reasonable argument for or against particular hypotheses or alternatives.

The acquisition of declarative knowledge is very much a constructive process that makes either implicit or explicit use of procedural knowledge. Of course students can memorize declarative knowledge, but such learning will not improve procedural knowledge. To teach science effectively teachers need to know how to help students participate in the constructive process, because doing so improves meaningfulness and retention of the declarative knowledge and increases consciousness and generalizability of the procedural knowledge. Although Anderson's Ms. Copeland showed an overreliance on meaningless (to students) textbook definitions (e.g., "Food refers to materials that contain energy . . .") and an underreliance on actual experience (e.g., she should have had the students actually grow plants under various conditions to test their alternative ideas about how plants obtain food), she nevertheless attempted to have her students participate in the constructive process.

HOW CAN STUDENTS DEVELOP SCIENTIFIC PROCEDURAL KNOWLEDGE?

A great deal has been written about the development of procedural/operational knowledge within the Piagetian tradition (e.g., Collea, Fuller, Karplus, Paldy, & Renner, 1975; Collette & Chiappetta, 1986; Inhelder & Piaget, 1958; Karplus et al., 1977). Piaget's stages of sensory-motor, preoperational, concrete operations, and formal operations are well known. Little argument exists over the validity of the notion of levels or phases in the development of procedural knowledge, but considerable controversy exists regarding the details.

In Piaget's theory the first stage of development is called the sensory-motor stage. During this stage, which lasts for about 18 months, children acquire such practical knowledge as the fact that objects continue to exist even when they are out of view (object permanence). In the next stage, called preoperational, which persists until around seven years of age, children exhibit extreme egocentricism and center their attention only on particular aspects of given objects, events, or situations. The major achievement during this stage is the acquisition of language.

At about age 7, children develop the ability to perform mental experiments; they can assimilate data from concrete experiences and arrange and rearrange the data in their heads. In other words, older children have a much greater mobility of thought than younger children. As Piaget explains this stage, "The operations involved . . . are called 'concrete' because they relate directly to objects and not yet to verbally stated hypotheses" (Piaget & Inhelder, 1969, p. 100).

The potential for the development of what Piaget calls *formal operational* thought presumably develops between 11 and 15 years of age. Piaget chose this name for his highest stage of thought because he believed thinking patterns were isomorphic with rules of formal propositional logic (cf. Piaget, 1957). This position is perhaps the most problematic in Piaget's theory. A long line of research indicates clearly that, although advances in reasoning performance do occur during adolescence, no one, even professional logicians, reasons with logical rules divorced from subject matter (Griggs, 1983; Lehman, Lempert, & Nisbett, 1988; Nisbett, Fong, Lehman, & Cheng, 1987; Wason & Johnson-Laird, 1972).

Reflectivity and the Internalization of Patterns of Argumentation

If the acquisition of formal logic does not differentiate the child's thinking from the adolescent's, what does? Lawson, Lawson, and Lawson (1984) hypothesized that the important shift is toward greater reflectivity due to adolescents' ability to ask questions of themselves, and to reflect on the correctness or incorrectness of answers to those questions in a hypothetico-deductive manner. This internalized hypothetico-deductive behavior involves the acquisition of linguistic skills associated with hypothesis-testing and leads ultimately to the development of hypothesis testing schemes and patterns of argumentation. In other words, prior to adolescence children raise questions and generate answers, yet have no systematic means of asking themselves if their answers are correct. So when left on their own, they generate ideas and for the most part use them for better or for worse. Without reflective ability, children confronted with complex tasks simply choose the most obvious solutions that pop into their heads and conclude that they are correct without consideration of arguments in favor or disfavor.

Kuhn, Amsel, and O'Loughlin (1988) reached a similar conclusion regarding the differences between child-like and adult-like thinking. They identified three key abilities that are acquired by some adults. First is the ability to think *about* a theory rather than thinking *with* a theory. In other words, the reflective adult is able to consider alternative theories and ask which is the most acceptable. On the other hand, the intuitive thinker merely has a "theory" and behaves as though it were true. Chamberlain (1897/1965) referred to these as ruling theories.

Second is the ability to consider the evidence as distinct from the theories themselves. For the child, evidence and theory are indistinguishable. In our experience perhaps the most difficult distinction to be made in the classroom is that between the words *hypothesis, prediction,* and *evidence* (Lawson, Lawson, & Lawson, 1984). Presumably this is because the words are essentially meaningless if one has never before tried to decide between two or more alternative explanations and thus has never before considered the role played by predictions and evidence. Third is the ability to set aside one's own acceptance (or rejection) of a theory in order to evaluate it in light of its predictions and the evidence.

Lawson, Lawson, and Lawson (1984) hypothesized that the ability to reflect on the correctness of one's theories arises as a consequence of the internalization of patterns of external argumentation that occurs with others when alternative theories are proposed. This hypothesis appears to be in essential agreement with Piaget's earlier thinking. Piaget (1928) set forth the hypothesis that the development of advanced reasoning occurred as a consequence of "the shock of our thoughts coming into contact with others, which produces doubt and the desire to prove" (p. 204). Piaget went on to state

> The social need to share the thought of others and to communicate our own
> with success is at the root of our need for verification. Proof is the outcome of
> argument. . . . Argument is therefore, the backbone of verification. Logical
> reasoning is an argument which we have with ourselves, and which produces
> internally the features of a real argument. (p. 204)

In other words, the growing awareness of and ability to use hypothetico-deductive thought during adolescence (defined as the ability to ask questions of oneself, generate tentative answers, deduce predictions based on those answers, and then sort through the available evidence to verify or reject those tentative answers, all inside one's own head), occurs as a consequence of engaging in arguments with other persons and listening to arguments of others in which alternative propositions (theories) are put forward and accepted or rejected on the basis of evidence and reason as opposed to authority or emotion.

No distinct age norms are suggested for passing from one level of thinking to the next, and I see no biological or psychological reason why children as young as, say, eight, could not reflect on their own thoughts, given an environment in which such reflective behavior was encouraged. Of course this represents just a beginning, and such children would still require considerably more time and experience to internalize the language of argumentation and develop the associated hypothesis-testing schemes. A dogmatic environment in which the relative merits of ideas are not discussed and rules are strictly and unthinkingly enforced would most likely retard the development of hypothetico-deductive thought.

Intuitive and Reflective Thought

This view of the development of procedural knowledge suggests that the terms *intuitive* and *reflective thought* are more descriptive of the intellectual changes that take place during adolescence than Piaget's terms *concrete* and *formal thought*. The child-like thinker is not conscious of the hypothetico-deductive nature of his or her thought processes, and therefore thinking is dominated by context-dependent cues and intuitions. Adult-like thinkers, on the other hand, have become conscious of their own thought patterns and have internalized powerful patterns of argumentation that allow conscious reflection on the adequacy or inadequacy of ideas prior to action. Reflective thinking is not based on formal logic, as Piaget claimed, but on alternative ideas, predictions, evidence, and arguments, all mediated by language.

Notice that we have argued that the reflective thinker has *internalized* important patterns of argumentation that the intuitive thinker has not. This raises the question of just how this internalization takes place. According to Piaget (1976) a process called *reflective abstraction* is involved in the development of procedural knowledge. Reflective abstraction involves the progression from spontaneous actions to verbally mediated rules that guide behavior. Reflective abstraction occurs only when people are prompted to reflect on their actions. The cause of this reflection is contradiction either by the physical environment or verbally by other people. The result of reflective abstraction is not only more accurate declarative knowledge but also greater skill in the procedures used to gain that knowledge. To teach science effectively, teachers need to know how to provoke students to reflect on the status of their own declarative and procedural knowledge.

WHAT TEACHING METHODS BEST FACILITATE SCIENTIFIC KNOWLEDGE ACQUISITION?

Essential Elements of Instruction

The previous discussion suggests that the following elements must be included in lessons designed to improve both declarative and procedural knowledge:

1. Questions should be raised or problems should be posed that require students to act based on prior beliefs (concepts and conceptual systems) and/or prior procedures.
2. Those actions must lead to results that are ambiguous and/or can be challenged or contradicted. This forces students to reflect on the prior beliefs and/or procedures used to generate the results.
3. Alternative beliefs and/or more effective procedures should be suggested.
4. Alternative beliefs and/or the more effective procedures should now be utilized to generate new predictions and/or new data to allow either the change of old beliefs or the acquisition of a new belief (concept).

Suppose, for example, that Ms. Copeland began her lessons on photosynthesis by posing this question to her students: What might be the food source for plants? Had she done this, she would have obtained several alternative hypotheses from the students, such as air, soil, water, sunlight, fertilizer, or perhaps the seed itself. She then should have provided the students with materials necessary to test these alternatives and challenged the students to do so. All that is really necessary for students to begin exploring these possibilities is for them to plant several seeds in soil, water them, and put them in the dark. Similar setups should also be prepared but left in the light. The growth of the seeds in the two conditions must then be measured and graphed until the plants in the dark stop growing and die. Had this been done, the students would have been left with the following facts: (1) Plants in light (with soil, air, and water) are green and sturdy and continue to grow, and (2) plants in dark (with soil, air, and water) grow rapidly at first, but are yellow and thin, and eventually droop and die.

What conclusions can be drawn from such a result? First, it is clear that light makes a difference. It is equally clear (from previous experiments) that water is necessary but not sufficient for sustained growth. What about soil? Previous experiments (plants grown without soil) indicate that soil is neither necessary nor sufficient. What about air? Since air was present in both light and dark conditions, all we can say is that air is perhaps necessary but certainly not sufficient for sustained growth. Thus, students using their own procedures and results are able to reflect on the adequacy or inadequacy of their own ideas. The teacher is even able to introduce new terms such as photosynthesis that can be defined in the context of the activity; that is, photosynthesis is the process whereby plants, utilizing the energy of light, are able to sustain life. But what do plants get from photosynthesis that keeps them alive? Once the hypothesis that plants produce food during photosynthesis is generated, it can easily be tested by testing for starch (food) in the leaves of plants in the light and in the dark. The net result of experiences such as these is (1) students become more knowledgeable about nature, (2) they become much better at generating and carrying out procedures used in gaining that knowledge, and (3) their new knowledge (both declarative and procedural) can then be applied in a variety of new situations.

The Learning Cycle

The main thesis thus far is that situations that allow students to examine the adequacy of prior beliefs (conceptions) force them to argue about and test those beliefs. When these beliefs are contradicted, students experience disequilibrium, which in turn provides the opportunity to acquire more appropriate concepts and become increasingly skilled in concept formation (e.g., reasoning patterns/forms of argumentation). The central instructional hypothesis is that learning occurs through a learning cycle that follows the three-phase sequence of (1) exploration, (2) term introduction, and (3) concept application (Science Curriculum Improvement Study, 1973).

During exploration, students often examine a new phenomenon with minimal guidance. The new phenomenon should raise questions or complexities they cannot resolve with their present conceptions or accustomed patterns of reasoning. In other words, it provides the opportunity for students to voice potentially conflicting, or at least partially inadequate, ideas. This can spark debate and analysis of the reasons for their ideas; that analysis can lead to an explicit discussion of ways of testing alternative ideas by making predictions. The results then can lead to rejection of some ideas and retention others, and also allow for a careful examination of the *procedures* used in the process. A key point is that initial exploration allows students to interact with the phenomenon in very personal ways, which can have a profound effect not only on their observational skills but on their hypothesis-generation and testing skills as well.

Three Types of Learning Cycles

Learning cycles can be classified as one of three types—descriptive, empirical-abductive, and hypothetico-deductive. The essential difference among the three is the degree to which students either gather data in a purely descriptive fashion (not guided by explicit hypotheses they wish to test) or initially set out to test alternative hypotheses in a controlled fashion. The three types of learning cycles represent three points along a continuum from descriptive to experimental science. They place differing demands on student initiative, knowledge, and reasoning skill. In terms of student reasoning, descriptive learning cycles generally require only descriptive patterns (e.g., seriation, classification, conservation), while hypothetico-deductive learning cycles demand use of higher-order patterns (e.g., controlling variables, correlational reasoning, hypothetico-deductive reasoning). Empirical-abductive learning cycles are intermediate and entail descriptive reasoning patterns, but generally involve some higher-order patterns as well.

In *descriptive* learning cycles, students discover and describe an empirical pattern within a specific context (exploration). The teacher gives it a name (term introduction), and the pattern is then identified in additional contexts (concept application). This type of learning cycle is called descriptive because the students and teacher describe what they observe without attempting to explain their observations. Descriptive learning cycles answer the question "What?" but do not raise the causal question "Why?"

Descriptive learning cycles help students observe a small part of the world, discover a pattern, name it, and look for the pattern elsewhere. Little or no disequilibrium may result, as students will most likely not have strong expectations of what will be found. Graphing a frequency distribution of the length of a sample of seashells will allow a teacher to introduce the term *normal distribution* but will not provide much argumentation among students. A descriptive learning cycle in skull structure/function allows the teacher to introduce the terms *herbivore, omnivore,* and *carnivore.* It also allows for some argumentation as students put forth and compare ideas about skull structure and possible diets. Yet seldom are possible cause-effect relationships hotly debated.

In *empirical-abductive* learning cycles students again discover and describe an empirical pattern in a specific context (exploration), but go further by generating possible causes of that pattern. This requires the use of analogical reasoning (abduction) to transfer terms and concepts learned in other contexts to this new context (term introduction). The terms may be introduced by students, the teacher, or both. With the teacher's guidance, the students then sift through the data gathered during the exploration phase to see if the hypothesized causes are consistent with those data and other known phenomena (concept application). In other words, observations are made in a descriptive fashion, but this type of learning cycle goes further to generate and initially test a cause(s).

Consider the empirical-abductive (EA) learning cycle called "What Caused the Water to Rise?" It requires students to do more than describe a phenomenon. An explanation is required, which opens the door to a multitude of misconceptions. The resulting arguments and analysis of evidence represent a near-perfect example of how EA learning cycles can be used to promote disequilibrium and the acquisition of conceptual knowledge and development of procedural knowledge.

To start, students invert a cylinder over a candle burning in a pan of water. They observe that the flame soon goes out and water rises into the cylinder. Two causal questions are posed: Why did the flame go out? Why did the water rise? The typical explanation students generate is that the flame used up the oxygen in the cylinder and left a partial vacuum, which "sucked" water in from below. This explanation reveals two misconceptions:

1. Flames destroy matter, thus producing a partial vacuum.
2. Water rises due to a nonexistent force called suction.

Testing these ideas requires hypothetico-deductive reasoning and the isolation and control of variables (see Figure 2.4).

The box on the left represents the key question raised. In this case it is "Why did the water rise?" The subsequent hypotheses, experiments, predictions, results, and conclusions follow the hypothetico-deductive if . . . then . . . and therefore . . . pattern of reasoning and require students to isolate and control independent variables in comparing water rise with one and four candles. As shown, the initial hypothesis leads to a false prediction, and thus must be rejected (reasoning to a contradiction). Students must now generate an alternative hypothesis or hypotheses and start over again until they have a hypothesis that is consistent with the data (i.e., not falsified).

The third type of learning cycle, *hypothetico-deductive*, is initiated with a causal question for which the students are asked to generate alternative explanations. Student time is then devoted to deducing the logical consequences of these explanations and explicitly designing and conducting experiments to test them (exploration). The analysis of experimental results allows for some hypotheses to be rejected and some to be retained and for terms to be introduced (term introduction). Finally the relevant concepts and reasoning patterns may be applied in other situations at a later time (concept application). The explicit generation and testing of alternative hypotheses through a comparison of logical deductions with empirical results is required in this type of learning cycle.

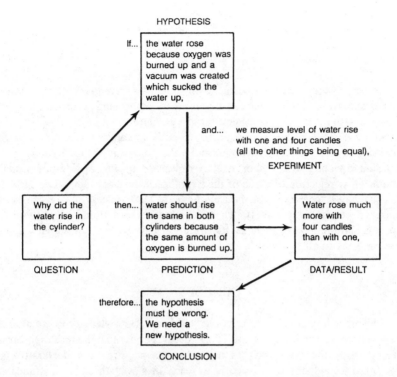

FIGURE 2.4: Hypothetico-deductive reasoning with isolation and control of variables.

Hypothetico-deductive cycles call for the immediate and explicit statement of alternative hypotheses to explain a phenomenon. In brief, a causal question is raised and students must explicitly generate alternative hypotheses. These in turn must be tested through the deduction of predicted consequences and experimentation. This places a heavy burden on student initiative and thinking skills.

Consider, for example, the question of water rise in plants. Objects are attracted toward the center of the earth by a force called gravity, yet water rises in tall trees to the uppermost leaves to allow photosynthesis to take place. What causes the water to rise in spite of the downward gravitational force? The following alternative hypotheses were generated in a recent biology lab:

1. Water evaporates from the leaves to create a vacuum that sucks water up.
2. Roots squeeze to push water up through one-way valves in the stem tubes.

3. Capillary action of water pulls it up like water soaking up in a paper towel.
4. Osmosis pulls water up.

Of course equipment limitations keep some ideas from being tested, but the "leaf evaporation" hypothesis can be tested by comparing water rise in plants with and without leaves. This requires the reasoning patterns of isolation and control of variables. The "root squeeze" hypothesis can be tested by comparing water rise in plants with and without roots; the "one-way valve" hypothesis can be tested by comparing water rise in right-side-up and upside-down stems. Results allow rejection of some of the hypotheses and not others. The survivors are considered "correct," for the time being at least, just as in "real" science, which of course is precisely what the students are doing. Following the experimentation, terms such as transpiration can be introduced and applied elsewhere, as in all types of learning cycles.

CONCLUSION

The preceding pages have presented a theory of knowledge construction and a compatible instructional theory. These theories argue that the most appropriate way, perhaps the only way, to help students acquire both declarative and procedural knowledge of science is to teach in a way that allows students to reveal their prior conceptions and test them in an atmosphere in which ideas are openly generated, debated, and tested, with the means of testing becoming an explicit focus of classroom attention. Correct use of the learning cycle teaching method allows this to happen. A considerable amount of research has been conducted that supports the notion that correct use of learning cycles in the science classroom is highly effective in helping students obtain the stated objectives.

To effectively teach science using these learning cycles, teachers need to know

- That science is a creative, hypothetico-deductive enterprise;
- That the central objective of teaching science is to help students develop creative and critical thinking skills;
- The major theories that constitute the structure of the disciplines within science;
- How to think scientifically;
- How scientific knowledge (both declarative and procedural) is acquired by students; and
- How to use learning cycles to guide students as they construct their own scientific knowledge.

Of course, it would help immensely if education policy makers knew this as well.

REFERENCES

Anderson, C. W., & Smith, E. R. (1986). Teaching science. In V. Richardson-Koehler (Ed.), *Educators' handbook: A research perspective* (pp. 84-111). New York: Longman.

Anderson, J. R. (1980). *Cognitive psychology and its implications.* San Francisco: W. H. Freeman.

Ausubel, D. P. (1963). *The psychology of meaningful verbal learning.* New York: Grune & Stratton.

Ausubel, D. P., Novak, J. D., & Hanesian, H. (1968). *Educational psychology: A cognitive view* (2nd ed.). New York: Holt, Rinehart and Winston.

Bolton, N. (1977). *Concept formation.* Oxford: Pergamon.

Bourne, L. E. (1966). *Human conceptual behavior.* Boston: Allyn & Bacon.

Bruner, J. S. (1963). *The process of education.* Cambridge, MA: Harvard University Press.

Burmester, M. A. (1952). Behavior involved in critical aspects of scientific thinking. *Science Education, 36*(5), 259-263.

Chamberlain, T. C. (1965). The method of multiple working hypotheses. *Science, 148,* 754-759. (Original work published 1897)

Collea, F. P., Fuller, R. G., Karplus, R., Paldy, L. G. & Renner, J. W. (1975). *Physics teaching and the development of reasoning.* Stony Brook, NY: American Association of Physics Teachers.

Collette, A. T., & Chiappetta, E. L. (1986). *Science instruction in the middle and secondary schools.* Columbus, OH: Merrill.

Educational Policies Commission. (1961). *The central purpose of American education.* Washington, DC: National Education Association of the United States.

Educational Policies Commission. (1966). *Education and the spirit of science.* Washington, DC: National Education Association of the United States.

Elementary Science Study. (1974). *Attribute games and problems.* New York: McGraw-Hill.

Gagné, R. (1970) *The conditions of learning* (2nd ed.). New York: Holt, Rinehart and Winston.

Green, J. C. (1958). *The death of Adam.* Ames: Iowa State University Press.

Griggs, R. A. (1983). The role of problem content in the selection task and in the THOG problem. In J. St. B. T. Evans (Ed.), *Thinking and reasoning: Psychological approaches* (pp. 16-43). London: Routledge & Kegan Paul.

Gruber, H. E., & Barrett, P. H. (1974). *Darwin on man.* New York: Dutton.

Hanson, N. R. (1958). *Patterns of discovery.* Cambridge: Cambridge University Press.

Hewson, P. W., & Hewson, M. G. A. (1984). The role of conceptual conflict in conceptual change and the design of science instruction. *Instructional Science, 13,* 1-13.

Holland, J., Holyoak, K., Nisbett, R., & Thagard, P. (1986). *Induction: Processes of inference, learning, and discovery.* Cambridge, MA: MIT Press.

Hume, P. (1896). *A treatise of human nature*. Oxford: Clarendon. (Original work published 1739)

Hurd, P. B., Bybee, R. W., Kahle, J. B., & Yager, R. E. (1980). Biology education in secondary schools of the United States. *American Biology Teacher*, 42(7), 388-410.

Inhelder, B., & Piaget, J. (1958). *The growth of logical thinking from childhood to adolescence*. New York: Basic Books.

Karplus, R. (1979). Teaching for the development of reasoning. In A. E. Lawson (Ed.), *1980 AETS Yearbook: The psychology of teaching for thinking and creativity* (pp. 150-173). Columbus, OH: ERIC/SMEAC.

Karplus, R., Lawson, A. E., Wollman, W., Appel, M., Bernoff, R., Howe, A., Rusch, J. J., & Sullivan, F. (1977). *Science teaching and the development of reasoning: A workshop*. Berkeley: Regents of the University of California.

Kuhn, D., Amsel, E., & O'Loughlin, M. (1988). *The development of scientific thinking skills*. San Diego: Academic Press.

Lawson, A. E. (1988). The acquisition of biological knowledge during childhood: Cognitive conflict or tabula rasa? *Journal of Research in Science Teaching*, 25(3), 185-199.

Lawson, A. E., Abraham, M. R., & Renner, J. W. (1989). *A theory of instruction: Using the learning cycle to teach science concepts and thinking skills*. Cincinnati, OH: National Association for Research in Science Teaching.

Lawson, A. E., & Lawson, C. A. (1979). A theory of teaching for conceptual understanding, rational thought and creativity. In A. E. Lawson (Ed.), *1980 AETS Yearbook: The psychology of teaching for thinking and creativity* (pp. 104-149). Columbus, OH: ERIC/SMEAC.

Lawson, A. E., Lawson, D. I., & Lawson, C. A. (1984). Proportional reasoning and the linguistic abilities required for hypothetico-deductive reasoning. *Journal of Research in Science Teaching*, 21(2), 119-131.

Lawson, A. E., & Thompson, L. D. (1988). Formal reasoning ability and misconceptions concerning genetics and natural selection. *Journal of Research in Science Teaching*, 25(9), 733-746.

Lawson, C. A. (1958). *Language, thought, and the human mind*. East Lansing: Michigan State University Press.

Lehman, D. R., Lempert, R. O., & Nisbett, R. E. (1988). The effects of graduate training on reasoning. *American Psychologist*, 43(6), 431-442.

Locke, J. (1924). *Essay on the human understanding*. Oxford: Clarendon. (Original work published 1690)

Lyell, C. (1830). *Principles of geology* (4th ed.). London: J. Murray.

Malthus, T. (1826). *An essay on the principle of population* (6th ed.) London: J. Murray.

Mayer, R. E. (1983). *Thinking, problem solving, cognition*. New York: Freeman.

Miller, G. A. (1956). The magical number seven, plus or minus two: Some limits on our capacity for processing information. *The Psychological Review*, 63(2), 81-97.

Nisbett, R. E., Fong, G. T., Lehman, D. R., & Cheng, P. W. (1987). Teaching reasoning. *Science*, 238, 625-631.

Novak, J. D., Gowin, D. W., & Johansen, G. T. (1983). The use of concept mapping and knowledge vee mapping with junior high school science students. *Science Education*, 67(5), 625-645.

Piaget, J. (1928). *Judgment and reasoning in the child*. Paterson, NJ: Littlefield Adams.

Piaget, J. (1957). *Logic and psychology*. New York: Basic Books.

Piaget, J. (1976). *The grasp of consciousness*. Cambridge, MA: Harvard University Press.

Piaget, J., & Inhelder, B. (1969). *The psychology of the child*. New York: Basic Books.

Posner, G. J., Strike, K. A., Hewson, P. W., & Gertzog, W. A. (1982). Accommodation of a scientific conception: Toward a theory of conceptual change. *Science Education, 66,* 211-227.

Resnick, L. B. (1987). *Education and learning to think*. Washington, DC: National Academy Press.

Science Curriculum Improvement Study. (1973). *SCIS Omnibus*. Berkeley, CA: Lawrence Hall of Science.

Shymansky, J. (1984). BSCS programs: Just how effective were they? *The American Biology Teacher, 46*(1), 54-57.

Simon, H. A. (1974). How big is a chunk? *Science, 183,* 482-488.

Smith, C. L., & Millman, A. B. (1987). Understanding conceptual structures: A case study of Darwin's early thinking. In D. N. Perkins, J. Lochhead, & J. C. Bishop (Eds.), *Thinking: The second international conference*. Hillsdale, NJ: Erlbaum.

Smith, E. L., & Anderson, C. W. (1984). Plants as producers: A case study of elementary science teaching. *Journal of Research in Science Teaching, 21,* 685-698.

Wason, P. C., & Johnson-Laird, P. N. (1972). *Psychology of reasoning: Structure and content*. Cambridge, MA: Harvard University Press.

Teaching Mathematics

The subject of mathematics has always suffered from its own multiple personalities. It is, on one hand, one of the most basic of the basic skills we expect of literate people, and at the same time one of the most esoteric and incomprehensible of academic disciplines, whose purpose is far from clear, even to those who pursue its outer edges. This remarkable range frequently leads to arguments over whether the school curriculum should concentrate on the basic skills of arithmetic or on the disciplinary skills of reasoning and problem solving. The purpose and role of elementary and secondary mathematics in the school curriculum are regularly challenged.

Yet, despite its multiple personalities, the authors who wrote about mathematics for this volume, Deborah Ball and Herbert Clemens, are in remarkable agreement as to what mathematics teachers should know and be able to do. Moreover, this agreement comes from authors who are themselves from different backgrounds and who have very different reasons for caring about this question. The first, Deborah Ball, is a teacher educator who also teaches third-grade arithmetic in an elementary school. The second is a mathematician housed in a university mathematics department. That these two authors come from such different backgrounds and yet reach such similar conclusions about the task of teaching mathematics is important in itself.

Their conclusions are even more important, for both suggest that mathematics need not be construed as either of these extremely different personalities, but instead as a way of reasoning about particular kinds of phenomena, ones that students *need to understand*. That is, students cannot adequately function if they memorize rules or accept mathematical propositions without asking questions. Moreover, both argue that mathematics is something that students *can* understand—it is not so esoteric or obscure that it is inaccessible, even to elementary students.

61

3

Teaching Mathematics for Understanding: What Do Teachers Need to Know About Subject Matter?

DEBORAH LOEWENBERG BALL

Mathematics education is in trouble in this country and the signs of it are everywhere. One recent outcry is the National Research Council (1989) report, *Everybody Counts*. The document opens with this assertion:

> Three out of four Americans stop studying mathematics before completing either career or job prerequisites. Most students leave school without sufficient preparation in mathematics to cope with either on-the-job demands for problem-solving or college expectations for mathematical literacy. . . . Our country cannot afford continuing generations of students limited by lack of mathematical power to second-class status in the society in which they live. (p. viii)

And, in his book, *Innumeracy*, John Paulos (1988) points out that "innumeracy, an inability to deal with the fundamental notions of number and chance, plagues far too many otherwise knowledgeable citizens" (p. 3). He suggests that, in fact, mathematical literacy is not seen as important by many well-educated people who are unashamed to flaunt their lack of mathematical understanding. "I just don't have a mathematical mind," is the common explanation.

The National Assessment of Educational Progress (NAEP) also supports these assertions (Dossey, Mullis, Lindquist, & Chambers, 1988). It is true that most students were accurate with simple number facts. However, beyond that the picture was bleak. Quite a few students lacked proficiency with basic computation and word problems. Only about half of the 17-year-olds and one-fifth of the 13-year-olds were able to apply mathematical knowledge to so-called moderately complex problems, such as calculating the area of a 6 x 4 cm rectangle or responding to a question like, "Which of the following is true of

87% of 10? (a) It is greater than 10; (b) It is less than 10; (c) It is equal to 10."
And almost none of the students at any age were able to solve multistep
problems (Dossey, Mullis, Lindquist, & Chambers, 1988). Although mathematical competence is an essential component of a good education, these results (as
well as many other indicators) suggest that many students are failing to learn
even rudimentary concepts about and procedures for working with quantities and
space. What they do learn, they learn without understanding. And, additionally
troubling, this failure is disproportionately distributed among African-American
and Hispanic students, as well as females.

Why is this? One route to making sense of this state of affairs is to try an
example on yourself, for you, too, are a product of U.S. mathematics education.
Do you remember how you were taught to divide fractions? Take the problem,
$1\frac{3}{4} \div \frac{1}{2}$. Do you remember how to do this—how to calculate the answer?
Traditionally this is taught via the rule "invert and multiply." In this case, that
means converting $1\frac{3}{4}$ to $\frac{7}{4}$, "flipping" $\frac{1}{2}$ to $\frac{2}{1}$ and multiplying the two numbers.
The result: $3\frac{1}{2}$.

Now, can you think of a situation in the real world for which $1\frac{3}{4} \div \frac{1}{2}$ is the
mathematical formulation? In other words, what does what you just did *mean*?
How do you get an answer like $3\frac{1}{2}$ for this?

Most commonly, people who are asked this make up a story something like
the following: "You have $1\frac{3}{4}$ pizzas and you want to share them equally between
two people." This seems to make sense because $1\frac{3}{4}$ pizzas are imagined as being
divided into four pieces each. Thus, if you divide seven pieces of pizza between
two people, each one gets $3\frac{1}{2}$ pieces of pizza. But this story represents $1\frac{3}{4} \div 2$,
not $1\frac{3}{4} \div \frac{1}{2}$. To divide something *in* half means to divide it into two equal parts
($\div 2$); to divide something *by* one-half means to form groups of $\frac{1}{2}$, as shown
in Figure 3.1. The $3\frac{1}{2}$ pieces of pizza in the common story that most people
construct represent $3\frac{1}{2}$ *fourths*, not $3\frac{1}{2}$ *halves*. An appropriate story should
actually be something like, "If you have $1\frac{3}{4}$ yards of fabric, how many half-yard
lengths can you cut?" Then the answer, $3\frac{1}{2}$ half-yard lengths, makes sense.

$4 \div \frac{1}{2} = 8$ $4 \div 2 = 2$

There are 8 halves in 4 wholes   There are 2 groups of 2 in 4 wholes

FIGURE 3.1. Dividing *by* $\frac{1}{2}$ **versus dividing** *in* $\frac{1}{2}$.

Why people who have "had" mathematics in school can get answers without knowing what they mean or what they relate to is due to the way mathematics is typically taught. Researchers who have studied math teaching and learning (e.g., Good, Grouws, & Ebmeier, 1983; Goodlad, 1984; Madsen-Nason & Lanier, 1986; Stodolsky, 1988) paint a picture that is all too familiar to anyone who has made his or her way through 12 years of public school: In most math classes, the teacher stands at the board, shows students how to go through the steps of a particular procedure, and then assigns practice exercises. For example, if the topic was division of fractions, students would be shown how to invert and multiply. They might be told that dividing by a fraction is "the same as" multiplying by its reciprocal and they would probably be reminded to convert mixed numerals to improper fractions. They would not be told why this procedure works nor how it relates to division with whole numbers. For the rest of the class time, the teacher would monitor students' work on these exercises. Then they would do 36, or 40, or 55 computations involving division of fractions. They might do a few story problems, although teachers often don't assign these because students find them frustrating.

Too rarely are procedures connected to their underlying conceptual foundations. Nor is relating the topic at hand to other topics common. For instance, in this example, few teachers would help students understand that division of fractions is no different from division of whole numbers, that in both cases the questions have to do with forming groups. Instead, mathematics tends to be presented in school in little airtight compartments, separated from one another in time and meaning. The school curriculum treats mathematics as a collection of discrete bits of procedural knowledge. This tendency to compartmentalize mathematical knowledge substantially increases what it takes to learn and to use mathematics. Each idea or procedure seems to be a separate case. Each requires a different rule, all of which must be individually memorized and recalled.

At the same time, traditional mathematics instruction makes little effort to relate mathematics to the learner, to help students engage in the questions and uses of the subject. Consequently, mathematics is not generally perceived as personally meaningful. Instead, it is something students do, a series of exercises that they complete. The teacher checks their work, marking errors. Often they are unsure whether they are right or not until they get their papers back.

All in all, this picture I am painting, one that is most likely familiar to you, helps to explain why many people who have "had" mathematics do not remember things that they were taught and, even more commonly, cannot make sense of situations, procedures, and answers involving quantities and space. (After all, the students who take the NAEP have *had* all that stuff on which they are being tested.) To quote the National Research Council (1989) report, "A mathematics curriculum that emphasizes computation and rules is like a writing curriculum that emphasizes grammar and spelling; both put the cart before the horse" (p. 44). Graduates of this typical mathematics teaching cannot (or do not try to) invent strategies to make sense, and they are likely to treat quantitative information as fact, exempt from critical examination and challenge. They rarely feel that they can assess the reasonableness of their own answers and are typically unsuccessful at applying procedures to solve problems. Many are left with feelings of inadequacy and anxiety about mathematics.

All this adds up to a system of exposing people to mathematics that is largely unsuccessful in empowering or inviting them to use or appreciate mathematics. How could we change these patterns of mathematical disenfranchisement? Clearly, we need to alter what goes on in mathematics classrooms. Students must develop sensible ways of dealing with quantity and space, using the tools of the domain in ways that they understand and that provide them with control over the reasonableness of their thinking. These tools include the concepts and procedures that have been developed over time by mathematicians; they also include processes of inventing, exploring, and justifying ways of making mathematical sense. The ability to perform arithmetical calculations simply will not suffice to equip today's (and tomorrow's) citizens. Instead, they must be able to sift through and appraise statistical information, assess relative probabilities, estimate and predict, perceive and interpret patterns, and, in general, have a well-developed sense of numbers, both large and small. To alter the portrait of mathematical illiteracy that we currently confront, the school and college curriculum—both what is taught and how it is taught—will need to undergo radical revision.

TEACHING MATHEMATICS FOR
UNDERSTANDING—ONE VIEW

To provide the reader with a picture of what this might look like, I turn next to my own third-grade classroom. I teach mathematics daily to a class of third graders in a local public elementary school. The students represent a substantial range of cultural, socioeconomic, and ethnic backgrounds and many speak English as a second language.

The children in this class have been learning about numbers and about number theory—for example, about even and odd numbers, about positive and negative numbers, about multiples and factors, and about place value in the base 10 numeration system for recording numerals. On the day I describe, they were investigating fractions as quantities and equivalent fractions as alternative representations of the same amount. The point of this story is to portray an alternative vision of mathematics teaching, a kind of teaching for understanding that aims to empower students to make sense of mathematics and to be able to reason with and about mathematical ideas themselves—precisely the kinds of capacities that the NAEP shows students are presently not developing.

Yesterday the class ended with one student, Jenny, asserting that $\frac{1}{2}$ "is not a number." She backed up her claim, pointing at the number line that runs around at the top of the classroom walls, "See? Look at our number line. There's no $\frac{1}{2}$ on there, just 2, 3, 4, and so on."

Because she wants the children to engage this assertion, the teacher decides to start class today by writing the following problem on the board:

> A man has 4 loaves of bread. He wants to share the bread equally among 8 of his friends. How much bread will he give each of his friends?

The third graders copy the problem into spiral notebooks. One hears some of them consulting with one another: "You can't *do* it. There isn't enough," and "How many slices are in the loaves?" Several are drawing large loaves of bread in their notebooks and beginning carefully to draw slices in the bread.

The teacher walks around, looking at what the children are doing, and occasionally stoops over to ask a question, such as, "How much bread is each one going to get?"

After about 10 minutes, the teacher asks, "Does anyone need more time to work on this? How many are ready to discuss?"

A few raise their hands as they continue carefully drawing smudgy lines in their loaves of bread.

A few minutes later, the teacher opens the discussion of the problem. "Would someone like to show their solution?"

James volunteers eagerly, "But I'm not sure if this is right."

He draws 4 large loaves on the chalkboard and proceeds to divide each loaf into 8 slices. Turning to the class, he announces, "Each friend should get 4 slices" (Figure 3.2).

Bridget's hand shoots up. "I challenge that. I think each friend gets 2 slices."

"Can you show that?" asks the teacher.

She draws 4 more loaves on the board and divides each into 4 slices. "You see? Two slices for each friend." She counts it out to prove she is right. "The first friend gets these 2; the second these 2, and so on" (Figure 3.3).

"This is confusing," says the teacher. "How can James come up with 4 slices each and Bridget 2 slices for the *same* problem?"

"Bridget's slices are bigger," observes one boy.

Another child is wildly flapping his arm, trying to be recognized. "I just said that each friend could have half a loaf."

"Can you write that number?" asks the teacher.

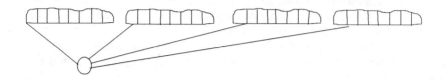

FIGURE 3.2: 32 slices of bread for 8 friends

He comes up and writes "$\frac{1}{2}$" on the board.

"And what amount of bread is James giving each friend?" asks the teacher.

There is a pause. She asks, "How much is one slice as James has cut it up?"

"One-quarter?" proposes a small girl.

"Can you write that?" asks the teacher.

Over the next few minutes, the teacher, with her questions, guides the class to understand that each of James' slices is $\frac{1}{8}$ of a loaf of bread because he has divided his loaf into 8 slices. The children write $\frac{1}{8}$, $\frac{1}{4}$, and $\frac{1}{2}$, noting that the slices of bread that the different children have made are different sizes and that the slices that are $\frac{1}{8}$ of the loaf are smaller than the slices that are $\frac{1}{4}$.

"Doesn't that seem weird?" asks the teacher. "How can $\frac{1}{8}$ be less than $\frac{1}{4}$? 8 is greater than 4."

"That's *easy*," says Sharon. "One-eighth is smaller because you have cut the loaf of bread into 8 pieces, not 4, so the pieces are smaller. That's why $\frac{1}{8}$ is smaller than $\frac{1}{4}$."

"What do the rest of you think about that?" asks the teacher.

"I agree with Sharon," says another girl. "If you cut a loaf of bread into 8 slices, of course the slices will be smaller."

The class proceeds to write a number to represent each child's solution to the bread problem: $\frac{1}{2}$, $\frac{2}{4}$, $\frac{4}{8}$. The teacher provokes the next problem with her next question: "Why do we have three different numbers for each of these?"

There is a brief moment of silence. Then several hands shoot into the air. One by one, different children give halting explanations—that "1 is half of 2, 2 is half of 4, 4 is half of 8, so they're really all the same" or "they're all ways of saying a half." One boy comes to the board and makes an elaborate explanation, using the drawings of loaves (Figure 3.4).

FIGURE 3.3: 16 slices of bread for 8 friends.

A lively discussion ensues, during which there is some confusion about the fact that $\frac{1}{8}$ is less than $\frac{1}{2}$, that $\frac{4}{8}$ is not more than $\frac{1}{2}$, and so on. The teacher orchestrates this discussion, asking people to speak up, monitoring who has the floor, asking for reactions from other students.

Gradually the children reach the conclusion that $\frac{2}{4}$ and $\frac{4}{8}$ are different ways of representing half a loaf of bread, that it depends on how many slices you make, but that 4 of the "skinny slices" (the eighths) are the same *amount* of bread as half the loaf, unsliced.

Near the end of class, the teacher asks the children if they can find the number on the number line that represents the number of loaves they started with. Several point to the 4. Then she asks if they can find the point on the number line that represents the amount of bread that each friend should get. Quite easily, someone uses the pointer to indicate a spot halfway between 0 and 1.

"That makes sense," he explains, "because it's more than 0 loaves but less than 1 whole loaf."

Just as class is ending, Erica raises her hand. "I noticed something. I think I have a conjecture," she says. "The reason that James' solution is $\frac{4}{8}$ is because it's $\frac{1}{8}$ from each loaf— $\frac{1}{8} + \frac{1}{8} + \frac{1}{8} + \frac{1}{8}$. You only have to add the 1's, not the 8's."

"Yeah!" exclaims one of the boys. "'Cause if you added the 8's, you'd get a much bigger number! Umm . . . $\frac{4}{32}$!"

"That's a very interesting conjecture," says the teacher. "Would you like to write that up and we can pursue it tomorrow? I'd like everyone to think about Erica's conjecture and see what you think. Does it make sense?"

Over the next few days the class solves and debates other problems like the loaf problem. They readily use drawings to convince themselves that $\frac{4}{32}$ is a much smaller number than $\frac{4}{8}$—in fact, that it represents the same amount of bread as $\frac{1}{8}$.

Compare this lesson with one you remember or one that your own child has experienced in school. Typically, fractions are presented as something new,

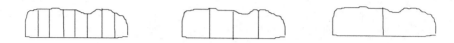

FIGURE 3.4: A start toward equating fractions.

unrelated to the children's previous work with numbers. Using pictures of circles (sometimes pies or pizzas), the children learn ways of naming an answer to the question, "How much is shaded?" They may not be too sure where that question came from or why they would want to answer it (except on a workbook page). They may learn that the "top number" in a fraction is called the numerator, the "bottom number" the denominator. Often, to simplify things, children work first only with unit fractions (e.g., $\frac{1}{3}$, $\frac{1}{5}$), later with other proper fractions, and still later with mixed numbers and improper fractions. Equivalent fractions and computation with fractions are also separate topics. Discussion or debate about ideas is rare.

What was going on in the lesson described above? With their eye on the basic problem—dividing one number by a larger number—the students were employing mathematical ideas and tools in their work, in contexts that made sense to them: pictures, the number line, stories about sharing bread. At once, they were engaged in opportunities to learn mathematics and to learn to *do* mathematics. As far as mathematical content is concerned, the students used and developed their understandings of fractions, of equivalent fractions, and of the correspondence between numeral and number. All these learnings are important for equipping children with a comfortable sense of numbers—their meanings and notations.

But there was more mathematics in the lesson than that. The idea that mathematics entails puzzles and uncertainties and that mathematical thinking involves questions as much as answers was represented in the problem of knowing whether Sharon's conjecture had exceptions to it. More than just getting right answers, doing mathematics in this classroom entails investigating, looking for patterns, framing and testing conjectures, arguing and proving. The search for patterns and formulating and testing their generalizability are at the heart of the students' activity.

The process of presenting and justifying solutions provides fertile ground for inquiry and arguments as children search for reasonable solutions that their peers will accept. The challenges they present to one another reveal the nature and power of proof—how one can persuade others in one's community of discourse that one's conjecture is reasonable or true (Lampert, 1988). These learnings are important as part of developing mathematical literacy, just as the ability to construct arguments, narrate events, or persuade, using written language, is part of written literacy. Neither knowledge of computational procedures nor knowledge of grammatical conventions alone is sufficient to equip learners with the power of literacy.

A significant feature of this classroom is that students are themselves sources of and validators of knowledge and insight. The teacher is not the only one who is able to determine if something makes sense. In this classroom students are helped to acquire the skills and understanding needed to judge the validity of mathematical ideas and results. These skills and understandings include specific knowledge—mathematical concepts and procedures; they also include the disposition to question and to examine mathematical claims and the confidence with which to do so. This matters; when mathematical answers are justified on the basis of the teacher's authority, learners may not develop the capacity to monitor the reasonableness of their thinking.

The teacher has a critical role to play in facilitating students' mathematical learning. She introduces a variety of representational systems (e.g., the drawings the children were using in this lesson) that can be used to reason about mathematics; she models mathematical thinking and activity, and asks questions that push students to examine and articulate their ideas. However, perhaps most significant in the classroom context is the teacher's role in guiding the direction, balance, and rhythm of classroom discourse by deciding which points the group should pursue, which questions to play down, and which issues to table for the moment—decisions that she makes based on her knowledge of mathematics as well as her knowledge of her students.

HOW CAN WE GET MATHEMATICAL UNDERSTANDING?

What would it take to turn more mathematics classrooms into places where teachers could help students acquire these kinds of skills and dispositions in mathematics, and where students would be more likely to develop power and confidence with the tools of mathematics, more inclined to engage in and use mathematics? A very big question, it goes beyond the boundaries of this chapter, for it involves change in patterns of thought about teaching and learning, which have their roots in our culture and in the organizational patterns of our schools (see, for example, Cohen, 1988). By no means unchangeable, these patterns demand serious consideration in their own right. In the pages that follow, I take up just one part of the question: What does a *teacher* need in order to orchestrate opportunities to learn mathematics with understanding, given the conception of understanding illustrated above? What does it takes to teach this or to teach like this?

Strategies for Change

The strategies for change focused on the teacher that are most often proposed include improving the materials that teachers have to use, training teachers in skills of effective teaching, and ensuring that teachers have adequate subject matter knowledge. Of the three, it is the third—teachers' knowledge of mathematics—that has been least well explored and defined. And the first two depend on it; alone, they cannot suffice to alter the patterns of traditional mathematics instruction.

Improve mathematics curriculum materials. Would it do to change the books that we use in mathematics classes? The books presently available focus on computational skills, omit other significant mathematics (such as geometry or probability), and represent math as recipe following. In the state of California, where a curriculum framework for mathematics teaching was developed to alter fundamentally the nature of school mathematics teaching and learning, the committee charged with state textbook adoption rejected all available textbooks the first time they were reviewed. Since then, several major publishers have worked hard to revise their textbooks in an effort to capture the lucrative California market. This struggle provides further evidence of how poor most available math curriculum materials are.

In any case, research on how teachers use textbooks suggests that providing better curriculum materials is necessary but insufficient as a solution. Teachers, as professionals, adapt and shape the content and approaches embedded in text materials, omitting sections they feel are unnecessary, dropping problems they see as irrelevant or too hard, and adding things they perceive as important (Schwille et al., 1983). These decisions are shaped by the teachers' own understandings and beliefs. No textbook can determine what goes on beyond the classroom door; nor, I contend, should it.

Equip teachers with more effective techniques. General concerns about what goes on in schools have led many to advocate programs aimed at improving teachers' technical pedagogical skills. The popularity of Madeline Hunter is evidence of the widespread belief that the way to improve schools is to train teachers to deliver instruction according to clearly specified principles (see Hunter, 1988-89; Mandeville & Rivers, 1988-89; Sparks, 1988-89). Yet using "advance organizers" and "response cues" for students can smooth classroom interactions without affecting the substance of what students are taught. Teachers can clearly "explain" the steps of a mathematical procedure without any focus on its meaning. In short, a teacher can be fabulously efficient, but whether she can design opportunities for her students to engage meaningfully in mathematical activity is a different issue, dependent on other knowledge, skills, and commitments.

Ensure that teachers have adequate subject matter knowledge. Neither the perfect textbook lesson nor a smooth procedure for calling on children will bail out the teacher who is confronted with a student who wants to know why, when he or she multiplies by a decimal, the answer is sometimes smaller (e.g., 4.06 x .5 = 2.03). Teachers must understand mathematics well themselves if they are to be able to respond to such a question—whether it is by directly answering or by reframing the question in a way that allows the student to figure it out on his or her own. They should understand the subject in sufficient depth to be able to represent it appropriately and in multiple ways. They need to understand the subject flexibly enough so that they can interpret and appraise students' ideas, helping them to extend and formalize intuitive understandings and challenging incorrect notions.

This argument—that content knowledge matters—is often met with a story of some high school teacher who, although holding a Ph.D. in topographical analysis, was completely unable to help sophomores learn algebra. This teacher, the story goes, had "too much" subject matter knowledge. This chapter argues that discussion about teachers' subject matter knowledge must turn from questions of "how much" to "what kind." More course work for teachers is *not* the solution, for college mathematics courses reflect the same patterns—if not worse—as those discussed above. Lecture, proof by coercion, and an emphasis on procedures, not meaning, permeate the pedagogy of higher education (Davis & Hersh, 1981; Kline, 1977). And instructors of undergraduate courses are often graduate students, not infrequently limited speakers of English. To dig into the question of "what kind" of subject matter knowledge teachers need in order to teach mathematics for understanding, I will address four dimensions of subject matter understanding: knowledge of the substance of mathematics, knowledge about the nature and discourse of mathematics, knowledge about mathematics in culture and society, and the capacity for what I will call pedagogical reasoning about mathematics.

Substantive Knowledge of Mathematics

Hardly anyone would argue with the claim that teachers need substantive knowledge of mathematics—of particular concepts and procedures (rectangles, functions, and the multiplication of decimals, for example). Most would agree that teachers' understanding should be both "flexible" and "deep," two vague but nice-sounding descriptors. I propose instead three specific criteria for teachers' substantive knowledge: correctness, meaning, and connectedness.

Teachers' substantive knowledge of mathematics should certainly be *correct*. Teachers should know that rectangles are plane figures with four straight sides and four right angles, and they should be able to correctly multiply 35.07 x .05. They should know that the places in our numeration system represent powers of 10 and that division by zero is undefined, and they should be able to distinguish between a variable and an unknown. This, for many people, defines knowing the content. This is, after all, the main focus of most tests—for teachers and for children. But "correctness" in mathematics is not always so straightforward. Are first graders *wrong*, for example, if they believe that 0 is the smallest number and that 3 is the next number after 2? Elementary classrooms are filled with "truths" that ultimately are not—for example, subtracting a larger number from a smaller one (e.g., 5 - 7) is impossible, you always get a smaller number when you divide and a larger number when you multiply, squares are not rectangles.

What is considered correct or incorrect depends on the domain, on the mathematical context in which people are operating. Ninth graders operating in the domain of rational numbers probably believe that there is no "smallest number" and no "next number" after 2. Does this make first graders wrong if they believe that 3 comes after 2? And then what happens if a pupil makes an assertion that presses on the boundaries of the current domain? Suppose a first grader claims that $2\frac{1}{2}$ is the next number after 2? Epistemological dilemmas such as this arise in everyday teaching; figuring out how to deal with them is central to teaching mathematics for understanding.

But correctness is not the only criterion. Teachers should not just be able to "do" mathematics; if they are to teach for understanding, they must also have a sense for the *mathematical meanings* underlying the concepts and procedures. Many children and adults go through mathematical motions correctly without ever understanding what they are doing or why. It is one thing to be able to get $3\frac{1}{2}$ as an answer to $1\frac{3}{4} \div \frac{1}{2}$; understanding the referent for the $3\frac{1}{2}$ entails knowing what it *means* to divide by $\frac{1}{2}$. Similarly, it is one thing to line up the numbers correctly on each line of the computation for a long multiplication problem; it is quite another to know *why* one is doing that.

Explanations of mathematics entail more than repeating the words of mathematical procedures or definitions. The statement, for example, that you "carry the 1" is not a mathematical explanation of regrouping in addition; neither, by itself, is the statement "7 ÷ 0 is undefined." To explain mathematics is to focus on the meaning, on the underlying ideas and concepts. To explain is to say *why*, to justify the logic, or to identify a convention.

Finally, however well explained or correct, mathematical knowledge is not a collection of disparate facts and procedures. The meaning of division of fractions can be *connected* to what it means to divide, for instance. Connections exist at multiple levels between and among ideas. Smaller ideas belong to various families of larger concepts; for example, decimals are related to fractions as well as to base 10 numeration and place value. Topics are connected to others of equivalent size; addition, for instance, is fundamentally connected to multiplication. Elementary mathematics links to more abstract content—algebra is a first cousin of arithmetic, and the measurement of irregular shapes is akin to integration in calculus. Mathematical ideas can be linked in numerous ways; no one right structure or map exists.

Despite this, mathematics is often delivered in school in small isolated packages. This makes it much harder to learn because there is so much more that must be remembered. In addition, treating mathematics as a collection of separate facts and procedures also seriously misrepresents the logic and nature of the discipline to students. If teachers are to break away from this common approach to teaching and learning mathematics and teach for understanding instead, they themselves must have connected rather than compartmentalized knowledge of mathematics.

The Nature and Discourse of Mathematics

A second component of subject matter knowledge consists of what I call knowledge about the nature and discourse of mathematics. In the example of teaching for understanding above, students were engaged in arguing about alternative mathematical hypotheses. They knew that their answers were subject to the scrutiny of their classmates as well as of their teacher. They understood that part of doing mathematics entails looking for patterns, trying to reach generalizations, challenging old assumptions, and formulating new ideas. These students' experience with mathematics is different from the usual. Typically, students experience mathematics as a series of rules to be memorized and followed, as a domain of clearly right and wrong answers (which are distinguished by the authority of the answer key), as a silent and private activity involving mostly calculation. Speed and accuracy are what count; justification and reasonableness play little role.

"So what?" one might ask. Perhaps the earlier example is a fairer representation of mathematics, but, some would argue, many students aren't going to be mathematicians and the goal for now is proficiency. However, it is not for us to decide who will one day want to pursue mathematics, and even proficiency is facilitated by helping students acquire control and power in the domain. When the answers seem arbitrary, when they reside in the teacher's head or in some book, when mathematics is a step-by-step routine, students are not likely to feel any sense of competence. Engaging students in mathematics, much as we already aim for genuine engagement in literature or writing, holds promise for the outcomes of formal mathematical study.

What do teachers need to know about the nature and discourse of mathematics? Do teachers need to become philosophers of mathematics? Again, the point is not how *much* but what *kind* of knowledge teachers need. I propose three aspects of understanding: one focused on answers, justification, and authority; another on mathematical activity; and another on the basis of mathematical knowledge—convention versus logic.

First, teachers need to consider what counts as an "answer" in mathematics. Typically, the question, "Is 124 even or odd?" is answered in classrooms with one word: "Even." Yet, to consider "even" an answer is to give short shrift to justification and to mathematical meaning. In mathematical discourse, justification is as much a part of the answer as is the answer itself. "Even, because half of 124 is 62 and even numbers are numbers that can be divided evenly in half," or "Even, because 123 is odd and 125 is odd and the pattern goes even-odd-even-odd," or "Even, because 100 is even, 20 is even, and 4 is even," are all possible alternative answers that contain a justification to establish the truth of the answer. Important to note here is that mathematical explanations necessarily rely on earlier assumptions or already established ideas (e.g., that even numbers are whole numbers that are divisible by 2 and that divisibility implies a whole-number quotient—i.e., the fact that $3 \div 2 = 1\frac{1}{2}$ does not mean 3 is divisible by 2).

How the truth or reasonableness of an answer is established in mathematics is a closely related issue. Typically, students know that their answers are right when they match those given in the back of the book or keyed in the teacher's guide or when the teacher says they are. In the discipline of mathematics, answers are accepted as true when others in the community, who share similar assumptions and core understandings, are unable to come up with viable counterevidence or refutations. Mathematicians do not look their conclusions up in books to see if they are right. Instead, they provide mathematical arguments designed to persuade others of their conclusions.

Classroom discourse aimed at emulating these patterns of discourse involves children in proposing solutions that (as described above) contain justifications that are subject to the scrutiny of the rest of the class. Suppose a student claims, for instance, that "115 is even because half of 100 is 50, half of 10 is 5, and half of 5 is $2\frac{1}{2}$—so half of 115 is $57\frac{1}{2}$." Instead of the teacher pronouncing this incorrect, other students can examine the claim and challenge it by pointing out that the requirement that an even number be divisible by 2 means that the result must be a whole number—thus 5 (and, hence, 115) is *not* even. Authority for reasonableness need not rest solely with the teacher. If justification is the basis for correctness, students gain control in mathematics—a control that can afford them competence, confidence, and enjoyment. And in everyday life there are no answer keys: Students must develop the capacity to assess the reasonableness of their own solutions.

A second aspect of mathematics that teachers need to consider explicitly is what "doing mathematics" entails. What do mathematicians do? Despite what generations of children have done in school in the name of mathematics, figuring columns of sums or performing long division is, at best, a pale shadow of "doing mathematics." Instead, mathematics consists of activities such as examining patterns, formulating and testing generalizations, and constructing proofs. The procedures one learns in school were generated as part of that activity and are now part of the accepted arsenal of mathematical tools. Becoming familiar with these tools is a critical part of learning mathematics;

using them in the context of mathematical activity affords them a more appropriate importance than when they *become* the point, as is too often the case.

Finally, mathematical knowledge is based on both convention and logic. This has implications for what can be derived logically (based, of course, on prior assumptions or previously established ideas) versus what could (at this point) be reasonably defined or handled in an alternative way and is, therefore, somewhat arbitrary. For teachers, distinguishing between the two is critical. For example, that our numeration system is based on 10 is arbitrary—we could just as well use a base 5 or base 12 system. That we use a procedure that involves crossing out 10s and "borrowing," or regrouping, in order to subtract is also a convention.

Other reasonable subtraction procedures can be (and have been) invented. However, that one "can't subtract up" in the subtraction problem

$$\begin{array}{r} 5\ 6 \\ -\ 2\ 9 \\ \hline \end{array}$$

is *not* merely a convention if we agree that subtraction is not commutative: 6 - 9 is not equal to 9 - 6. This distinction is important with respect to the question of authority and its relationship to learning mathematics. Children can establish for themselves, for example, that if they "subtract up" they will obtain

$$\begin{array}{r} 5\ 6 \\ -\ 2\ 9 \\ \hline 3\ 3 \end{array}$$

a result that will not correspond to what they get when they take 29 objects away from 56.

"Invert and multiply" is also erroneously perceived to be an arbitrary convention of procedure. However, multiplication and division are *logically* reciprocal: $6 \div 2$ produces the same result as $6 \times \frac{1}{2}$, for example. Confronted with $6 \div \frac{1}{2}$, and considering what it means to divide, students can figure out that this is asking how many *halves* there are in 6. Since there are two halves in each whole, then there will be 6×2, or 12, halves in 6. When teachers confuse knowledge based on convention with knowledge that is logically derivable, the nature of mathematics becomes muddled.

Sometimes rules refer to ideas or procedures that can be figured out logically (e.g., "division by 0 is undefined; $\frac{0}{0}$ is considered indeterminate," or "when you multiply by 10, just add a zero"). And sometimes students are asked to figure out things that are purely arbitrary, given their own mathematical development (e.g., that the number 1 is not classified as a prime).[1] The major issue here is for teachers to realize how much of what pupils learn *is* derivable and logical, not arbitrary and conventional. When students can derive and justify ideas mathematically, they are better equipped to access the underlying meanings and less likely to conceive of particular mathematical ideas as "something you just have to remember."

Knowledge About Mathematics in Culture and Society

If teachers are to play a role in reversing the patterns I described at the beginning of this chapter, then they need additional knowledge of mathematics, knowledge that is more contextual than disciplinary. They need to understand, at least broadly, the role played by mathematics in our society and in everyday life, about the evolution of mathematics as a field of human inquiry, and about the achievement and participation problems that plague school mathematics. Nothing is more often trivialized in school than so-called "applications" of mathematics. Students are asked to calculate amounts that no one would ever calculate—exactly or at all—in everyday life and, in general, to use mathematics in ways that misrepresent its uses and applications. Who, for example, after cooking breakfast, subtracts the number of eggs cooked from the original number of eggs in order to figure out how many eggs are left? Wouldn't most people simply count the eggs remaining? Probability has applications that go beyond coin tossing. Measurement is critical in many familiar undertakings; graphing relationships is a useful tool in making decisions.

Applying mathematics to real situations also involves framing a problem to which mathematics can contribute—figuring out a question, setting the constraints, deciding on the precision needed. Would an estimate suffice? What order of magnitude matters? For example, trying to figure out how much to charge for handmade stationery involves deciding on a desirable profit margin, estimating total costs, assessing the market, and so on. If teachers are to help students learn mathematics in ways that allow the students to make connections to everyday life, they themselves must know more about mathematical connections and applications. They need to have an awareness of how mathematics is used in a wide variety of settings and endeavors—including uses that are recreational and intellectual as well as practical. Just as we want students to read because reading is inherently worthwhile, so should mathematical play and intellectual inquiry be legitimate goals of mathematics education.

Teachers also need some awareness of the evolution of mathematical ideas across history and in different cultures. In teaching numeration, for instance, it may be useful to understand that human beings have sought and constructed a wide variety of systems of counting and recording quantities, of which our base 10 positional system is one. How are Roman numerals different as a system? Zero, as a numeral to represent nothing, was a later invention. Knowing about the Mayans and why zero became important to them is useful both in understanding positional numeration[2] as well as in helping students see and value that many peoples have contributed to the development of mathematics.

This year, in my own class, I used the Egyptian invention of fractions to provide a real context for developing an understanding of rational numbers. My third graders actually faced some of the same puzzlements confronted by others over three thousand years ago—how to distinguish between slices of bread from a loaf that has been cut into eight slices and slices from an identical loaf that has been cut into four slices. In each case we can say that we have *one slice*, but the amounts of bread are clearly different. In developing ideas about eighths and fourths, these eight-year-olds not only learned to write $\frac{1}{8}$ and $\frac{1}{4}$ to correctly represent the quantities, but they could also explain clearly that $\frac{1}{8}$ was obviously *less than* $\frac{1}{4}$. Connecting what students learn and how they learn it to the historical development of mathematics connects them in a fundamental way to the growth of knowledge as a constructive process of continual invention and revision. Furthermore, when teachers know about the alternative ways in which different peoples have worked with notions of quantity and space, they can use that knowledge to enhance students' sense of pride in their heritage.

Finally, mathematics is a key filter in U.S. secondary schools and, thus, a critical determinant of students' futures. While some students take four years of math in high school, often through calculus, many others drop out formally after the ninth grade. Of those who elect to end their study of mathematics, many dropped out in spirit years earlier, while still in elementary school. They have come to see themselves as bad at math, as not mathematically inclined. They aspire to futures that do not require mathematics. The fact that these students are also disproportionately African-American, Hispanic, and female is a serious issue.

If teachers are to alter this pattern, they need to be aware of factors that contribute to it: the patterns of interaction in classrooms, the cultural stereotyping of "math types," the sources and power of encouragement or discouragement to study mathematics, the kinds of applications that predominate in math texts and math classrooms, linguistic differences, and differences in basic cultural assumptions or understandings, for example. A good example of the last factor was told to me by my colleague Bill McDiarmid, based on his experience with Yup'ik Eskimo children in western Alaska. In this culture, dividing a catch or a kill equally means that each hunter's share is based on his or her *need*. Conceiving of "equal" portions in the mathematical sense—as portions that are the same in quantity—is at odds with cultural assumptions. This does not imply that Yup'ik children should not learn the mathematical concept of "equal," but a teacher who is aware of this different basic understanding would be able to approach it with sensitivity, offering the mathematical concept as a different way of thinking about "equal" in another context.

Pedagogical Reasoning in Teaching Mathematics

So far, this chapter has addressed some of the kinds of knowledge about mathematics that teachers need in order to teach mathematics for understanding. I have outlined various aspects of mathematics that teachers should understand. Unlike some current arguments, however, I have not proposed that teachers should have a repertoire of representations—of examples, explanations, activities—that they can use to teach mathematics. While I do think such a repertoire is essential, I chose for this chapter to focus on what teachers need to know about the *subject matter* of mathematics. Partly this is because I think that this question typically gets little or superficial consideration, and partly it is because teaching is dynamic. Teachers, from moment to moment, ask and answer questions, interpret students' understandings, provide illustrations or analogies, decide to drop or add examples from the text, make decisions to follow or drop a tangent, and so on. If we want teachers who can, in the thick of things, manage the mathematics of their classrooms in ways that allow students to learn with understanding, we need to pay close attention to what teachers know and how they draw upon that knowledge in this dynamic environment.

Teachers' everyday work consists of activities as various as choosing a worksheet, using the teacher's guide to plan a lesson, responding to a student's question, examining students' written work, developing an example or explanation, assessing what students understand. Take developing an example or explanation. Suppose you are teaching fifth grade and you want to help students understand multiplication of decimals. You remember that when you were taught, your fifth-grade teacher told you to forget about the decimal points and just multiply the numbers as though they were whole numbers:

$$
\begin{array}{ccc}
4.06 & \longrightarrow & 406 \\
\underline{\times\ .5} & & \underline{\times\ \ 5} \\
& & 2030
\end{array}
$$

Then you were to count the number of decimal places in the original problem and place the decimal point that many spaces over in your answer: 2.030. Now, you could just use this explanation as is, but you have a sense that it doesn't focus on the underlying meaning. Why does it work to add up the number of decimal places? And what does 4.06 x .5 mean? What could you do? Your substantive knowledge—what you understand about multiplication and about decimals—will shape what you come up with. A teacher who is trying to teach for understanding should know more than that the answer is 2.030.

Take the common task of planning a lesson from a textbook. Teachers should be both able and inclined to appraise the adequacy of a textbook's presentation of multiplication of decimals. Does it emphasize rules and steps over the meaning of the operation? How appropriate are the activities it suggests in terms of engaging pupils in genuine discussion? Does it show any connection between the multiplication of decimals and any context in which this might come up—and, if so, is the context sensible or silly? Appraising and modifying textbook lessons depends on the teacher's own understanding of the content.

Students ask questions all the time in classrooms: "Is zero even or odd?" "When you multiply 4.06 x .5, why is the answer smaller?" They make claims: "Zero is a multiple of 5." "I have a new way to do this problem." "This triangle has a perimeter of 3 centimeters" (Figure 3.5).

Deciding how to respond to students' questions, claims, and puzzlements has important consequences for what students learn about both the substance and the nature of mathematics. Should the teacher respond—and, if so, should it be with a question, with an explanation, or with a suggestion that the comment be put aside for the moment? And, if the decision is to respond, what should the teacher do or say? Perhaps the comment should be opened up to the class. While there is no single best course of action, these are crucial questions.

Teaching for understanding entails keeping a wide range of considerations in mind: about the substance of the content, about the ways in which the nature and discourse of mathematics are represented, and about social and cultural aspects of mathematics. Teachers' capacity and inclination to weave together these different considerations is a critical part of teaching mathematics for understanding, one that goes beyond simply knowing or being aware of certain things. We need to concern ourselves with the extent to which mathematical considerations affect teachers' pedagogical reasoning. For example, it may be helpful to tell second graders who are learning to subtract with regrouping ("borrowing") that "you can't subtract a larger number from a smaller one."

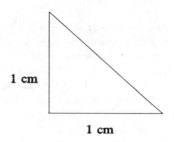

1 cm

1 cm

FIGURE 3.5 What is the perimeter?

However, a teacher who neither sees nor cares that he or she is passing on an ultimately false idea, seems to fail to consider the consequences for students' later learning. There is no right answer to these dilemmas in teaching; teachers must make those judgments themselves. However, concerns for making the content "fun" or "easy" for students often overshadow mathematical considerations. In the example given above, it matters little whether the teacher is aware of negative numbers, if he or she does not at least weigh that as one consideration in the decision about how to teach second graders to "borrow." It also matters little whether the teacher knows one or more excellent concrete models for subtraction with regrouping. Instead, what matters is the extent to which he or she is disposed to consider mathematics in choosing pedagogical courses of action.

CONCLUSION

Although something called "subject matter knowledge" is widely acknowledged as a central component of what mathematics teachers need to know, little agreement exists about what this means or how to tell whether teachers have it. Course work, grades, and test scores are the most frequent surrogates for subject matter understanding. These surrogates result in a superficial definition of subject matter knowledge, one that focuses mainly on the correctness of teachers' substantive knowledge. This chapter links the argument about what teachers need to know about mathematics to current concerns for improving the teaching and learning of mathematics. Hopes for interrupting the vicious cycle in mathematics education and altering the outcomes of school mathematics teaching depend, at least in part, on a closer and more serious consideration of the mathematics that teachers need to understand, as well as how, when, and where they can acquire this kind of understanding and how we can assess it.

NOTES

1. If primes are the numbers whose only factors are 1 and themselves, then 1 appears to be prime. If, however, all numbers can be expressed uniquely as the product of primes—the fundamental theorem of arithmetic—then the set of primes cannot include 1 (otherwise this theorem does not hold, for 6 could be expressed as 2 x 3 x 1 x 1 or 2 x 3 x 1 or 2 x 3, and so on). This dilemma illustrates the systemic interrelatedness among ideas in the various territories of mathematical knowledge.

2. A *positional numeration system* is one in which the position of a numeral also determines its value—for example, the 3 in 39 is worth more than the 3 in 53. Contrast this with the Roman numeration system, which is not fundamentally positional—for example, X is consistently worth 10. Zero is important in a positional system—for instance—to mark a difference between 1 and 1_0.

REFERENCES

Cohen, D. K. (1988). Teaching practice: Plus ça change . . . In P. Jackson (Ed.), *Contributing to educational change: Perspectives on research and practice*. Berkeley, CA: McCutchan.

Davis, P., & Hersh, R. (1981). *The mathematical experience*. New York: Houghton Mifflin.

Dossey, J., Mullis, I., Lindquist, M., & Chambers, D. (1988). *The mathematics report card: Are we measuring up? Trends and achievement based on the 1986 National Assessment*. Princeton, NJ: Educational Testing Service.

Good, T., Grouws, D., & Ebmeier, H. (1983). *Active mathematics teaching*. New York: Longman.

Goodlad, J. (1984). *A place called school: Prospects for the future*. New York: McGraw-Hill.

Hunter, M. (1988-89). "Well-acquainted " is not enough: A response to Mandeville and Rivers. *Educational Leadership, 46*(4), 67-68.

Kline, M. (1977). *Why the professor can't teach: Mathematics and the dilemma of university education*. New York: St. Martin's Press.

Lampert, M. (1988, November). *The teacher's role in reinventing the meaning of mathematical knowing in the classroom*. Paper presented at the tenth annual meeting of the North American chapter of the International Group for the Psychology of Mathematics Education, De Kalb, IL.

Madsen-Nason, A., & Lanier, P. (1986). *Pamela Kaye's general math class: From a computational to a conceptual orientation* (Research Series No. 172). East Lansing: Michigan State University, Institute for Research on Teaching.

Mandeville, G. K., & Rivers, J. L. (1988-89). Effects of South Carolina's Hunter-based PET program. *Educational Leadership, 46*(4), 63-66.

National Research Council. (1989). *Everybody counts: A report on the future of mathematics education*. Washington, DC: National Academy Press.

Paulos, J. A. (1988). *Innumeracy: Mathematical illiteracy and its consequences*. New York: Hill and Wang.

Schwille, J., Porter, A., Floden, R., Freeman, D., Knapp, L., Kuhs, T., & Schmidt, W. (1983). Teachers as policy brokers in the content of elementary school mathematics. In L. Shulman & G. Sykes (Eds.), *Handbook of teaching and policy* (pp. 370-391). New York: Longman.

Sparks, G. M. (1988-89). Caution! Research results ahead. *Educational Leadership, 46*(4), 64.

Stodolsky, S. S. (1988). *The subject matters: Classroom activity in math and social studies*. Chicago: University of Chicago Press.

4

What Do Math Teachers Need to Be?

HERBERT CLEMENS

Here's a problem:

$$\frac{21}{1320} + \frac{12}{1255} = ?$$

Give your answer as a fraction in lowest terms.

What is your reaction? My guess is that the reaction of many grade school teachers would be something like, "Those numbers are too big, and, anyway, what book did that problem come from?"

Here's another problem:

$$\frac{21^{-2}}{7^{-3}} \div \frac{\frac{1}{7} - \frac{4}{21}}{1 + \frac{5}{7}} = ?$$

Give your answer as a fraction in lowest terms.

What is your reaction? Perhaps this time the first comment of elementary school teachers might be, "We're not supposed to know this, are we?" As a mathematician with absolutely no formal training in education, I can only guess at what a teacher's reaction to these problems would be, but I can tell you for sure what my first reaction is, namely, "I can do these problems!" Would I like to do 50 of these kinds of problems? Probably not. (Maybe I wouldn't even like to do five, but one or two would be okay.) When pressed by the chemistry of a school classroom to reach out to kids, my next reaction might be (and often has been)

> We can probably fool around with this big messy problem and pull together some interesting things about math. In fact, I can probably use this problem to explain some things better than the book can . . . let's see how would I start . . . it doesn't

84

matter if that approach doesn't work for some of the kids . . . after I read their minds a bit, I'll reorganize the problem with them in a way that works for them.

I like teaching and I like the way I teach; otherwise I wouldn't have written this chapter. So, to begin my answer to the question posed in the title, the first thing I think a math teacher must be is what I like to think I am (on my good days), and that is *unafraid*. To explain a bit more, let's ask the reverse question, What does it mean to be afraid? It means being anxious when confronted with that which is unknown or unfamiliar; it means jumping to the assumption, "I cannot deal with this new person or thing, and so this encounter is going to be a negative, defeating personal experience." If that's what we mean by being afraid, then many school teachers I know are afraid of math.

What else awould a teacher be? Again, let's pose a question: Are the above problems "fun"? Quite frankly, no. Can learning to solve them be fun? Maybe in one specially configured circumstance, yes, but not over the long haul. The numbers are big, the necessary multiplications and additions get very boring very quickly (unless we use a calculator), and, all in all, there are a lot more fun ways to spend an afternoon. I'm much too pseudo-sophisticated and cynical to be won over by the "math-is-fun" crowd. Interesting? Quite often, yes. But fun? No. Doing math is a lot like developing a spiritual component to life—when you are young and immature you do it because your parents force you to; when you grow up you understand its importance in your own life and you do it in your own personal way. The enterprise of mathematics is too basic and important, with too much beauty, history, and depth, to be trivialized into "fun and games."

So the second thing a math teacher must be is what any good cleric must be, namely, *reverent*. If we are good math teachers, then by our demeanor and way of talking about it, we reflect respect and reverence—not some ostentatious false piety, but a belief that the enterprise is worth it. True respect and reverence for mathematics, as for religion, rests on the belief that its content is solid enough to be doubted, questioned, probed, and attacked. The outcome is usually that the basic truths are unmoved, but that the individual who has the integrity and intelligence to question, probe, and attack has learned and grown in the process. We cannot expect young, immature minds to be capable of appreciating much of the beauty and depth, but we really must configure experiences—even when we have to force them a bit—that open up for our children the opportunity to appreciate these things in adult life. The question, "We're not supposed to know this, are we?" is the mathematical equivalent to some of the questions that were current during my adawescent religious training, like "What kind of a sin is it to French kiss for one minute and 30 seconds?"

What comes next in this scout's oath of math teacher virtues? I'd say it's the realization that, in the area of mathematical culture, the United States is an underdeveloped nation. All measures of the ability of our school children and general populace to deal with mathematics rank us far down on the roster of nations. Our power in advanced research and technology is derived increasingly from scholars who receive their basic education in other mathematically developed countries. So our math teachers, and all the rest of us, should be *humble*. We're a poor mathematical nation, we're ignorant, and the most important first step in attacking ignorance is to admit to ourselves that we are ignorant. In the fight for mathematical literacy, we're the underdogs. This may give us energy and determination, which is all to the good, but it should also induce a certain quiet sense of shame, and of admiration of those who do better than we do.

What's next? Let's go back to the reaction "I can do this problem."

$$\frac{21^{-2}}{7^{-3}} \div \frac{\frac{1}{7} - \frac{4}{21}}{1 + \frac{5}{7}} = ?$$

In fact, this problem is a terrific opportunity! It is complicated, like most interesting things, and it demands that we analyze it, break it up into simpler "steps." For example, I can work with

$$\frac{\frac{1}{7} - \frac{4}{21}}{1 + \frac{5}{7}}.$$

I know that I don't change the big ratio if I multiply it by

$$1 = \frac{21}{21}.$$

This problem is an opportunity to talk about clever ways to write the number 1. Many, many complicated fraction problems get a lot simpler if one writes "one" in a helpful way, but learning how to do that comes from "getting the hang of it," not from learning a bunch of rules. So a math teacher must be *opportunistic* and must pick the right moment to do the right thing.

In order to exploit opportunities, a math teacher must be *versatile*. Children are so different, one from another, in the ways they think, visualize, and learn. A teacher doesn't need one technique to teach fractions or place value; he or she needs three or four. He or she needs a file cabinet full of different materials, needs to be able to keep two or three different approaches going at the same time in the same lesson, and needs to have alternative approaches available if the current one isn't working. In my experience, no particular technique for presenting a given lesson on a given day reaches more than four or five students out of a group of 24. (Fortunately it's not always the same group of four or five!)

All these virtues are part of feeling in control of one's math. All good math teachers are *in control* of their math—ultimately this is reflected in the ability to change the rules if they need to and to be able to satisfy themselves and others as to whether the change is legitimate. To give a couple of very concrete examples of what I mean by being "in control," we might write, "there is a number whose square is -2," or we might write, "10101 = 21." Both of these are perfectly good mathematical statements if we explain them appropriately.[1] So we drive the mathematics, not the reverse. We're better than the book, or at least we can be, if we put our minds to it!

So far I've said nothing about what mathematics a math teacher should know, and that's not because I think that the question is unimportant. I believe I have mentioned those qualities, or lack thereof, that distinguish teachers, and the population in general, in mathematically developed countries from those in our own country. Empirical evidence indicates that these factors may be relevant to math education.

But what about subject matter? It is very appealing to think that there is a set of quantitative skills that we can give to math teachers and, together with some good teaching technique, they will do the job. There are some problems with that. For example, the little I know about research in math education says that better results come from teachers who inspire and who command respect for their quantitative ability than from teachers who know some particular type of mathematics, however enlightened and well designed.

This is not to say that the teacher's command of the subject is unimportant—it is essential. I can't imagine a teacher who is not bright and well trained in math feeling in control, opportunistic, and unafraid! But the criteria for subject matter should be its mathematical integrity and its relevance to quantitative experiences and questions that are natural to human beings. This leaves a lot of latitude in choosing subject matter. Basic quantitative insights and techniques, well exercised in any of a number of settings, are readily transferable by students, whereas the most enlightened and carefully drawn set of mathematical facts, in the hands of those with little insight, is a dangerous weapon! So math teachers have to have a feeling for math—there's just no substitute for that, which may say more about those we should pursue to become math teachers than it does about what particular mathematics they should learn.

EXAMPLES OF ELEMENTARY SCHOOL MATHEMATICS

That said, I'll tell you what math I would talk about if I were teaching in elementary school. But I want to insist that another choice made by someone else can be equally valid, with equal mathematical integrity and equal relevance to quantitative experiences and questions that are natural to human beings. Let me list four areas of knowledge that I would like children to understand before they leave grade school:

1. Place value, the base 10 number system
2. Operations with fractions
3. Estimating, approximation, margin of error
4. Lengths, areas, and volumes

I'd like to make some comments on each of these areas and to give some examples "at the high end" of what I would like teachers and students to know about them.

Place Value

"10101 = 21." If that equation makes sense to you, you know more about place value than I want children to know and about as much as I'd like most teachers to know. The left side of the above equation is, let's say, Mayan, and the right side is the equivalent phrase in English. The intellectual (mathematical) content of the two phrases is the same—it's just that, by historical accident, people counted with their arms in the land where the Mayan language developed, but they counted with their fingers in the land where English developed (see Figure 4.1).

Any difference between the two columns in Figure 4.1 has about as much to do with mathematics as the differences between good translations of *Brothers Karamazov* into, say, Spanish and French. I'd like teachers to understand that our decimal system is one of several languages with which we can express mathematical ideas, just as English is one of several languages with which we can express poetic ideas. Mathematical notation *does* affect mathematical thought, facilitating some concepts and obscuring others—if you doubt that, just try to do a large multiplication problem using Roman numerals. But there is a fundamental difference between the concepts themselves and the system we use to express them.

Operations with Fractions

The problem "6 ÷ 2 = ?" means "How many 2's are there in 6?" So too, "$\frac{1}{2} \div \frac{2}{9}$ = ?" means "How many $\frac{2}{9}$'s are there in $\frac{1}{2}$?" The latter is a problem about halves and ninths. Figure 4.2 shows a suitable model of the number 1 in which we can easily see the halves and ninths of it.

Figure 4.2 produces a graphical approach to solving $\frac{1}{2} \div \frac{2}{9}$. Using "invert and multiply" yields the same answer, but without a concrete referent: $\frac{1}{2} \div \frac{2}{9} = \frac{1}{2} \times \frac{9}{2} = \frac{9}{4}$, or $2\frac{1}{4}$. I would like a fifth-grade math teacher to be

How to add:
When you get 2 in a column replace it with 1 in the column to the left.

How to add:
When you get 10 in a column replace it with 1 in the next column to the left.

Multiplication table:

	0	1
0	0	0
1	0	1

Multiplication table:

(Remember third and fourth grade)

Sample problems

```
  10101
×    11
  10101
 10101
 111111
```

Sample problems

```
  21
×  3
  63
```

```
        1010.1
10 ┊ 10101.0
      10
       010
        10
        010
        10
```

```
       10.5
2 ⟌ 21.0
     2
     010
     10
```

FIGURE 4.1: The left-hand column is in Mayan, the right-hand column is the exact translation of the same mathematics into English.

able to make the entire journey, without skipping any of the necessary transitions, from the lesson in Figure 4.2 to the rule of "invert and multiply."

Perhaps calling for the depth of knowledge and understanding necessary to make such a journey implicitly advocates the introduction of "math specialists" to teach fifth- and sixth-grade math. At least there should be one teacher in any given school who can make the journey.

Why do I think that understanding operations with fractions is so important? I guess it's because of my experience teaching mathematics at the college level.

Calculus becomes a memorization game instead of a learning experience because students don't understand algebra. Algebra becomes a memorization game instead of a learning experience because students don't understand fractions. For example,

$$\frac{1}{x} + \frac{1}{y} = \frac{(y+x)}{xy}$$

Is this equality correct? If so, why? If not, why not? This is just adding fractions by finding a common denominator, or, if you want, just multiplying

$$\frac{1}{x} + \frac{1}{y}$$

by 1 in a fancy way

$$1 = \frac{xy}{xy}$$

so that

$$\frac{1}{x} + \frac{1}{y} = 1 \times \left(\frac{1}{x} + \frac{1}{y}\right)$$

$$= \left(\frac{xy}{xy}\right) \cdot \left(\frac{1}{x} + \frac{1}{y}\right)$$

$$= \left(\frac{xy}{xy}\right) \times \left(\frac{1}{x}\right) + \left(\frac{xy}{xy}\right) \cdot \left(\frac{1}{y}\right)$$

$$= \left(\frac{y}{xy}\right) + \left(\frac{x}{xy}\right)$$

$$= \frac{y+x}{xy} .$$

Squint a little bit, see 3 instead of x and 5 instead of y, and you have a problem in adding fractions. If you know how to add fractions with unlike denominators, you know how to do this algebra problem. There is no other area of elementary school mathematics more intimately related with what comes later.

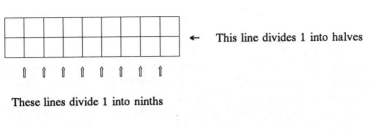

← This line divides 1 into halves

These lines divide 1 into ninths

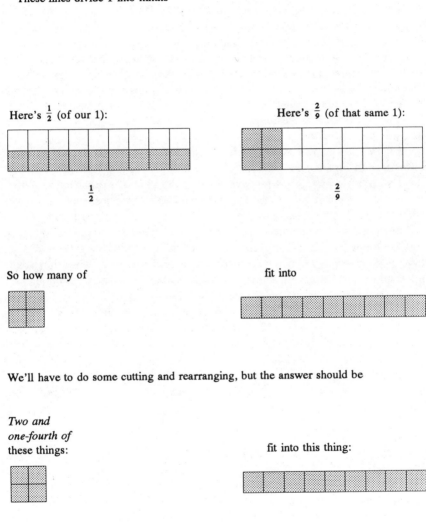

Here's $\frac{1}{2}$ (of our 1):

$\frac{1}{2}$

Here's $\frac{2}{9}$ (of that same 1):

$\frac{2}{9}$

So how many of   fit into

We'll have to do some cutting and rearranging, but the answer should be

Two and one-fourth of these things: fit into this thing:

FIGURE 4.2   How many $\frac{2}{9}$'s are in $\frac{1}{2}$?

Estimating

Lest this turn into a math lesson that doesn't know when to stop, I'll combine items 3 and 4 on my list and integrate my example of the type of estimation I find useful with the type of geometry I find useful (see Figure 4.3).

Children should be accustomed enough to estimating size to look at Figure 4.3 and decide that it will take less than 4 cans to paint the inside of the circle, and to give convincing reasons why it will take more than 2 cans. But suppose I wanted to know the answer to within one decimal place. What does that mean? What sort of strategy might I use to get the answer within the desired margin of error? These are fundamental questions about human quantitative experience. The questions are deep, interesting, yet accessible. Learning to deal with them successfully is easily transferable to other quantitative situations. Maybe they also give us a chance to meaningfully touch some of the concepts of higher math in a way accessible to children.

Figure 4.4 shows some useful strategies for the particular problem introduced in Figure 4.3.

I've tried to pick just a few examples of the kind of mathematical skills I think a math teacher might aim for. Even in these examples, there are many ways to deal with them successfully. There are many ways to teach about them, and many ways to think about them, that have mathematical value and integrity and that prepare children for quantitative success. Any way that gets children to think is good—there are no end of good ways. Good teachers, when they aren't too tired or overburdened, will find the way that is most natural to them.

Do my choices of examples mean that I don't think rote arithmetical skills are important? No, I don't think that at all. It should go almost without saying that kids have to be able to do the traditional computations such as adding, subtracting, multiplying, and dividing whole and decimal numbers with several digits, and do these computations rapidly and accurately. That's the base; those are the calisthenics; you have to do the calisthenics and keep doing them to stay in shape, or you can't play the game. But you also have to play the game, not just do calisthenics!

SOME FUNDAMENTAL QUESTIONS

I've tried to give a feel, by example, for the kind of mathematical acumen an elementary school math teacher should have and the kind of mathematical goals he or she might well have for students. It doesn't make sense for me to try to outline an entire curriculum—the National Council of Teachers of Mathematics (1989) has recently done that far better than any of us could. And besides, as I tried to stress at the outset, it's not always the particular topic or

If it takes one can of paint to paint the inside of this square

estimate how many cans of paint it takes to pain the inside of this circle:

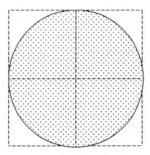

In other words, estimate the value of the number π.

FIGURE 4.3: An estimation problem.

approach that matters most. For me the more fundamental questions are as follows:

Does the subject matter have some mathematical integrity?
Does it have beauty and order?
Does it respond to a quantitative issue that is natural and basic for us humans?
Can this teacher teach it with conviction, and with some feeling for its essence?

1. It is sufficient to solve "one-fourth" of the problem:

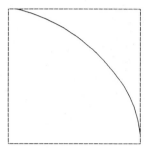

2. A fine grid will help:

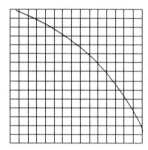

3. If it takes one can of paint to paint the big square, how much paint does it take to paint one of the tiny squares? (There are 19 in each direction.)
4. How many tiny squares lie entirely inside the quarter-circle?
5. Use this information to give a lower estimate for the amount of paint needed to paint the quarter-circle.
6. How many tiny squares completely cover up the quarter-circle?
7. Use this information to give an upper estimate for the amount of paint needed to paint the quarter-circle.
8. How far is your lower estimate from your upper one? So how close are you to the exact value of one-fourth π?
9. Now multiply your estimates by four. What happens to your margin of error?

FIGURE 4.4: Finding a more precise estimate.

A PROFESSION IN DANGER

Finally, why in the world does a research mathematician, with a safe and comfortable job at a nice university, worry about grade school math? I suppose there are some selfless, noble motives that one could cite, but for many of us the issue is more crass and mundane than that. Our profession is currently in danger, and the danger is directly traceable to the fact that our culture no longer values what we do. Our schools reflect our culture and they transmit its message too—go to school and get training so you can get a job and make money, preferably a lot of money. Worry about training, but don't worry about education, that's too impractical for all but the ivory tower types. Get grades, not ideas.

So we have to import our scientists from other countries, and even that is becoming more difficult as career opportunities for those people increase in their home countries. Our university students complain that their math teachers don't speak English. Of course not, when the students' own older brothers and sisters, and fathers and mothers, can't compete for university teaching positions because of inferior scientific qualifications!

All aspects of mathematics, from grade school to advanced research, develop together, or in the end none develop. Some of us find mathematics exquisitely beautiful, the quantitative equivalent of the best poetry and literature. And if history is any guide, future generations will often find mathematical theory, developed now for aesthetic reasons, astoundingly useful. But the entire enterprise is threatened from within because it is not valued by our young, and we mathematicians share the blame for that. We are often intellectual "yuppies," concentrating only on that which is at the pinnacle, because that's where the personal rewards are, but forgetting to attend to the base. Together, let us attend to the base lest the entire structure crumble!

NOTES

1. Mathematicians understand the square root of -1 to be written as i. So the square root of -2 is $i\sqrt{2}$ [because $(i\sqrt{2})^2 = i^2(2)$, or $2(-1)$, or -2]. The second statement has to do with expressing the same quantity in different number systems. In this case, twenty-one is represented in base 2 as 10101, where the places are worth, from right to left, respectively: $2^0, 2^1, 2^2, 2^3, 2^4$. Thus 10101 equals $(1 \times 2^4) + (0 \times 2^3) + (1 \times 2^2) + (0 \times 2^1) + (1 \times 2^0)$, or $16 + 0 + 4 + 0 + 1$. In base 10, the places are worth, from right to left, respectively, $10^0, 10^1, 10^2, 10^3$, and so on, so twenty-one is represented as 21 because it's $(2 \times 10^1) + (1 \times 10^0)$, or $20 + 1$.

REFERENCES

National Council of Teachers of Mathematics, Commission on Standards for School
    Mathematics. (1989). *Curriculum and evaluation standards for school mathematics.*
    Reston, VA: Author.

Teaching History and Social Studies

The term *social sciences* is used to refer to a number of disciplines, represented in universities by departmental units and recognized among scholars not only by the content they study but by their methods of inquiry, rules of evidence, and ways of forming problems. The relationship between these social sciences and the school subject *social studies* is far from clear. Moreover, more than most school subjects, social studies are imbued with community values and cultural norms. It is the special burden of teachers in these fields not only to bridge the school subject and the discipline, but to bridge them both with community and cultural expectations as well.

The awkward relationship between school subjects and disciplines is not unique to the social sciences; we have seen similar tensions in virtually every other subject. But the value-laden content and moral overtones that accompany social studies probably distinguish this subject from other school subjects and provide a special challenge for social studies teachers. Addressing the teaching of these unusual subjects are Suzanne Wilson and James Banks, both of whom would like their subject to be taught better than it now is. Both want the subject to be meaningful; both want it to be intellectually serious. But they differ in how to get there from here.

The first view, presented by Suzanne Wilson, concentrates on teaching history. Wilson would redefine history for students, so that it is not a list of names and dates, but instead a way of trying to understand events, one that uses particular methods of inquiry and is guided by particular rules of evidence, but that yields multiple and evolving interpretations, rather than fixed, definitive conclusions, about the events it seeks to understand. The second author, James Banks, reminds us that there are other aspects to social studies—that social values and cultural perspectives are inescapable parts of social sciences and that these perspectives necessarily limit the potential of each social science. History, for instance, tends to focus on white European males, while anthropology tends to focus on other groups. Because each social science is imbued not only with its own methodology and content but also with its own perspective, teachers need both to understand and to teach these subjects together rather than separately.

5

Parades of Facts, Stories of the Past: What Do Novice History Teachers Need to Know?

SUZANNE M. WILSON

There appears to be reason for concern. American students believe that Arizona is the capital of Pennsylvania. They think that the Great Depression took place *before* World War I and that the New Deal had something to do with the purchase of Alaska. They certainly don't know the names of all of our presidents; as a matter of fact, some of them don't know there was a president named Harding. This frightening lack of knowledge about the past has been thoroughly documented, most notably in the results of the National Assessment of History and Literature reported by Ravitch and Finn (1987).

Although not as well known, similarly depressing reports have been made of history teaching. Teachers talk; students record dates, names, events. Occasionally, the march through endless lectures is broken with a filmstrip. Seldom are students engaged in critical thought; for many of them, class remains the place where they memorize dates, storing yet more worthless information in the corners of their minds reserved for school knowledge. They have little understanding of the potential that such knowledge holds for them, what meaning it has, how they might use it. Consequently, students have no sense of themselves as historical beings, individuals whose lives are determined, to some extent, by where they came from.

Consensus seems to be, then, whether one is talking about what students learn in history class or about how students are taught, that history teaching and learning are in desperate straits. Although teachers are but part of the current problem, in this chapter I focus on the knowledge, skills, and dispositions that beginning history teachers in secondary schools need if they are to change current practice. For the purposes of my argument, I draw many examples from the teaching of U.S. history since it is a mainstay in the elementary and secondary school curriculum. However, I believe the points I make about U.S. history teachers and teaching are more generally applicable to many courses housed under the title of social studies.

WHAT SHOULD STUDENTS LEARN IN HISTORY CLASS?

Implicit in any evaluation we make of the quality of teaching and learning is a set of assumptions about what students should learn in school. That is, our disdain for what students are not presently learning in high school history classes is, in large part, determined by what we think they *should* be learning. Yet there is little consensus, even among experts, concerning what secondary history education is about. The field has a history of its own, one that is largely characterized by disagreements about the content of the social studies curriculum. Shouldn't history teachers, some individuals ask, teach students citizenship values? "No!" others argue, "history teachers should teach the subject matter—American, African, ancient, European, third world history." The arguments continue, opinions and positions abound, and history teaching is alternatively characterized as values clarification, critical thinking, issue-oriented and thematic, or discipline-grounded.

But the camps that various social studies educators have defined for themselves are unproductive illusions, false dichotomies in a sense. There is no need for either-or choices in social studies—one doesn't have to teach about American history *or* about citizenship, one needn't teach about critical thinking *or* the history of third world nations. History teachers, like any other teachers, have multiple agendas and responsibilities. Yes, they are supposed to teach their students to be good citizens; yes, they are supposed to help students clarify their values; yes, they are supposed to hand down to students the history of our past, as well as the histories of other peoples.

Those goals are not antithetical. Rather, they may all be different ways of talking about the same set of concerns—that our schools are in the business of producing an educated citizenry, a citizenry that knows enough about the past to have a sense of itself as a body politic that has evolved out of a set of social, cultural, political, and economic traditions. Moreover, an educated citizen knows how to think analytically and critically. All goals can be achieved if we represent the disciplines being taught with integrity. As they teach students about the American Revolution, history teachers can teach students to think critically. Students can learn both the content—the Boston Tea Party and the Intolerable Acts, Sam Adams and the Committees of Correspondence, Lexington and Concord—and historical analysis—examining different interpretations of the same set of characters and events, weighing the evidence presented by historians and source materials, discussing the strengths and weaknesses of various accounts.

Good history teachers can and do teach students both the subject matter of the course and how to think critically about themselves, their values, the world around them, and their place in that world. And educating students about their past in this way, empowering them to think critically about the present by asking questions and being skilled in answering them, is a form of citizenship education. Such students have the knowledge and skill to examine the status quo, actively participate in changing what needs to be changed, and defending what needs to be protected and nurtured.

SO WHAT IS GOOD HISTORY TEACHING?

The image of good teaching on which this chapter is based is one that is grounded in subject matter. It is a disciplinary conception of history teaching that presupposes that one major goal for teaching history is the communication of historical knowledge—the central facts, concepts, and ideas of the discipline—and the nature of the methods employed by historians, for example, the role played by interpretation and narrative. This conception also presupposes that knowledgeable teachers can use their knowledge of history to further other goals—developing critical thinking skills, teaching students to communicate effectively, and helping students identify and clarify their values, thus contributing to the schooling of an educated citizenry. By claiming that students should learn about the more interpretative aspects of history, I am not suggesting that we revisit the "new history" curricula of the 1960s. Developing an awareness in students of the nature of historical knowledge is not equivalent to making students into "little historians." History teachers may have students "do" history in order to develop a sense for the interpretative nature of historical knowledge, even though they are not committed to producing miniature Beards or Bailyns. Teachers may engage students in activities that *resemble* history, helping them develop patterns of reasoning that are appropriate in asking and answering questions of a social nature, without assuming that all of their students will become professional historians.

Historical knowledge is, at its heart, interpretive. Teachers need to communicate that to students. The nature of historical knowledge has implications for the pedagogy of history. If students are constantly told information, an implicit message may be sent that there is something absolute or final about the material being presented. It is not sufficient for history teachers to be good story tellers, for the stories of the past are not settled. Sometimes teachers may tell stories, but at other times they may want students to write their own accounts or to read various conflicting accounts, so that students can see the different perspectives taken by a range of scholars on a single event. At other times, teachers may engage students in debates or discussions, asking them to support a position using evidence and logical argument. Whenever and whatever they choose to teach, history teachers must simultaneously consider the content, the instructional strategies most appropriate for teaching that content, and the knowledge and experiences their students bring with them.

Good history teaching, then, requires teachers who are knowledgeable about the subject matter, who are skilled at creating educational settings in which students may acquire similar understandings, and who constantly reflect on the interaction of concerns for content, students, and goals. In the following section of this chapter, I describe a series of lessons planned by Sean, a first-year teacher. Because good teaching requires intentional action, I will describe both the teacher's instructional strategies and his rationale for his choices. Following this brief description of Sean, I explore the kinds of knowledge and understanding Sean possesses about history and about teaching that allow him to think and to act in the way that he does.

SEAN: LEARNING TO TEACH THE GREAT DEPRESSION

Sean knew a little about the Depression and New Deal from a few classes he had taken in history and political science as an undergraduate. He knew, for example, that Franklin Roosevelt was a controversial figure, that the stock market crash did not cause the Depression but was symptomatic of larger economic problems, and that the New Deal consisted, in part, of a series of legislative acts that were designed to stimulate the economy and reform some of its ills, all while providing relief to some sectors of the American public.

Sean was pretty sure that his students would have little knowledge of either the crash or the New Deal and had several goals for this unit. He wanted students to learn about Roosevelt's personal and political history; to understand the destitute conditions many people endured during the Depression and Dust Bowl; to learn about some of the personalities of the time—Eleanor Roosevelt, Frances Perkins, Harold Ickes, Father Coughlin, Huey Long, John Lewis, among them; and to understand the controversy associated with Roosevelt's administrations.

Noting that the authors of the American history textbook he had been assigned focused primarily on political issues and debates during the New Deal, and that they appeared to be Roosevelt loyalists, Sean went back to several texts he had read as an undergraduate for information he could use to augment the rather one-sided and underdeveloped textbook account. In addition to using historical and political science texts, he went to Terkel's (1970) *Hard Times*, Steinbeck's (1939/1967) *The Grapes of Wrath*, and a collection of Margaret Bourke-White's photographs.

The unit Sean eventually taught consisted of a number of activities. During the first four days of the unit, he delivered a set of mini-lectures on various aspects of the crash, Roosevelt, and his New Deal legislation, supplemented with teacher-led discussions of issues such as laissez-faire capitalism, social insurance, labor and unionization, and the Dust Bowl. During these classes, Sean was the center of attention, monitoring how and when the conversations progressed, asking students questions about the topics covered in the textbook reading, tying in current events when appropriate. During several other classes, which focused on the social and cultural history of the period, Sean constructed small-group activities for his students in which they alternatively examined slides and photographs of Dust Bowl farmers, soup lines, and Hoovervilles; read excerpts from *The Grapes of Wrath* and *Hard Times*; and listened to music of the period. Asked why he included these lessons, Sean explained

> When kids are taught that history is only what happened in the presidential elections and in Washington, D.C., they think, "Oh well, no wonder history means nothing to me. There's stuff that's happening there [in Washington] and I don't know about it either. No big deal." I think they need to see how common Americans are affected and affect decisions that have been made. I want them to understand what *life was like*. I want them to understand that history is more than elections. It's a way of thinking, of acting. It's about ways of life.
>
> I want them to connect in some way to the material and not just read it and digest it and spit it back. I want them to *become* the material, if only for a moment. I think that kids think that all history is is a bunch of stuff that already happened that was sort of inevitable. That history is just sort of stuff that happened. They say, "This already happened. There is *nothing* we can do about it." I also tend to think that they look at the present-day world as history. It's stuff that is going on and there is nothing they can do about it. I want to get them out of this passive role.

In addition to his lectures and small-group activities, Sean included a lesson called "You Are the President," in which he presented students with the problems Roosevelt faced during the Depression and asked students to generate their own solutions. Asked why such an activity was important, Sean said

> I put them in Roosevelt's shoes because then when I talk about what actually happened, it's not just history, it's not just something that happened 50 years ago. Instead, it's "Well, how did I do?!?! How would *I* have done if I was president of the United States then?" I think that that would engage them a little bit more.
>
> This activity puts students in the shoes of people of the time. Now historians will tell you that that's a problem because we think differently now and kids don't necessarily understand that, but I say, "What's more important here?" I think my job is to get them excited about history so they'll go on to learn more.

Sean concluded his unit on the Depression and New Deal with two activities: a debate and a whole-class discussion of the success of the New Deal. The debate Sean organized his class around concerned the question, "Was the New Deal *new*?" He assigned all the students to sides and presented them with some materials he had found to help them prepare to support one or the other position. After two days of debate and conversation, Sean led a large-group discussion with his students concerning the range of interpretations about the success of the New Deal.

In this class, he presented students with three alternative perspectives on the question, "Did the New Deal work?" in which one historian claimed that Roosevelt had saved the country, another historian suggested that World War II, not the New Deal, pulled the country out of the Depression, and a third historian suggested that Roosevelt failed to save the country because he did not take advantage of the fact that he could have made some significant and radical changes in our political, economic, and social structure had he been so inclined. The class then discussed these three perspectives, and Sean ended the period by suggesting that students should draw their own conclusions based on the three arguments.

It is clear that Sean, even though he is only a novice at teaching, is thinking about subject matter, students, learning, and teaching as he considers what and how he should teach. But what does Sean have to know in order to make pedagogical decisions wisely? What knowledge, skill, and dispositions are necessary for him to make the appropriate instructional choices?

WHAT DO BEGINNING TEACHERS NEED TO KNOW?

The list of understandings and abilities that teachers should possess is endless. Rather than delineate a complete list, I will discuss two aspects of the knowledge of beginning teachers: subject matter knowledge and subject-specific pedagogical knowledge. Within each of those dimensions, I propose that we focus on two features of beginning teachers' knowledge.

Subject Matter Knowledge

Proposition 1: Social studies teachers should know one subject matter within the social studies deeply. Good teachers are dedicated to exposing their students to the richness and wonder of the subject matter they teach. Good history teachers, for example, want their students to understand that history is interesting and exciting, full of fascinating stories and colorful people. They also want their students to understand themselves as persons placed in a context that has been developed and shaped by what has gone before. Teachers who themselves do not understand history in this rich sense cannot help students develop such understandings.

But what does it mean to have deep or rich knowledge of something? Deep knowledge of the "stuff" of American history is not easily measured. It is not simply a matter of *more* knowledge, that is, the ability to recite more dates, recognize more names, recall more events. Rather, it is an elaborated understanding of historical phenomena. There are at least four qualitative dimensions along which we can consider depth of historical knowledge.

First, depth of knowledge can be described as *differentiated,* that is, teachers can understand the main components and subcomponents of a concept or event. For example, an American history teacher can know that there were three major aspects of the Social Security Act as it was proposed in the New Deal: aid to senior citizens, unemployment insurance, and aid to dependent children. Differentiated knowledge of the subject matter, then, means that a teacher perceives and understands the components, dimensions, or features of a particular idea in a social science. In other words, the teacher has skeletal knowledge of the concept or idea.

Differentiated knowledge of the subject matter is essential for teaching. Teachers need to be able to represent the subject matter to students accurately. A teacher whose knowledge of social security is limited to the fact that each month a portion of his or her salary is withheld for social security may fail to communicate to students that social insurance as embodied by the Social Security Act is a much larger issue than the social security checks that retired persons receive. Clearly, without differentiated knowledge, teachers would not be able to distinguish what was important to teach about the subject matter, to separate the wheat from the chaff, so to speak.

A second aspect of deep historical understanding is how *qualified* the knowledge is. Qualification reflects an awareness of the fact that historical knowledge is contextualized and underdetermined. These two factors frequently lead historians to qualify their explanations of the past, by explicitly stating that the conclusions they draw are bound both by the contexts within which events took place and by the undetermined nature of their work.

One of the ways that historical content gets simplified on its way into classrooms is by the neglect of contextual information. In many textbooks, for example, the New Deal is portrayed as an innovative, bold, and radical program of legislation proposed by President Roosevelt with the help of his Brain Trusters. But many measures that Roosevelt took were based on programs that had long before been implemented in European countries. It is unlikely that this information could be found anywhere in the textbooks. Sean knew this and purposefully provided students with information about alternative interpretations of F.D.R. and the "innovations" of his administration. Similarly, many textbooks fail to state explicitly that their content is knowledge as it can best be determined presently. Material in textbooks is *not* presented as interpretation but as hard, cold fact. Students, for example, read about the causes of the French Revolution and are seldom told that there is disagreement among scholars about what the actual causes were, how they were related to one another, and how they interacted. Students who never learn to treat texts as sources of information rather than authorities, are seriously limited in their ability to think critically about the information that they are presented with (Wilson, 1988).

Historians entertain many hypotheses and search for the complete set of causes that contributed to a phenomenon, and the process of developing an interpretation involves selecting, sorting, and sequencing those causes, as well as establishing priorities among them. But the prioritizing of one cause over another does not lead historians to the conclusion that their candidate for primacy is the *sole* cause. Most remain humble enough to acknowledge the existence of other, albeit in their opinion less central, causes. Teachers must have qualified knowledge of the subject matter they teach if they are to expose their students to the nature of understanding and knowledge.

A third characteristic of deep knowledge of the subject matter is how *elaborated*, or detailed, a teacher's understanding is. This dimension recognizes that teachers can possess knowledge of an event, person, concept, or idea that goes beyond the skeletal information associated with differentiated knowledge of subject matter. Details play an important role in the social sciences, often providing new insights into old questions and allowing social scientists to generate more refined or, sometimes, novel explanations for phenomena. In other words, knowledge of detail often correlates with knowledge of the complexity of the problems that historians wrestle with, an understanding of the subtle distinctions that make the obvious not so obvious. An extended example from an American history class will illustrate this point (Davidson & Lytle, 1986).

Most students of colonial history know that the Jamestown colony had a high death rate throughout its early years; for example, despite the fact that over 3,750 settlers migrated between 1619 and 1621, the population of the colony hovered around 700. An astute student would be able to generate a number of valid reasons for this phenomenon: inadequate housing, disease, contaminated wells, poor diet.

The factors I have listed are all reasonable; in fact, all of them contributed to the startling death rate, which was somewhere between 75% and 80%. But if one knows two other details, the picture changes. First, the death rate during the plague epidemics in Britain in the fourteenth century never exceeded 50%. It is puzzling that Jamestown would have had a death rate higher than that of the worst years of the plague. Second, there was a law that required Virginians to plant corn. Another anomaly: In a colony where people were starving and corn could be grown easily and efficiently, why would the government mandate the planting of corn?

Knowledge of these details (and others) and the paradoxes that they create when placed against the dire conditions in Jamestown led historians to discover that Virginians were funneling all their physical and financial resources into the cultivation of tobacco. To shorten, and assuredly oversimplify, the example, what one can conclude is that the reasons for the extraordinarily high death rate of the Jamestown colonists were not all dependent on the fact that the colonists were "fighting the elements." Rather, the colonists were themselves contributing to the inflated death rate by the conscious decisions they made about how to invest their time, energy, and resources.

Even this oversimplified example serves to demonstrate how complicated and complex historical phenomena are. There are levels of understanding in any historical problem, and knowledge of details is essential for acquiring knowledge of those multiple levels. In the case of Jamestown, knowledge of the high death rate and the horrendous conditions leads to one kind of understanding; knowledge of a few details, like the law about planting corn, sharpens and changes (to some extent) that understanding.

Granted, not all details are equally relevant. But weighing the relative value of details is a slippery issue—the salience and significance of details are dependent on a plethora of variables, including the questions being asked and the context in which the phenomenon took place. It may very well be true that I don't need to know whether Huey Long had a pet; yet, it is essential that I know that Nixon had a dog if I am to understand his "Checkers" speech. Additionally, teachers often use such details to motivate students. Students care more about Gentleman Johnny Burgoyne when they hear about the wagonloads of French champagne. In the midst of misery, here is a man who is eating and drinking as well as King George. Good teachers use such enlivening detail to capture the fancy of their students.

A final dimension of deep understanding of the subject mater is *integration* or relatedness. In the social sciences there are many ways in which ideas or phenomena can be interrelated. I will use two types of relationships as examples: causal and thematic. Within the field of history, for instance, events and people can be integrated by looking at causal relationships between them. Events or figures can be interpreted to represent similar issues or ideas, thus providing another way of integrating historical knowledge. I discuss each relationship in turn.

Some historians claim that the study of history is the study of causes. Frequently, they look for cause by asking why: *Why* did Roosevelt win the election of 1932? *Why* did the British Empire expand in the ways that it did? *Why* does apartheid exist? But historians seldom find one answer to their question. Instead, they find multiple and competing candidates for their construction of causal explanations. Subsequently, they arrange the causes, constructing interpretations. Cause, then, and historians' interpretation of causality, are central to history. If a teacher makes the claim that he or she has knowledge of history, it follows that the teacher must be aware that questions of cause, purpose, and motive are central to historical understanding.

But the phenomena examined by historians are related in ways other than causation. Another type of integration is related to the thematic or categorical relationships between ideas or phenomena. Events, ideas, and people can *represent* particular issues or phenomena or themes, and what makes them significant is their representativeness. For example, Sean knew that James Farrell and John Steinbeck were both authors who used their fiction to showcase and protest hardships weathered by American families during the Depression. He used this knowledge in selecting the types of literature he wanted students to read during the unit on the Depression.

Similarly, Sean knew that the Unemployment Relief Act, which created the Civilian Conservation Corps, represents a type of relief legislation that Roosevelt pushed through Congress during the First New Deal, while the Tennessee Valley Authority Act is an example of reform legislation. Because he knew that these pieces of legislation stood for different aspects of Roosevelt's New Deal—relief versus reform—Sean selected them, from the morass of acts, agencies, and laws presented in the textbook, as *representing* central issues. Thus, students learned that these acts were *meaningful*, that they represented issues, and did not think of them simply as floating facts to be memorized for no particular reason. Nor did the students memorize seemingly endless lists of the alphabet soup legislation of the New Deal. Sean's knowledge the subject matter allowed him to *select* the appropriate material to have students learn.

Proposition 2: History teachers should be knowledgeable about the nature of each of the disciplines that constitute the social studies. A central dilemma in the certification of social studies teachers is that most teachers are certified to teach not one subject, but many subjects, when they receive their social studies credential. It is possible for a teacher to become certified to teach any social studies class without ever having taken a course in American history. It is not unusual for new teachers to teach courses that they have not had since they themselves were in elementary or secondary school. Such certification practice flies in the face of our commitment to subject matter knowledge in teachers.

If we take seriously the notion that teachers must have rich subject matter knowledge, we cannot expect that social studies teachers can or will know equally well anthropology, sociology, political science, economics, American history, world history, western European history, psychology, and the other subjects that are included in social studies. It is impossible for one teacher to know, in the kind of depth I have described, all of the social sciences that make up the high school social studies curriculum. Yet most social studies teachers are required to teach multiple subject matters, sometimes even in the same course.

There are at least two solutions to the dilemma. We could call for narrowing the focus of certification within the social studies, certifying teachers to teach one subject matter, not many. This solution would not be practical for the hundreds of small high schools in our country where teachers routinely must teach multiple courses. Alternatively, we could continue to certify teachers for all of the social studies but require that every teacher proclaim a specialty. Teachers would be required to exhibit deep subject matter knowledge within their specialty and a more superficial understanding of the other content areas they might be assigned to teach.

Among the understandings one might require on this other level might be knowledge of the similarities and differences across the social sciences, that is, what makes economics different from political science, history different from anthropology. But this requirement cannot be fulfilled by new teachers reciting dictionary definitions of the different social sciences. Anthropology is more than the study of human beings; sociology, more than the study of society and institutions of social order; psychology, more than the study of the self. Each of these disciplines is characterized both by the questions pursued by its members and the methods used to answer those questions. Social studies teachers need to understand the nature of knowledge and work in each of the subjects they teach, for at least two reasons.

First, although there is always the potential that over time, teachers will learn more about the subject matters they teach, misconceptions about those subject matters may be obstacles to future learning. For example, in working with novice teachers, we have found that those who believed that history was fact, even when exposed to interpretations in history, did not recognize them for what they were (Wilson & Wineburg, 1988). In a very real sense, their ignorance closed off possible doors to future learning. On the other hand, Sean knew that there were certain things he didn't know about the New Deal. For example, he was not aware of alternative interpretations of Roosevelt's leadership, but his knowledge of history led him to believe that there were multiple perspectives on how good a president Roosevelt was. Consequently, he looked through his books for information about varying accounts and found them. In contrast, Fred, a novice teacher who believed that history was fact, would not even know to pursue this possibility. In this way, Sean's knowledge of the nature of history facilitated his continued learning. Conversely, Fred's ignorance impeded such learning. When certifying beginning teachers, we are forced to assume that there are many things that teachers will learn from experience in classrooms. But making this assumption does not free us of the responsibility for priming them for that learning.

The other reason history teachers should know about the social studies is that they should have a sense of where students have come from and where they are going. Knowing, for example, that students will be taking a course in economics in their senior year, an American history teacher can lay some foundational knowledge about the relationship between economics, politics, culture, and industry in the United States. Alternatively, when the class discusses bank crises, stock market crashes, or the federal reserve system, history teachers can introduce vocabulary that will facilitate future learning. Teachers who know where their students have been and where they are going are better prepared to treat those students as people who have already learned a great deal about history and social sciences, and who will be learning more in the future.

But knowledge of history and social sciences is not sufficient for teaching. Each of us has encountered brilliant historians who had little capacity to teach. Knowledge of the subject matter is necessary to teaching but it is not sufficient. History teachers also need to know *how to teach* history. Such a complex capacity involves many types of knowledge, skill, and disposition, but in this chapter I concentrate on one kind of understanding, subject-specific pedagogical knowledge. Such understanding is the joint product of concerns about teaching, learners, and subject matter.

Subject-Specific Pedagogical Knowledge

Subject-specific pedagogical knowledge, alternatively called pedagogical content knowledge (Shulman, 1986; Shulman & Sykes, 1986; Wilson, Shulman, & Richert, 1987), is an understanding of how to teach particular subject matters to learners to meet certain goals. Subject-specific pedagogical knowledge has many dimensions. For beginning teachers, two important aspects of knowing history for the purposes of teaching include knowing how to transform the subject matter for teaching and knowing how to analyze and use curricular materials appropriately.

Proposition 3: History teachers should know how to transform the subject matter. Teaching history is not equivalent to knowing history: A third party, the learner, is always present in teaching. Good teachers know that students have beliefs, knowledge, skills, preconceptions, and experiences that affect what they learn. The story one student hears and takes away from history class will be much different from the story another student hears. Teachers who have subject-specific pedagogical knowledge know many things about how students typically construct their understandings about the history they are taught. Such teachers know about the most common misconceptions students have about revolution, about leadership, about chronology, about government. Moreover, these teachers consider students' beliefs and interests as they decide how to present the content to students. This process of thinking about the subject matter and about the learner and making decisions about how best to teach can be called a process of *transformation*. In transforming the subject matter into educational experiences for students, teachers create *representations* of history

(Shulman, 1987; Shulman & Sykes, 1986; Wilson, Shulman, & Richert, 1987; Wineburg & Wilson, in press). Talking about the relationship between England and the colonies in terms of a mother and child is one representation of that relationship. Other illustrations, metaphors, examples, and analogies might cast the relationship in a different light, providing yet other representations.

Sean's instruction included a number of representations. His "You Are the President" activity presented students with information about the problems that the nation suffered during the Depression in a format that made students reflect on how they might solve such dilemmas. In this way, he tried to transform historical information about the New Deal into an experience that would appeal to students and engage their thinking. In much the same way, he decided to have students debate the question, "How new was the New Deal?" Such an activity required that students learn information that would help them develop their arguments, as well as requiring that students develop logical arguments in response to the question. By engaging students in such a task, Sean was also trying to communicate to students the underdetermined nature of history—that the answer to the question, "Was the New Deal really new?" is not an unequivocal "Yes!" or "No!" but a matter of interpretation. In both of these cases, we can see Sean struggling with transforming information about the Depression and the New Deal into instructional representations of the material. As he did so, his concerns for content—what he wanted students to learn about history, for students—what they already knew or believed or valued, and for purposes—teaching students to develop arguments, use materials, and appreciate the value of knowledge of the past, all contribute to his pedagogical reasoning (Wilson, 1988).

Teachers must have a repertoire of such representations, for all students do not have the same prior experiences and will not respond equally to a single representation. So while historians can write one explanation, teachers must generate multiple representations in response to students' questions and concerns. Sean is beginning to accumulate a collection—the mini-lectures, the large-group discussions and questioning, the debate, the "You Are the President" activity, the small-group work with photographs, music, and literature—of instructional representations of the Depression and New Deal.

We cannot expect beginning teachers to have the wealth of representations that an experienced teacher may have accumulated over many years of practice. Nor can we expect their representations to be fully developed or finely tuned. However, it is essential that they be predisposed toward transforming the subject matter in ways that capitalize on what students already know and believe. They also need to have the skills and understandings necessary to generate such representations and to evaluate representations that they acquire from other sources, such as other teachers or curriculum materials.

Proposition 4: History teachers should know how to evaluate curricular materials critically. I make this claim for a very simple reason. It has been well documented that the textbook remains a central teaching tool and source of information for social studies teachers (Shaver, Davis, & Helburn, 1979a, 1979b). Unfortunately, analyses of social studies textbooks, like those done by FitzGerald (1979) and Gagnon (1987, 1988), suggest that the history represented in textbooks bears little relation to other histories. The information presented in textbooks is often oversimplified, seldom current, and sometimes false.

If textbooks do not present truth, if some of them present pablum instead of history, teachers who treat textbooks as knowledge run the risk of teaching untruths to their students. I highlight teachers' use of textbooks here as an illustration of the larger issue: Much of what finds its way into high school history classes, either in the form of textbooks or other curricular materials, is not the subject matter to be taught. It is history revised, to paraphrase FitzGerald. Teachers must know how to appraise textbooks critically, using them as resources, not as the sole determinants of content or pedagogy.

I will revisit the example of Jamestown to make this point. Todd and Curti (1986), authors of one of the most popular textbooks in the United States at this time, provide the following depiction of Jamestown:

> **Better times at Jamestown.** Slowly, after 1610, the conditions [in Jamestown] began to improve. Much to everyone's surprise, tobacco saved the colony. . . . By 1619 there were more than 1,000 colonists in Virginia and most were raising tobacco. . . . The directors of the London Company, encouraged by Virginia's growing prosperity, sent out hundreds of new settlers. Some of them started an ironworks on the James River. Others planted olive trees and laid out vineyards, but most of the newcomers cleared a piece of land and began to grow tobacco.
>
> Then disaster struck. Nearby Indians had become alarmed at the rapid growth of the colony. On March 22, 1622, Indians attacked the outlying farmhouses, killed 347 settlers, including John Rolfe, and burned most of the buildings. (pp. 24-25)

Textbook authors have to simplify American history; it would be impossible to provide all the information and current thought that exists about the history of the United States in one book, even if there were several volumes. The account of Jamestown that Todd and Curti present is accurate—after 1610, conditions *did* begin to improve, the population of the colony *did* grow, most of the colonists *were* raising tobacco. But a teacher who knew that the colonists were so busy putting all their resources into tobacco planting for profit that they failed to grow enough crops to feed the colony would be able to and might choose to help students understand that, while tobacco was a saviour in some ways, tobacco was the devil in others. A teacher who knew that 3,570 settlers were sent to the colony between 1619 and 1622 and that the population of Jamestown in 1622 was about 700 (which is what it was in 1619 prior to the importation of these settlers) would also know that 3,500 settlers disappeared. If that teacher also knew that no significant portion of them returned to England or migrated to other colonies, and that the Indians killed 347 of them in the 1622 incident, he or she would know that 3,000 colonists died in some other way over that time span. The incident reported in the text accounts for only 10% of the total deaths. Clearly, teachers' knowledge of subject matter and subject-specific pedagogy are critical to their ability to evaluate textbooks. Teachers with little subject matter knowledge, for example, might become victims of their limited sources. Unaware of the problematic nature of the content of history texts, they might choose to teach as truth what they have read. Novices in the subject matter, that is, may not be able to differentiate when a textbook account is accurate and when it is not.

I close this discussion with a warning. It is dangerous and presumptuous to assume that the types of knowledge—deep subject matter knowledge and subject-specific pedagogical knowledge—described here are the result of the completion of an undergraduate degree in history and a teacher education program. Many undergraduates never learn to think about history in the rich and flexible ways that I have described. That kind of knowledge cannot be acquired by taking a series of survey courses, nor is it the result of the kind of teaching documented by Boyer (1987). Yet many states have responded to the claim that teachers need to have more content knowledge simply by increasing the number of required courses teachers take in the content areas that they intend to teach. This is a shortsighted and superficial response to a substantive and substantial problem.

Likewise, the pedagogical reasoning required to generate instructional representations and the subject-specific knowledge needed for teaching are not results of all teacher education programs. For any set of claims we make about what teachers need to know, we must also consider when and where they acquire these understandings. In the case of history teaching, the picture is grim.

CONCLUSION

The current practice of teaching history at schools and universities exerts a powerful influence on future generations of history teachers. Our future teachers have few models of good teaching to use as touchstones, and the certification of beginning teachers' knowledge alone is not likely to be a sufficient counterforce, even if it were substantially reformed. Tomorrow's teachers are today's students, sitting in school and university classrooms where much pedestrian teaching takes place. The schooling system feeds itself, maintains itself. What is required is not learning from experience, but breaks with experience—the experience of mediocre teaching that too often greets the student. An agenda to improve the quality of history teaching and learning for teachers and students alike must have two aspects.

First, the teaching of history in our schools and universities must be honored and improved. At the elementary and secondary level this means strengthening teachers' connections to and identification with history. At the university level, this means strengthening historians' connections to and identification with teaching. If such symmetry is not pursued, then little progress will be made. At issue is whether historians and history teachers form one or two professions. Here too the tendency is to pull apart that which is better joined—the school to the university, teaching to scholarship.

The best history teachers in our schools know a great deal about teaching. They can profit from the connection to historical scholarship. Historians stay abreast of and contribute to research, but typically fail to learn much about teaching. The first aspect of reform, then, must encourage status-equalizing opportunities for historians and history teachers to learn from one another, so that research and teaching may be mutually informative and educative, so that a common professional identity may begin to form.

The second aspect concerns the formal preparation of history teachers, encompassing the standards framework, the university course work, and the structure of opportunity for practice and induction in the schools. Teacher educators also belong within the profession of history teachers. They will be responsible for much of the research on teaching and learning history, and should work closely with colleagues in history departments on the preparation of teachers and the improvement of teaching. This means establishing closer collaboration across departments within the university and between universities and schools. Rather than regarding the university curriculum as a zero-sum contest for control of credit hours, historians and history educators should work together to strengthen the intellectual content and the integration of course work for prospective teachers.

State standards should likewise begin to focus on pedagogical and curricular knowledge of history. A promising lead in this regard is the emerging work of the National Board for Professional Teaching Standards. This body was established in 1987 to develop procedures for the voluntary certification of teachers. This group is engaged in a national and comprehensive reform effort that involves the certification of teachers using alternative and innovative assessments, as well as calling for the changes in schools and schooling necessary to support accomplished teaching.

Research and development work underway on innovative assessments has begun to suggest promising approaches that states might draw upon, and the Educational Testing Service has already announced a multiyear effort to reform the National Teachers Examination to accommodate these emerging developments. So it appears that promising changes are getting underway, changes that will more centrally emphasize deep knowledge of subject matter and subject-specific pedagogical knowledge.

States also should press forward with plans to create induction experiences for beginning teachers. A sensible approach might involve providing the first-year history teacher with a reduced load, assistance from a mentor teacher, and a continuing seminar at a nearby university. Such structural arrangements may be set in the context of extended teacher education and/or licensure requirements, for the supervision of initial practice provides a performance base for evaluation. Here too, however, standards and criteria must emphasize subject matter teaching in addition to generic teaching skills. Beginning teachers understandably are concerned with the management aspects of teaching, but evidence also suggests this preoccupation can drive out attention to the teaching of subjects. States can begin to support teachers in ways that will correct this imbalance.

When we consider what beginning teachers need to know, we must consider a multitude of contexts that affect the answer to that question. We must consider the knowledge about history and about teaching that beginning teachers have been exposed to; we must consider when and how beginning teachers' knowledge is assessed; we must consider the very real demands of schooling; and we must consider our conceptions of the process of learning to teach. Policy makers who are concerned with improving one piece of the teaching puzzle—the knowledge of beginning history teachers—but who ignore such considerations of these other pieces ensure the demise of their own efforts.

REFERENCES

Boyer, E. L. (1987). *College: The undergraduate experience in America.* New York: Harper & Row.

Davidson, J. M., & Lytle, M. H. (1986). *After the fact: The art of historical detection* (Vol. 1, 2nd ed.). New York: Knopf.

FitzGerald, F. (1979). *America revised: History schoolbooks in the twentieth century.* Boston: Little, Brown.

Gagnon, P. (1987). Democracy's untold story. *American Educator, 11,* (2) 19-25, 46.

Gagnon, P. (1988, November). Why study history? *The Atlantic Monthly,* pp. 43-66.

Ravitch, D., & Finn, C. E., Jr., (1987). *What do our 17-year-olds know?: A report on the first national assessment of history and literature.* New York: Harper & Row.

Shaver, J. P., Davis, O. L., Jr., & Helburn, S. W. (1979a). An interpretive report on the status of precollege social studies education based on three NSF-funded studies. In *What are the needs in pre-college science, mathematics, and social sciences education? Views from the field* (Document No. SE 80-9). Washington, DC: National Science Foundation, Office of Program Integration, Directorate for Science Education.

Shaver, J. P., Davis, O. L., Jr., & Helburn, S. W. (1979b). The status of social studies education: Impressions from three NSF studies. *Social Education, 43,* 150-153.

Shulman, L. S. (1986). Those who understand: Knowledge growth in teaching. *Educational Researcher, 15,* 4-14.

Shulman, L. S. (1987). Knowledge and teaching: Foundations of the new reform. *Harvard Educational Review, 57,* 1-22.

Shulman, L. S., & Sykes, G. (1986, March). *A national board for teaching?: In search of a bold new standard.* Paper commissioned for the Task Force on Teaching as a Profession, Carnegie Forum on Education and the Economy.

Steinbeck, J. (1967). *The grapes of wrath.* New York: Viking. (Original work published 1939)

Terkel, S. (1970). *Hard times.* New York: Pantheon Books.

Todd, L. P., & Curti, M. (1986). *Triumph of the American nation.* Orlando, FL: Harcourt.

Wilson, S. M. (1988). *Understanding historical understanding: Subject matter knowledge and the teaching of U.S. history.* Unpublished doctoral dissertation, Stanford University.

Wilson, S. M., Shulman, L. S., & Richert, A. E. (1987). "150 different ways" of knowing: Representations of knowledge in teaching. In J. Calderhead (Ed.), *Exploring teachers' thinking* (pp. 104-124). Eastbourne, England: Cassell.

Wilson, S. M., & Sykes, G. (1989). Toward better teacher preparation and certification. In P. Gagnon (Ed.), *Historical literacy.* New York: Macmillan.

Wilson, S. M., & Wineburg, S. S. (1988). Peering at American history through different lenses: The role of disciplinary knowledge in teaching. *Teachers College Record, 89,* 525-539.

Wineburg, S. S., & Wilson, S. M. (in press). The subject matter knowledge of history teachers. In J. Brophy (Ed.), *Advances in research on teaching: Vol. 2. Teachers' subject matter knowledge and classroom instruction.* Greenwich, CT: JAI Press.

6

Social Science Knowledge and Citizenship Education

JAMES A. BANKS

In her carefully conceptualized, interesting, and well-crafted chapter, Suzanne Wilson identifies and describes two main types of knowledge that history teachers need: (a) subject matter knowledge and (b) subject-specific pedagogical knowledge. With the use of a vivid case study and rich exchanges, she successfully illustrates the importance of these two forms of knowledge for effective social studies teachers. Because her chapter is successful in attaining its major goals, my comments are designed primarily to extend the scope of the discussion by focusing on issues related to the knowledge of social studies teachers that she discusses only briefly, and to present different perspectives on other issues that she discusses in more depth.

WHAT SHOULD STUDENTS LEARN?

In a potentially significant but overly brief section of her chapter, "What Should Students Learn in History Class?" Wilson discusses the various debates over goals and rationales in social studies education—for example, whether the social studies should focus on the social sciences, value education, citizenship transmission, or reflective citizenship. She devotes little analytical attention to the serious debates over rationales and goals in social studies education and, perhaps unwittingly, dismisses a rich, historical, and sophisticated body of literature in social studies education that deals with rationales and goals (Atwood, 1982; Barr, Barth, & Shermis, 1977; Engle, 1960; Hunt & Metcalf, 1955; Shaver, 1967, 1977). She calls these debates "unproductive illusions, false dichotomies in a sense." She reaches this conclusion because she believes that these debates over conflicting rationales and conceptions can be resolved by the implementation of an eclectic version of the social studies that incorporates a number of important curriculum elements, characteristics, and goals. She writes, "Those goals are not antithetical. Rather, they may all be different ways of talking about the same set of concerns."

The succinct treatment of conflicting conceptions and rationales in social studies education is a serious problem in Wilson's chapter. This is the case not only because a knowledge of the conflicting goals and conceptions in social studies education is an important kind of pedagogical content knowledge that teachers need in order to reflectively choose a rationale to guide their instructional decisions, but also because teachers who have an eclectic rationale for social studies teaching are rarely effective in the classroom. These teachers are like the jockeys who try to run their horses in several directions at the same time. Effective social studies teachers must embrace and reflectively derive a clear, coherent, and consistent rationale for teaching (Goldmark, 1968; Newmann, 1975, 1977). Confusion about goals and attempts to teach using an eclectic rationale often result in the kind of deadly, boring, and nonreflective social studies teaching that Wilson and other researchers have described and documented (Goodlad, 1984; Shaver, Davis, & Helburn, 1979). Newmann (1977) states that a comprehensive rationale should state positions in "seven problem areas: curriculum goals, nature of learning, definition of community, citizenship and other goals of schooling, schools and other social agencies, authenticity, and diversity" (p. 11).

An example using two hypothetical teachers who embrace different and conflicting rationales for social studies teaching will illustrate my point. Ms. Hinkle is a high school social studies teacher who endorses a "citizenship transmission" rationale for teaching (Barr, Barth, & Shermis, 1977). She believes that the primary goal of the social studies should be to help students inculcate the "right" values and historical facts so that they will become loyal and unquestioning citizens of the nation-state. Such students will become deeply loyal but will not question national policies and decisions. They will view questioning the national government as unpatriotic.

In her teaching of history, Ms. Hinkle is likely to emphasize the glorious aspects of the U.S. past, no matter how much subject matter knowledge she has mastered. Ms. Hinkle may have mastered as much subject matter knowledge as Wilson thinks is desirable, yet it is highly unlikely that she will become a reflective and creative teacher like Wilson's Sean. When teaching, she will mediate the subject matter knowledge she has acquired. Her selection and presentation of this knowledge will reflect the vision of the kind of citizens she wants to socialize—namely, those who are nonreflectively loyal to the nation and who accept, without question, the "official" version of the U.S. past, present, and future. Such citizens will engage in adulation of the nation-state without reflection.

Neither subject matter nor pedagogical knowledge is sufficient to substantially change the way Ms. Hinkle teaches. She needs to examine alternative and conflicting conceptions of social studies education, to analyze their assumptions and purposes, and to reflectively derive a rationale for social studies teaching that is coherent and consistent. Only then will she be able to select social science content, methods, and teaching strategies in a deliberate and reflective way. Knowledge of conflicting rationales, goals, and visions in social studies education, and the opportunity to reflectively derive a clarified philosophical position with regard to the goals and purposes of that education, is essential in a teacher education program and a prerequisite to reforming social studies teaching in the nation's schools. Teachers' visions, goals, and purposes for teaching cogently influence how they select and interpret social science knowledge, the knowledge they select to teach, the knowledge they choose not to teach, how they mediate and interpret knowledge (Parker, 1987), and how they interact with students when discussing the knowledge they teach. The selection and interpretation of knowledge is essential in social studies teaching.

Ms. Hinkle endorses a citizenship transmission conception of social studies education. Another teacher, Ms. Cortes, endorses a rationale of social studies education that we may call "reflective citizenship." She believes that the major goal of social studies education should be to create reflective citizens who can and will actively participate in the reformation of society to make it more just and consistent with the ideals Myrdal described as American Creed values (Myrdal with Sterner & Rose, 1944). Helping students to hear and understand the voices of women, people of color, and workers will be much more important to Ms. Cortes than to Ms. Hinkle. Ms. Cortes, unlike Ms. Hinkle, is likely to view historical literacy as "a struggle for voice." In this conception of historical literacy,

> All students will deal with the fact that their voices differ from one another's, from their teachers', from their authors'. All learners will somehow cope with the issue of translating their many voices, and in the process they will join in creating culture (and history), not simply receiving it. (Starrs, 1988)

SOCIAL STUDIES VERSUS HISTORY

The bulk of Wilson's chapter is devoted to a discussion of the knowledge needed by effective history teachers. I am going to take what is perhaps an iconoclastic view in a volume on the knowledge base of teaching. I think we ought to educate social studies teachers rather than history teachers. History and the other social sciences are distinguished from the social studies in several important ways. We should not make the mistake, in our quest to infuse the social studies curriculum with sound historical knowledge, of assuming that the social studies are the social sciences simplified for pedagogical purposes (Shaver, 1967; Wesley, 1937). We have often made this mistake in the past and have created social studies curricula that do not deal with the important concerns of students and of society.

The social sciences and the social studies differ significantly in aim or purpose. The main goal of the social sciences is to build theoretical knowledge (Merton, 1968; Zetterberg, 1965). Consequently, social scientists devote their attention to the building of empirical propositions. Homans (1967) states that the major aim of any science, including the social sciences, is discovery and explanation:

> Any science has two main jobs to do: discovery and explanation. By the first we judge whether it is a science; by the second, how successful a science it is. Discovery is the job of stating and testing more or less general relationships between properties of nature. (p. 7)

Homans contends that history is a science like the other behavioral sciences, not because of its results but because of its aims.

While the aim of the social sciences is to build theory that explains human behavior, the major aim of the social studies is to prepare reflective citizens who can participate effectively in public discourse and deliberations and who can act to improve society and make it more consistent with humane values, such as equality, justice, and human dignity. The aim of social scientists is achieved when they explain and predict behavior. However, this is where the aim of social studies educators begins. Social studies educators must help students to make reflective and humane decisions by synthesizing and using the knowledge derived by social scientists (Banks with Clegg, 1990; Engle, 1960; Shaver, 1967). Decision making and citizen action are the chief aims of social studies education. The main components of decision making are scientific knowledge, value analysis and clarification, and the synthesis of knowledge and values. Consequently, the analysis of moral and public issues is an essential component of social studies education (Oliver & Shaver, 1966). An important kind of pedagogical knowledge that social studies teachers need is knowledge of theories of moral development, value-inquiry strategies, and decision-making models and techniques. They also need to know how social science knowledge can be used to help solve important public problems faced by citizens in a democratic nation-state.

Social science knowledge is an important part of an effective social studies curriculum. However, the ways in which social science knowledge is interrelated and used in interdisciplinary ways to inform effective decisions and citizen action should be emphasized in social studies teaching. Homans (1967) states that the social sciences are a single science. He states, "These sciences are in fact a single science. They share the same subject matter—the behavior of men. And they employ, without always admitting it, the same body of general explanatory principles" (p. 3). The inventory of scientific findings compiled by Berelson and Steiner (1964) supports Homans' claim.

Teachers need knowledge of the ways in which the social sciences are interrelated and should be able to view issues, concepts, and problems in an interdisciplinary way. Teachers also need an interdisciplinary orientation to the social sciences because disciplinary boundaries are often blurred in the real world of the schools as units are taught that include insights and perspectives from several different disciplines. Sensitive to the nature of the social sciences and to the real world of the schools, Wilson wisely devotes an important part of her chapter to the need for history teachers to have some knowledge of each of the social and behavioral sciences (Proposition 2).

THE LIMITATIONS OF THE DOCUMENTARY RECORD

To become effective social studies teachers, teachers must understand the way in which knowledge is constructed in history and the other social sciences, how knowledge reflects the social context in which it is created, and why significant knowledge gaps exist in the history of some groups, such as African-American women, child laborers, and migrant workers. Effective teachers must understand, and must help their students to understand, what we do not know as well as what we know about the past. Much of the history of Indians and African-Americans, and especially Indian and African-American women, is lost, perhaps forever. Teachers need to understand that important aspects of some peoples' history is lost, as well as why there are significant gaps in the documentary record. Case studies can be used to illustrate the "lost, stolen, or strayed" aspects of history. We have rich accounts of the Lewis and Clark expedition from their diaries, but only sketchy information about York, the African-American who accompanied them and who, as far as can be determined, played an important role in the success of the expedition (Logan & Winston, 1982).

African-American historians in Washington state are trying to construct the history of Marcus Lopez, believed to be the first black to settle in the Pacific Northwest. However, they have been able to construct only a sketchy portrait of this early African-American pioneer. Lerner (1972), who has done pioneering research on the history of women, points out that the "limitations of the available documentary record . . . result in omissions and a middle class bias" (p. xxii). Rich historical documents exist describing the life of the rich, the powerful, and those who won wars and battles. However, the life of the poor, the victimized, and the vanquished is as voiceless in historical documents as it is in contemporary life. If teachers and their students are keenly aware of the limitations of historical and social science knowledge, they will be able to use it more effectively to make sound decisions on public policy issues.

We should be educating social studies rather than history teachers for several reasons that are related to (a) the nature of the social science disciplines, (b) the goals and purposes of social studies education in a democratic society, and (c) the realities of schools. I discuss each of these reasons below.

THE SOCIAL SCIENCE DISCIPLINES

The social science disciplines are interconnected rather than separate and discrete. Increasingly, historians are using concepts from disciplines such as sociology, psychology, and anthropology. Concepts from these disciplines have enriched the historical study of women (Cott & Degler, 1987), people of color (Gutman, 1976), and workers (Terkel, 1972). History has always been highly interdisciplinary. Traditional history emphasized concepts from politics, political science, economics, and the military.

The social science disciplines do not consist of unique content, but are formalized and unique ways to view and understand human behavior. To gain a comprehensive understanding of human behavior and of problems and issues in society, students must be helped to view them from the perspectives of several social science disciplines, as well as from the perspectives of philosophy and the arts (Engle & Ochoa, 1988). To view issues and problems from the perspective of a single discipline will result in only a partial understanding of human behavior.

THE GOALS AND PURPOSES OF THE SOCIAL STUDIES

The major aim of the social studies should be to help students become reflective decision makers and civic actors who can and will participate in the transformation of society—that is, to make it more democratic and just (Banks, 1988; Banks with Clegg, 1990). To make reflective decisions on and to take effective action related to complex social issues and problems such as sexism, racism, nuclear proliferation, and homelessness, students must view these problems from the perspectives of different disciplines, as well as from the perspectives of the groups who are the main victims of these problems, such as women, people of color, poor people, and people who are powerless and marginalized (Banks & Banks, 1989). Disciplines such as anthropology and sociology have a better record than history (and political science) of giving voice to voiceless groups such as women, African-Americans, and workers. While all disciplines, including anthropology and sociology, reflect the ideologies and perspectives of the powerful groups within a society (Berger & Luckmann, 1966; Mannheim, 1936), history has been and is used more frequently than anthropology and sociology by dominant groups to reinforce their hegemony and to make powerless groups docile and content with the status quo. In recent years, both the Soviet Union and Japan have rewritten their history textbooks to make them more congruent with the prevailing views and ideologies of dominant and powerful groups in society.

It is interesting to speculate why dominant groups frequently use history, rather than anthropology or sociology, to reinforce prevailing political and economic ideologies. This may result in part from the nature of inquiry in history and from the way in which it evolved. History, especially in its infancy, often told the stories of great nations by focusing on the leaders and military battles that made the nations great. The story of the conquered, the victimized, and the common people is rarely told in the narrative histories that document the growth of expanding empires.

Anthropologists, in contrast to historians, were deeply concerned with the stories and cultures of common people and ethnic groups, when their discipline emerged in the United States. Leading U.S. anthropologists, such as Boas, Benedict, and Mead, were also interested in using anthropological research as an antidote to the racism that was rampant during the World War II period (Benedict, 1941; Pelto & Muessig, 1980). Race relations research was also of paramount concern to sociologists such as Robert E. Park and his colleagues in the "Chicago School" of sociology at the University of Chicago during the 1930s and 1940s (Lyman, 1972). Early courses in black studies drew heavily upon concepts and data from sociology when the black studies movement gained momentum in the 1960s and 1970s. The only course offered on many U.S. college and university campuses in the early 1950s and 1960s that dealt with race relations was usually taught in the department of sociology. Although black historians such as George Washington William, W. E. B. DuBois, Carter G. Woodson, and John Hope Franklin had created rich scholarship in African-American history, it had been largely ignored by white, mainstream historians until the civil rights movement of the 1960s and 1970s (Meier & Rudwick, 1986).

Because of the way that history is often used and misused by dominant groups within a society, we ought to be somewhat skeptical of the strident call by conservative popular writers and historians for more history in the schools, and particularly for more factual history. This call has been made by such popular writers as Hirsch (1987) and Ravitch and Finn (1987). Rarely do these writers address such issues as the perspectives from which "more history" will be told, its purposes, and whose interests will be served by the teaching of more factual history in the schools. Aronowitz and Giroux (1988), in a thoughtful and important review of books by Bloom (1987) and Hirsch (1987), suggest that these books are part of a neoconservative political scheme that perpetuates a "public philosophy informed by a crippling ethnocentrism and a contempt for the language and social relations fundamental to the ideas of a democratic society" (p. 194). They also point out that the neoconservative critics of the school curriculum

> espouse a view of culture removed from the trappings of power, conflict, and struggle, and in doing so . . . attempt to legitimate a view of learning and literacy that not only marginalizes the voices, languages, and cultures of subordinate groups but also degrades teaching and learning to the practice of implementation and mastery. (p. 183)

The knowledge in the social studies curriculum should liberate and empower students rather than contribute to their victimization and oppression. A social studies curriculum that includes content, insights, concepts, and perspectives from a range of disciplines is more likely than a curriculum that focuses heavily on history, especially facts and historical trivia, to help students become effective civic actors and decision makers. Historical knowledge taught in the schools should be enriched with concepts from the other social sciences, such as anthropology and sociology. Concepts from the behavioral sciences will enable students to better understand the experiences and voices of groups that school history often neglects, such as women, people of color, and workers.

THE REALITIES OF SCHOOLS

Schools are not organized and do not function in a way that makes it possible for teachers to be narrow disciplinary specialists and experts. When I was teaching fifth grade at the Francis W. Parker School in Chicago we planned and implemented an interdisciplinary curriculum. This interdisciplinary curriculum framework resulted in effective and stimulating teaching and learning. Interdisciplinary teaching often occurs at the elementary level, but less frequently at the high school level because many secondary teachers view themselves as history or political science teachers rather than as social studies teachers.

Many high school teachers try to maintain tight disciplinary identities and affiliations even though such affiliations are inconsistent with the culture of the public schools. The disciplinary identifications of social studies teachers may partially explain why such a small percentage of them are members of the National Council for the Social Studies, compared with the much larger percentage of English and language arts teachers who are members of the National Council for Teachers of English.[1] Disciplinary divisions and identities have made it difficult for social studies teachers to unite and to speak professionally with one voice.

The way we educate social studies teachers contributes to the disciplinary Balkanization among them. In the next and final part of this chapter, I will briefly describe a way to educate social studies teachers that will help them to attain broader disciplinary perspectives as well as contribute to the weakening of disciplinary identifications and boundaries. I perceive such boundaries as a negative influence on effective social studies teaching and learning. We need to educate teachers in a way that maintains the integrity of the specific disciplines, yet helps teachers to gain the knowledge and insights needed to teach school subjects in an interdisciplinary way.

A THEMATIC APPROACH TO EDUCATING
SOCIAL STUDIES TEACHERS

We can help social studies teachers to acquire the interdisciplinary knowledge, skills, and attitudes needed to implement a social studies curriculum that emphasizes decision making by requiring them to participate in a year-long interdisciplinary seminar focusing on enduring social issues and problems. The issues selected for study should be ones that have been of concern to humans in the past, that are of concern today, and that will be important concerns in the future. The specific issues chosen for study should be selected by an interdisciplinary team that would participate in teaching the seminar and by the education faculty involved in the teacher education program. The interdisciplinary seminar would be team taught by a historian, a sociologist, an anthropologist, a philosopher, and a literature specialist. While the students would study the structure of the major social science disciplines (i.e., their key concepts, theories, and research methods), the focus of the seminar would be on how each of the social science disciplines can contribute to the understanding and the solution of enduring human problems and issues. The roles that citizens in a democratic nation-state can and should play to help solve these problems would also be highlighted. The seminar might focus on issues such as

1. The quest for freedom
2. Leadership and social change
3. The development, use, and control of technology
4. Immigration, migration, and population change
5. Peoplehood, cultural identity, and nationalism
6. Magic, science, and religion: the quest for explanations
7. Cooperation and conflict in human societies

SUMMARY

In this chapter, I have tried to extend the scope of Wilson's chapter by discussing in more detail points she treated briefly and to present a different perspective on several of the important issues she raised. An essential kind of pedagogical content knowledge teachers need to acquire is knowledge of the conflicting conceptions, rationales, and aims in social studies education. They also need an opportunity to examine these conflicting visions and rationales in a critical and probing way and to reflectively derive a coherent and consistent rationale that can guide their selection of goals, content, and teaching strategies.

I contend that the main goal of the social studies should be to help students acquire the knowledge, attitudes, and skills needed to make reflective public decisions and participate effectively in the reformation of society to make it more consistent with the nation's idealized values—namely, the American Creed. Such citizens can best be developed by teachers who are educated to be social studies teachers rather than history teachers. Social studies teachers should be educated in a way that enables them to acquire an in-depth understanding of the structure of the social sciences and of how social science knowledge can be used to improve the human condition. A social studies teacher education program should also help teachers to become sensitive to the ways in which social science knowledge has been and often is used to reinforce dominant group hegemony, ideologies, and institutions. I am proposing that an important component of the education of social studies teachers consist of a year-long interdisciplinary seminar that examines a series of persistent and enduring social issues and problems. Concepts, insights, and understandings from a wide range of disciplines must be brought to bear on human problems in order to educate students so that they have the knowledge, will, and commitment to help make our nation and world more humane.

NOTES

1.   In 1989, the National Council of Teachers of English had 102,000 members, while the National Council for the Social Studies had 25,000 members. See Burek, Koek, & Novallo, 1989, pp. 797,877.

REFERENCES

Aronowitz, S., & Giroux, H. A. (1988). Schooling, culture, and literacy in the age of broken dreams: A review of Bloom and Hirsch. *Harvard Educational Review, 58,* 172-194.

Atwood, V. A. (Ed.). (1982). Historical foundations of social studies education [Special issue]. *Journal of Thought, 17*(3), 1-141.

Banks, J. A. (1988). *Multiethnic education: Theory and practice* (2nd ed.). Boston: Allyn & Bacon.

Banks, J. A., & Banks, C. A. M. (Eds.). (1989). *Multicultural education: Issues and perspectives.* Boston: Allyn & Bacon.

Banks, J. A., with Clegg, A. A., Jr. (1990). *Teaching strategies for the social studies: Inquiry, valuing, and decision making* (4th ed.). New York: Longman.

Barr, R. D., Barth, J. L., & Shermis, S. S. (1977). *Defining the social studies* (Bulletin 51). Washington, DC: National Council for the Social Studies.

Benedict, R. (1941). Race problems in America. *Annals of the American Academy of Political and Social Sciences, 216,* 73-78.

Berger, P. L., & Luckmann, T. (1966). *The social construction of reality.* Garden City, NY: Doubleday.

Berelson, B., & Steiner, G. A. (1964). *Human behavior: An inventory of scientific findings.* New York: Harcourt.

Bloom, A. (1987). *The closing of the American mind. How higher education has failed democracy and impoverished the minds of today's students.* New York: Simon & Schuster.

Burek, D. M., Koek, K. E., & Novallo, A. (Eds.). (1989). *Encyclopedia of Associations 1990* (Part I, 24th ed.). Detroit, MI. Gole Research Inc.

Cott, N. F., & Degler, C. N. (1987). Women in history: Mainstream or minority? In G. N. Grob & G. A. Billias (Eds.), *Interpretations of American history* (5th ed., pp. 79-124). New York: The Free Press.

Engle, S. H. (1960). Decision making: The heart of social studies instruction. *Social Education, 66,* 301-304.

Engle, S. H., & Ochoa, A. S. (1988). *Education for democratic citizenship: Decision making in the social studies.* New York: Teachers College Press.

Goldmark, B. (1968). *Social studies: A method of inquiry.* Belmont, CA: Wadsworth.

Goodlad, J. I. (1984). *A place called school.* New York: McGraw-Hill.

Gutman, H. G. (1976). *The black family in slavery and freedom 1750-1925.* New York: Vintage.

Hirsch, E. D., Jr. (1987). *Cultural literacy: What every American needs to know.* Boston: Houghton Mifflin.

Homans, G. C. (1967). *The nature of social science.* New York: Harcourt.

Hunt, M. P., & Metcalf, L. E. (1955). *Teaching high school social studies: Problems in reflective thinking and social understanding.* New York: Harper & Row.

Lerner, G. (1972). *Black women in white America: A documentary history.* New York: Vintage.

Logan, R. W., & Winston, M. R. (1982). *Dictionary of American Negro biography.* New York: Norton.

Lyman, S. M. (1972). *The Black American in sociological thought.* New York: Capricorn Books.

Mannheim, K. (1936). *Ideology and utopia: An introduction to the sociology of knowledge.* New York: Harcourt.

Meier, A., & Rudwick, E. (1986). *Black history and the historical profession 1915-1980.* Urbana: University of Illinois Press.

Merton, R. K. (1968). *Social theory and social structure* (3rd ed.). New York: The Free Press.

Myrdal, G., with Sterner, R., & Rose, A. (1944). *An American dilemma: The Negro problem and modern democracy.* New York: Harper & Row.

Newmann, F. M. (1975). *Education for citizen action: Challenge for secondary curriculum.* Berkeley: McCutchan.

Newmann, F. M. (1977). Building a rationale for civic education. In J. P. Shaver (Ed.), *Building rationales for citizenship education* (Bulletin 52, pp. 1-33). Washington, DC: National Council for the Social Studies.

Oliver, D. W., & Shaver, J. P. (1966). *Teaching public issues in the high school.* Boston: Houghton Mifflin.

Parker, W. C. (1987). Teachers' mediation in social studies. *Theory and Research in Social Education, 15,* 1-22.

Pelto, J., & Muessig, R. H. (1980). *The study and teaching of anthropology.* Columbus, OH: Merrill.

Ravitch, D., & Finn, C. E., Jr. (1987). *What do our 17-year-olds know? A report on the first national assessment of history and literature.* New York: Harper & Row.

Shaver, J. P. (1967). Social studies: The need for redefinition. *Social Education, 31,* 588-592.

Shaver, J. P. (Ed.). (1977). *Building rationales for citizenship education* (Bulletin 52). Washington, DC: National Council for the Social Studies.

Shaver, J. P., Davis, O. L., Jr., & Helburn, S. W. (1979). The status of social studies education: Impressions from three NSF studies. *Social Education, 43,* 150-153.

Starrs, J. (1988). *Cultural literacy and black education.* Paper submitted to James A. Banks as a partial requirement for the course, EDC & I 469, University of Washington, Seattle.

Terkel, S. (1972). *Working.* New York: Avon.

Wesley, E. (1937). *Teaching social studies in high school.* Boston: D. C. Heath.

Zetterberg, H. L. (1965). *On theory and verification in sociology* (3rd ed.). Totowa, NJ: Bedminster.

Teaching Writing

Until recently, writing has been a stepchild in arguments about school curricula. Among advocates of basic skills, writing takes a backseat to reading and arithmetic, and becomes more prominent only when it is converted to punctuation, grammar, or spelling. But among advocates of a more rigorous curriculum, writing often takes a backseat to mathematics and science. Indeed, the nature of writing is itself open to question. It is not really a subject in the sense that other school subjects are, but, like reading, is a tool used to study and understand other subjects. Yet it is not a skill that can be acquired through repetitive drills, for writing can derive only from the author's own personal and intellectual investment.

What, then, must a writing teacher know or be able to do in order to teach writing? Three authors have tried to answer this question for us. The first answer, put forward by Tom Romano, argues that the most important thing for teachers of writing is that they themselves be writers. In fact, Romano coins the term *teacher-writers* to emphasize the importance of this feature of writing teachers. The second author, George Hillocks, adds to Romano's proposal by synthesizing research literature in the field of writing, much of which suggests specific content and pedagogy that should be part of instruction in writing. Finally, John Gage adds yet another dimension by pointing out that there are several schools of thought in this field, and that teachers need to maintain a critical attitude toward competing theories of writing and of writing pedagogy. Teachers need to be able to examine all sides of an issue and to try different ideas in their classrooms and with their colleagues.

7

Musts for Writing Teachers—Report from the Classroom

TOM ROMANO

> Do not think the youth has no force,
> because he cannot speak to you and me. Hark!
> in the next room his voice is sufficiently
> clear and emphatic.
> *Ralph Waldo Emerson, "Self-reliance"*

The room where I spend much of my time is the room where I write. Books. Desk. Chairs. File cabinets. Computer. I'm at home in this room. Before I began writing this chapter, however, I went to another room that is important to me—"the next room," the place where I have taught English to teenagers for 17 years, the place where they have read and written and talked. My classroom. I wanted to learn what my students thought writing teachers must know. In matters of education the voice of youth is usually ignored and rarely sought. I didn't want to perpetuate such error.

And it is error. To teach without listening to students is foolhardy. We learn how to teach better, with more accuracy, insight, and relevance, if we listen to those who learn with us, whether they are first graders or graduate students. I asked my tenth and twelfth graders to write about this question: What things must a writing teacher know in order to teach writing well and help teenagers become better writers? Their responses form the core of this chapter.

"Teachers," writes Aimee, "should be experienced writers so they can understand what their students have to go through to write an interesting paper. They wouldn't have to be genius college professors to teach good writing. They just need to be loyal writers." Not necessarily even published writers. Just loyal ones who do enough writing about personally and professionally important topics to see writing from the inside, to know which strategies for teaching writing ring true and which clang.

LITERATURE AND WRITING COURSES

English teachers traditionally get most of their training in literature classes. They are studiers of literary artifacts. Rarely are they makers of literary artifacts. Instead of writing literature, they write *about* literature: Renaissance literature, Victorian literature, romantic American literature. While enriching and essential to making prospective English teachers well read, such study does not make them excellent teachers of writing.

It makes them amateur critics equipped to evaluate the literary artifacts of professionals. Different reading skills and sensitivity, however, are demanded of those who would read the unfinished writing of secondary school students, who would nurture their growth as writers, as thinkers. Teachers need to know, as Kristine says, "how to help students on difficult spots." Timely instruction or reassurance may be all a student needs on her way to developing a draft.

"A writing teacher," notes Bryan, "must be able to feel what the student is trying to say; that teacher must be able to connect with the words on the page. He or she must be able to identify what works and what doesn't work in a story. It is important for a teacher to be able to sense if a small composition might be a doorway to a gigantic story that lies hidden." Teachers must know how to read evolving writing, writing that isn't there yet, but could be. This is a different skill from merely knowing how to criticize. Reading student writing means being sensitive to the nascent, the embryonic, the possible.

Prospective teachers need plenty of experience in writing courses, those in which instructors respect individual voices and help each writer gain sophistication and versatility in the use of written language. If students—near-teachers—leave college seeing themselves only as critical readers, and not also as writers, many of them will fall easily into an elitist view of written language, one that pigeonholes the writing of students as second rate.

"English teachers should have experience with lots of different styles of writing," acknowledges Rosanna, "and they shouldn't be prejudiced about a student's writing." Our schools house students of great diversity. The range of education, culture, and intellect is incredible. There are students whose reading is so vast, whose home life so literate, whose facility with language so accomplished, and whose motivation so high that they already possess literary voices. And there are students whose reading is so meager, whose home life so aliterate, and whose motivation so low from repeated educational defeats that their written voices are at best halting, at worst mute.

But both extremes and all those between them have places in our democracy, are entitled to speak, "each," as Walt Whitman (1855/1981) put it, "singing what belongs to him or her and to none else" (p. 14). And those varied voices, the literary as well as the nonliterary, can develop in skill under the guidance of teachers who accept them without prejudice and who know writing from the inside. To know writing from the inside, writing teachers must write. So imperative is it that they be loyal writers, as Aimee said, that I would call this brand of educator a *teacher-writer*, the two nouns bonded by a hyphen. Teachers who write, writers who teach. Teacher-writers put pen to paper frequently, and for more reasons than writing comments on student papers and jotting bathroom passes.

Teacher-writers know the transformative power of writing. They know that writing, as Donald Murray (1985) has written, "is a satisfying human activity that extends both the brain and the soul. It stimulates the intellect, deepens the experience of living, and is good therapy" (p. 73). Teacher-writers try their hands at various modes of writing, become learners in many genres: essays, letters, poetry, fiction. Through such experience, teachers learn the "territory" of writing both "intellectually and emotionally" (p. 74). Teacher-writers, as Stephanie understands, "know the *pains* of writing. Beginnings, endings, writer's block, a thousand rough drafts."

Teacher-writers speak from knowledge born of doing. "The teacher needs to be able to write and create so he can show the tools of the trade," writes Eric. Teacher-writers can show these tools of the trade because they use them. They know what it's like to draft five leads in order to find one that's suitable. They know firsthand the faith it takes to head into a topic and trust the generative powers of mind, imagination, and language to produce writing.

POWER OF CLASSROOM COMMUNITY

Teacher-writers also must understand the sustaining power of a classroom community. Although a good deal of writing is done alone—the writer left to the solitary harmony of eye, mind, and hand—teacher-writers recognize the immense value of the social aspect of learning to write. In *Language Stories and Literacy Lessons* (Harste, Burke, and Woodward, 1984) Jerome Harste notes,

> Discussion with neighbors prior to, during, and after involvement [in writing] are not disruptions to the process, but a natural part of the process itself. Successful writers use friends in order to discuss where they might go next and what arguments still need to be developed, and to verify for themselves that their writing has the effect they desire. Opportunity to build from the natural support of the classroom should be part of the language arts. (p. 214)

Teacher-writers know that students need not be lone wolves, uncommunicative, talking with no one about their writing. "An English class always comes across as just writing and reading," Karen explains, "but I think it should be writing, reading, and more discussion (here's a word I learned in English: confer). Students should be able to confer." Writing is a social act; writers seek to reach others.

Developing a sense of audience is crucial to learning to write. Stories, poems, plays, and essays are not created perfunctorily. They are aimed at flesh-and-blood readers. In the writing class, students read the evolving writing of their peers. They reveal what they've understood, ask genuine questions, and may offer suggestions. When writers are involved in making meanings, in plumbing the depths of their thought and language, conferring with others helps them to see with different eyes.

Gaining the response of others and learning to gauge the needs of audience are reasons enough for students to share writing with peers, but there is another: "Sharing writing," Jeff argues, "gives students the satisfaction that this piece was not written for just another grade." When students have worked hard creating with language, that work deserves a time of group acknowledgment. Writing must not merely be handed to the teacher for marking and handed back to students for filing. Student writing needs to be celebrated.

TEACHER-WRITERS AS RESPONDENTS

Teacher-writers are key models of sensitive responders and appreciative celebrants. By their intent listening, their genuine interest, their desire to help without bullying, teacher-writers demonstrate to every member of the writing class the respect that all writers need in order to risk learning and to grow. "A teacher has to remember when he was a teenager and what he was thinking," writes Carrie. "Nine out of 10 [teenagers] are thinking about what they're going to do for the weekend or how much their paycheck will be for the week."

If teacher-writers expect to communicate with teenagers, they must remember their own teenage mind. They have to remember adolescence with compassion, have to feel anew the sting of self-consciousness, the ache of being jilted, the desperate need to be accepted. When teenagers are asked to write their truths, as they must again and again, matters of personal significance arise. Students may be writing about the role of women in Hawthorne's *The Scarlet Letter*. They may be writing about the death of their beloved grandfather. In either case, the topics should be inextricably bound to the writer. Effective writing rarely comes without deep involvement.

And although writing can be improved and rhetorical strategies can be taught, students first need to be safe, need to know that their teacher respects the personal level of the writing. The writer and the writing cannot be divorced. "Writing is the writer. It embodies her voice, her passion, her thinking, her intellect, her labor, and, on some occasions, her very soul" (Romano, 1987,

p. 125). Teacher-writers must be sensitive, but not to language alone. They must be sensitive to people. Teacher to student. Person to person. Writer to writer.

SENSITIVITY TO RISK

This respect and sensitivity extend also to the realm of risk and error, two concepts whose relationship either enhances learning or sabotages it. Teacher-writers understand that risk and error are companions of learning. To become more accomplished writers, students need to risk trips into new territory, need to try the untried.

Although students work to perfect many skills and become proficient in routine matters of writing, they also need to attempt the new—new genres, new strategies, new words. And teacher-writers must understand that risk—and the errors that attend risk—are to be applauded. When students take risks, that means they are in the midst of learning. And teacher-writers must know that when students risk trying new skills, they may temporarily regress in old skills that seemingly had been mastered.

Holly, for example, was a bright sophomore I taught one semester. She saw topics for writing all around her. She wrote fluently and took pleasure in creating her vision in essays, narratives, and poems. About 12 weeks into the semester, she boldly entered new territory, began writing fiction, a genre she hadn't tried before. Her short story ran 12 pages, about 3,000 words, three times longer than anything she'd written before—a breakthrough for her. The final draft of her short story, however, was plagued by comma splice errors. On previous pieces Holly had appeared to have that particular punctuation malady under reasonable control; but on this piece, this brand-new, all-consuming attempt, Holly's attention to the editing skill of marking off sentence boundaries had lapsed.

I was disturbed by the comma splices and knew I'd have to reteach her the concept of sentence sense, but I knew something else too: I knew that the comma splice relapse was minor compared with the great strides Holly had made as a writer. She had managed so many new, complex skills in this notable first effort in fiction. She had developed believable characters and had carried forth a narrative with a fine interplay of description and dialogue; she had created a plausible plot and worked out a satisfactory resolution. These are no mean feats for a high-school sophomore. Comma splices or no, this 15-year-old was on her way to becoming a capable, independent adult writer.

TEENAGERS MORE THAN PROOFREADERS

Teacher-writers know that surface manuscript errors—those of spelling, punctuation, and usage—must be kept in perspective. It is easy to become fanatical about eradicating surface errors. They are oh-so-obvious. But when teachers lose perspective on this matter, they elevate copyediting to the ultimate concern. And this unwarranted elevation relegates other matters of composition—crucial ones—to inferior positions. Teacher-writers cannot let that happen because

- Developing the confidence to write fat first drafts is more important than spelling
- Learning to focus writing is more important than good margins
- Becoming proficient at revising writing for clarity and vividness and a rhythmical, readable style is more important than avoiding comma splices.

Teacher-writers must understand that they are teaching teenagers to be more than proofreaders. They are teaching them to be writers, critical thinkers who take responsibility for the totality of their work. Writers make language and meaning choices, then they evaluate them. And based on that evaluation they make their next move. Certainly teachers must work patiently with students to teach them the copyediting skills needed to prepare manuscripts. But that is only part of a teacher-writer's role. We have all read enough insurance forms and administrative reports to know that perfectly edited manuscripts alone do not ensure good writing.

Nor does a flawless mastery of grammar. Should teacher-writers know grammar, the how of language? Of course they should, to a degree. But they don't need to know grammar as deeply as linguists or editors. They *do* need to know, however, that teaching formal grammar does not improve students' writing. In his book *Research on Written Composition: New Directions for Teaching,* George Hillocks (1986) examined 20 years of writing research. On the longtime tradition of teaching grammar, Hillocks writes,

> None of the studies reviewed for the present report provides any support for teaching grammar as a means of improving composition skills. If schools insist upon teaching the identification of parts of speech, the parsing or diagramming of sentences, or other concepts of traditional school grammar (as many still do), they cannot defend it as a means of improving the quality of writing. (p. 138)

Teacher-writers need to know punctuation, grammar, and usage in order to show students how to make purposeful use of them within the context of their writing: how a colon or a dash, for example, can abruptly halt a sentence and signal importance to the detail that follows; how a fragmentary sentence can emphasize an idea; or how diction affects tone. Was the spy terminated? Or was the foreign visitor murdered?

Teacher-writers know that the process of learning to employ the rules of written language and to utilize their flexibility is affected by culture and experience. It is a lifelong process that most of us will never master completely. And it is a process best undertaken with curiosity and a sense of humor. I observed a high school junior, on one occasion, write about the extinction, millions of years ago, of that marvel of reptilian evolution—the poor, doomed "Dinah Shore." And I have seen the marks of my copyeditor pointing out to me the difference between *complement* and *compliment*. Curiosity and sense of humor. My teaching is complemented by them. And so is my learning.

WRITING LIVES IN THE BIG WORLD

Teacher-writers must understand that writing lives in the big world. Writing is not a snapshot; it is a mural. The literate world we want students to inhabit contains many kinds of writing, everything from folktale to rap. Within its borders are light verse and letters and literary analysis. But many secondary school English curricula do not reveal writing as a big world mural, so heavily do they emphasize literary analysis to the virtual exclusion of every other genre.

Literary analysis is surely one valuable kind of writing, but not the only kind, and certainly not of such eminence that English curricula should make it the sole focus of interest. If teacher-writers want students to value writing, to readily use it for personal expression, then students must get chances to write far more than literary analyses. Students must see themselves as potential creators of all kinds of writing, not just the kind that is about someone else's writing. I want students to write poems, fiction, persuasive essays, drama, memos, reviews, letters of love, complaint, and praise. I want to enfranchise students as creators of literary artifacts.

Teacher-writers can start granting validity to all forms of writing by making no condescending distinction between expository writing and so-called "creative writing," as if the latter were some airy-headed, nebulous genre that involves no rigor in diction, syntax, logic, selection, analysis, and synthesis. If anything, teacher-writers must show students how creativity—the merging of intellect and imagination—infuses all genres in the big-world mural of writing.

Teacher-writers must know that writing—like woodworking, swimming, and gardening—improves with plenty of real practice. Composing occasional isolated paragraphs or even more substantial pieces only once in every six-week grading period will not provide enough practice to improve skills, strengthen voices, and make easy and familiar the immersion into written composition. Teacher-writers know that class time is invaluable and, therefore, no use of it surpasses that of students bent to paper, writing their meanings in individual voices, especially in a democracy that thrives on freedom of expression.

CONNECTION BETWEEN READING AND WRITING

The literacy coin has two sides. Writing is one side. Reading is the other. Teacher-writers know that without reading there is little reason to write, and without writing there is no reason to read. "What makes a story, poem, or book good is its ability to interest the reader," writes Mike. "In teaching teenagers who don't really know exactly how to trap a reader's interest, a teacher should encourage a young writer to read different assortments of writing."

Teacher-writers must be wide readers.

Although it is important that teacher-writers know traditional literature, they must also be readers of contemporary literature. Contemporary literature offers a virtual seminar in effective writing techniques. Teacher-writers can bring them into the classroom to teach students rhetorical strategies, like using a very short sentence to end a passage pointedly or employing the "power of threes" to create strong, memorable repetition—three parallel sentences, three rhythmical phrases, three revealing words. The voices of contemporary literature are those of our time. Like students, those voices are gloriously diverse. And they are the voices I want my students to learn from.

There is another kind of contemporary literature teacher-writers must know, one that connects directly with teenagers. It is the literature written for young adults, typically referred to as YA literature or adolescent literature. The best writers are voracious readers. And teacher-writers want students to read. It is through wide reading that students can learn a love for language, a sense of story and persuasion, a feel for the written word.

This young adult literature is not second rate, by any means; it is high quality. In her comprehensive and powerful book about teaching literacy to adolescents, *In the Middle,* Nancie Atwell (1987) argues,

> The last 20 years have witnessed an explosion in the number of novels and short stories written expressly for young adults, adolescent literature of such breadth and depth no teacher need ever apologize for building a curriculum around kids' responses to their own books. Much of the writing—I'm thinking of Robert Cormier [1974, 1988], Lois Lowry [1977, 1978], Susan Beth Pfeffer [1980, 1987], Madeleine L'Engle [1962], Robert Lipsyte [1967, 1977]—is exquisite. (p. 161)

The key to this young adult literature is the direct appeal of its characters and subject matter to adolescents. In it they can find characters at or near their own age confronting the problems of the world. Young adult literature is the surest bet to get students hooked on reading. The more young adult literature teacher-writers know, the better their chances of luring students to literacy.

PROFESSIONAL DEVELOPMENT

The teaching of writing is an exciting profession. Researchers are going into real classrooms and examining how students best learn to write. University researchers like Donald Graves (1983, 1984), Jane Hansen (1987), and Glenda Bissex (1980) and excellent classroom teachers like Susan Stires (1988, 1989), Carol Avery (1987, 1989), and Linda Rief (1985, 1989) have conducted research and published their findings in books and articles. Such reading is not only informative and stimulating, but also vitally necessary to ongoing professional development.

Teacher-writers need to know that continued growth in their field will help keep them vibrant in the classroom. In addition to doing professional reading, teacher-writers may also grow professionally by attending national, regional, state, and local conferences sponsored by the National Council of Teachers of English, the Modern Language Association, and many universities and colleges. At such conferences participants can be introduced to new skills and approaches to teaching writing and can be inspired by the best thinkers in the profession. And teacher-writers working critically and creatively may more actively join this sharing of ideas by proposing their own presentations for these conferences. All this professional activity serves to reinvigorate teacher-writers and to reaffirm their commitment as members of a community dedicated to quality literacy instruction.

ENVIRONMENT OFTEN ANTITHETICAL
TO GOOD LEARNING

They will need such reinvigorating. Often the environment for teaching writing is antithetical to what we know would make for good learning. Many secondary teachers struggle to teach writing under the burden of six classes a day with as many as 25 or 35 students in each class. And administrators rarely look upon teachers as reflective professionals who need reasonable workloads and time built into the school day for intellectual interaction with colleagues to discuss research, debate issues, and collaboratively explore problems and propose solutions. More often, teachers are viewed as hired hands who don't really need to think, who need only keep the corral locked and the beasts within orderly and able to jump through standardized testing hoops that do not measure actual ability to initiate written text.

Although this issue is crucial and realistic, and a part of the present territory that teacher-writers will enter, I don't want to conclude with that point. It leaves the written word, and I want to end by returning to it. The one thing I would have every teacher-writer know—not tacitly, but overtly, not theoretically, but experientially—is this: The act of writing is an act of thinking. Here's how Peter Elbow (1983) described this relationship between language and thought:

> Once you get yourself writing in an exploratory but uncensored fashion, the ongoing string of language and syntax itself becomes a lively and surprising force for generation. Words call up words, ideas call up more ideas. A momentum of language and thinking develops and one learns to nurture it by keeping the pen moving. (p. 39)

Obvious? For years it wasn't obvious to me. And I've loved writing since I was 12. I have taken pleasure in the quiet thrill of a story, a line of argument, or a personal realization forming under my pen. I have taken pleasure in thinking. And the best language, the best ideas often occurred unexpectedly as I was actually putting words on paper. Teacher-writers must put this concept of "writing as thinking" to work for themselves by writing. And they must trust in it passionately enough to allow the concept to go to work for their students.

"Let students write," says Troy. "A writing teacher's main goal should be to open up the channels in each of his students to let them put their ideas and emotions and personality on paper." Krissy provides a different slant to this. "The most important thing that a teacher should tell his students," she writes, "is to not be afraid. He should stress to the students that if you think you have something then go with it."

Like Krissy, I believe it comes down to courage. But I would try to persuade her that teacher-writers must not just *tell* students to be courageous. Teacher-writers must *be* courageous. It takes courage to enter a profession that is perpetually underfunded, undervalued, and often undermined. It takes courage to work with other human beings and believe that your skills will help them become better writers. And whether teachers are in their classrooms or at their writing desks, it takes courage to remain open to all possibilities and yet maintain enough faith in themselves to understand clearly, without doubt, when they really have something. And it takes courage to go one step farther, to *act* upon that understanding, or as Krissy recommends, to "go with it."

REFERENCES

Atwell, N. (1987). *In the middle: Writing, reading, and learning with adolescents.* Portsmouth, NH: Heinemann.

Avery, C. (1987). Laura's legacy. *Language Arts, 65,* 110-111.

Avery, C. (1989). From the first: Teaching to diversity. In J. Jenson (Ed.), *Stories to grow on: Demonstrations of language learning in K-8 classrooms* (pp. 37-55). Portsmouth, NH: Heinemann.

Bissex, G. (1980). *Gnys at wrk: A child learns to write and read.* Cambridge, MA: Harvard University Press.

Cormier, R. (1974). *The chocolate war.* New York: Dell.

Cormier, R. (1988). *Fade.* New York: Delacorte.

Elbow, P. (1983). Thinking by teaching writing. *Change, 15*(6) 37-40.

Emerson, R. W. (1934). Self-reliance. In H. H. Clark (Ed.), *Ralph Waldo Emerson: Representative selections, with introduction, bibliography, and notes by Frederick I. Carpenter* (pp. 89-113). New York: American.

Graves, D. (1983). *Writing: Teachers and children at work.* Portsmouth, NH: Heinemann.

Graves, D. (1984). *A researcher learns to write: Selected articles and monographs.* Portsmouth, NH: Heinemann.

Hansen, J. (1987). *When writers read.* Portsmouth, NH: Heinemann.

Harste, J. C., Burke, C. L., & Woodward, V. A. (1984). *Language stories and literacy lessons.* Portsmouth, NH: Heinemann.

Hillocks, G., Jr. (1986). *Research on written composition: New directions for teaching.* Urbana, IL: ERIC Clearinghouse on Reading and Communication Skills.

L'Engle, M. (1962). *A wrinkle in time.* Farrar, Strauss & Giroux.

Lipsyte, R. (1967). *The contender.* New York: Bantam.

Lipsyte, R. (1977). *One fat summer.* New York: Harper & Row.

Lowry, L. (1977). *A summer to die.* Boston: Houghton Mifflin.

Lowry, L. (1978). *Find a stranger, say goodbye.* Boston: Houghton Mifflin.

Murray, D. M. (1985). *A writer teaches writing* (2nd ed.). Boston: Houghton Mifflin.

Pfeffer, S. B. (1980). *About David.* New York: Dell.

Pfeffer, S. B. (1987). *The year without Michael.* New York: Bantam.

Rief, L. (1985). Why can't we live like the monarch butterfly? In D. Graves, T. Newkirk, & J. Hansen (Eds.), *Breaking ground* (pp. 133-146). Portsmouth, NH: Heinemann.

Rief, L. (1989). Seeking diversity: Reading and writing from the middle to the edge. In N. Atwell (Ed.), *Workshop I.* (pp. 13-24) Portsmouth, NH: Heinemann.

Romano, T. (1987). *Clearing the way: Working with teenage writers.* Portsmouth, NH: Heinemann.

Stires, S. (1988). Reading and talking: Special readers show they know. In N. Atwell & T. Newkirk (Eds.), *Understanding writing* (pp. 207-214). Portsmouth, NH: Heinemann.

Stires, S. (1989). Thinking throughout the process: Self-evaluation in writing. In J. Jenson (Ed.), *Stories to grow on: Demonstrations of language learning in K-8 classrooms* (pp. 71-95). Portsmouth, NH: Heinemann.

Whitman, W. (1981). "I hear America singing." In *Leaves of Grass* (p. 14). Franklin Center, PA: The Franklin Library. (Original work published 1855)

8

The Knowledge Necessary to Teach Writing Effectively

GEORGE HILLOCKS, JR.

Teachers of writing ought to be writers, just as teachers of piano ought to be pianists. Teachers of piano need not be great concert pianists, but we expect them to play, with more than mediocre facility, at least some works of Bach, Brahms, Chopin, Liszt, Mozart, Beethoven, and Debussy. So, we should also expect the teacher of writing to write on a variety of topics and in a variety of genres (personal essays, stories, arguments, analyses, poems) if for no other reason than to know what it is like to write them. At the same time, we expect the skilled piano teacher to have a body of knowledge about music theory, the techniques of piano playing, and piano music—knowledge that can be brought to bear in teaching. Similarly, the teacher of writing requires a body of knowledge about writing and the teaching of writing. What that body of knowledge encompasses, however, is not so clear.

In order to examine the knowledge necessary to teach writing effectively, we need to address two enormously complex questions: (a) What does *writing* encompass? and (b) What is involved in the effective teaching of writing? Although we do not have the knowledge to provide definitive answers, recent research and theory provide frameworks for addressing both.

THE TERRITORY OF WRITING

Research and theory over the last 20 years or so have expanded the territory of writing to include not only the nature and quality of written products but the processes involved in bringing them into existence. A number of researchers have concentrated on what might be called the general writing process. Others have examined specific subprocesses used in generating form and content. Instructional studies have provided insight into the differential effects of focusing on various kinds of knowledge in the teaching of writing. Taken together, these studies indicate that, for effective teaching, the territory of writing includes knowledge of the general writing process, knowledge of processes for producing particular kinds of discourse, and knowledge related to developing content.

General Writing Process

A number of researchers and theorists have argued for the primary importance of what I will call the general writing process (e.g., Calkins, 1983; Graves, 1983). These researchers and theorists emphasize the need for generating ideas before writing (prewriting), drafting, receiving feedback from real audiences of peers, revising, editing, and finally publishing the writing by sharing it with audiences in a variety of ways. Anyone who writes knows the importance of these general processes for writing. However, many youngsters do not know this.

Every fall for the last eight years, a small group of prospective English teachers and I have taught a group of seventh graders in the Chicago public schools. Every year during the first writing these students do for us, five or six bottles of "whiteout" appear. The youngsters bend closely over their work, meticulously using the whiteout to eradicate errors, improve handwriting, correct spelling, and even space words more adequately. This year, one girl used whiteout seven times in a single line. Clearly, these students have much to learn about the writing process. They need to know that writers produce preliminary lists and drafts, scrap entire passages, cross out words, insert material using arrows or asterisks, and revise several times before achieving what they desire.

At the same time, learning to engage in the general writing process does not entail learning the particular strategies necessary for effective writing. For example, *Time*'s cover story for February 6, 1989 (Church, 1989), on the use of weapons by citizens, points out the difficulty of "writing a definition of paramilitary weapons that would distinguish them from some types of semiautomatic hunting rifles," precisely the kind of definition necessary for effective legislation prohibiting the sale of such weapons. If the writer of such a definition does not know what criteria are, how to generate them, and how to use examples to illustrate them, no amount of prewriting, drafting, revising, and editing will help produce an effective definition that can pass the muster of legislative action.

Process and Specific Writing Tasks

It seems almost intuitively obvious that the processes required in drafting a narrative about personal experience will differ markedly from those involved in writing an extended definition for a piece of legislation or an argument to convince someone to vote for that legislation. Carl Bereiter (1980) suggests a model, which I have adapted in Figure 8.1, for examining the subprocesses involved in specific writing tasks. This figure represents levels of decision making in the composing process.

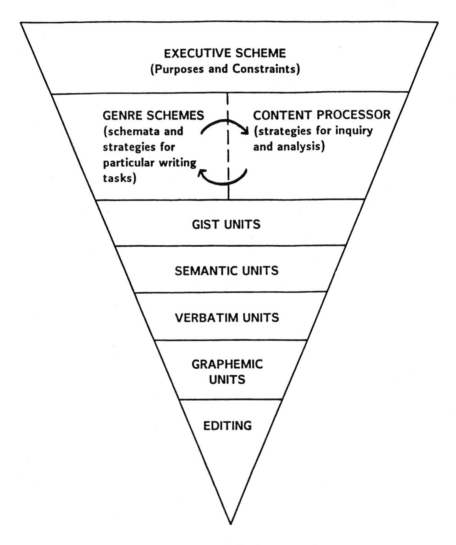

FIGURE 8.1: Decision-making levels in the composing process.

Purposes and Constraints

At the top of this inverted triangle are the purposes and constraints that control the production of a piece of writing. The purposes in writing are ordinarily both substantive and affective; that is, a writer usually wishes to make a point about some subject and to elicit some response from an audience. In technical writing, for example, the writer may wish the audience to examine each piece of data in a detached fashion, assessing its value along with the conclusions reached by the writer. In a narrative about personal experience, in contrast, the writer may wish to evoke empathy from the audience.

Some kinds of writing may not be purposive in this sense at all. Statements by such writers as Blake, Conrad, Tolstoy, and T. S. Eliot suggest that sometimes the writer produces almost compulsively without a conscious notion of purpose. A. E. Housman (1938), for example, writes of downing a pint of beer at luncheon, resuming his walk on Hampstead Heath, and having two stanzas of a poem "bubble up" from "the pit of the stomach." The third stanza came "with a little coaxing after tea." Of the fourth stanza, he says, "I had to turn to and compose it myself, and that was a laborious business. I wrote it thirteen times, and it was more than a twelvemonth before I got it right" (pp. 49-50).

The first three stanzas produced by Housman seem to have been composed without concern for an audience's response. For such material, the usual criteria for judging writing (which derive from the audience/writing relationship) are irrelevant. Housman's concern for getting the fourth stanza "right" suggests that, by that point, he did have a purpose and, therefore, criteria in mind. It may be that writing sometimes begins without a conscious purpose but takes one on as the writer becomes aware of subconscious goals.

The constraints under which writers work include the time available, their perceptions of their own involvement in the communication situation, and, most important, the audience. Audiences that writers encounter in the real world vary along certain key continua: close and intimate to distant and unknown; uninformed to highly knowledgeable; accepting to skeptical. Sometimes, in an effort to develop their students' confidence as writers, teachers try to restrict the audience dimensions of a classroom to the known, accepting, and friendly. But writers in the real world need strategies for dealing with skeptical audiences as well.

Genre Schemata and Discourse Knowledge

The purposes and constraints under which a writer works influence decisions about what Bereiter (1980) calls "genre schemata." A schema may be defined as a patterned set of categories used to organize and interpret incoming information and to guide subsequent verbal and nonverbal behavior. An example of genre schemata that has been carefully researched by psychologists is that of the story schema (Stein & Glenn, 1979; Stein & Trabasso, 1982). Work on the analysis of schemata that control conceptions of argument has also begun (McCann, 1989; Stein & Miller, 1988). Although we have much to learn about genre schemata, writers appear to elect (or invent), early in the composing process some schema that is suitable to their purposes. Accordingly, a writer's knowledge or conception of the schema will guide the production of a particular piece. If a writer's schema for argument is limited, so will be his or her particular arguments.

Genre schemata may be the most important part of a writer's knowledge of discourse, for they come into play early in composing and guide everything that follows. Syntactic knowledge, another part of discourse knowledge, does not come into play until after the level of gist units, chunks of discourse envisioned but without the benefit of specific words and sentences. The discourse knowledge having to do with the conventions of mechanics, spelling, and usage appears not to come into play until the production of graphemic units and editing (see Figure 8.1). Ironically, the discourse knowledge that receives most attention in schools (certain limited conceptions of grammar and conventions of usage and mechanics) has the least impact on the final form of written compositions. It would seem that enhancing discourse knowledge at the level of genre schemata would do much more to improve writing.

One objection to teaching knowledge about discourse at the level of genre schemata is that it leads to formulaic writing. At one level, writers probably use relatively formulaic patterns to help them generate pieces of discourse, for example, some business letters, some memos, letters of recommendation (Anderson, 1985), and the five-paragraph theme that Emig (1971) found her students using. At another level, however, discourse knowledge appears to operate in the composing process in a way that is not at all formulaic.

An example appeared in a study my students and I conducted a few years ago. We asked the youngsters attending a summer writing workshop at the University of Chicago to do the following: "Write about an experience, real or imaginary, that is important to you for some reason. Write about it so specifically that someone else reading what you have written will see what you saw and feel what you felt." Of the 40 students writing in a large classroom, my graduate students and I observed a stratified random sample of 19 during the writing. As each of the youngsters concluded his or her writing, one of the graduate students took the writer to another room to talk about what had just been written. The first questions in the interview asked the writers what they considered writing about before they actually began writing. Eighteen of the 19 students observed considered content of some kind first. That is, they thought of a summer vacation, a trip to an amusement park, a school-related adventure, or some other specific experience.

One 14-year-old boy, however, said that he did not know what he was going to write when he began. He did, however, know the kind of story he wished to write—one that would be mysterious and puzzling and that would have a surprise ending, "a twist," he called it. The story begins with the line, "Where's the floor?" He chose that line, he says, because he thought it would get people's attention. He claims he did not know what would come next, that for him writing the story enabled him to discover what would happen next.

The story develops in the first-person narrative as a nightmarish dream sequence and ends with a double ironic twist. The writer in his interview was able to describe the kind of story he wanted to write in his own words and to compare what he had done with certain stories by Edgar Allan Poe. When the story was rated holistically, it received the highest rating from three raters. Here was a complex first-person narrative with ironic twists written in 50 minutes by a young man who claimed that he did not know what the content of the story would be when he began it. Here is a case in which discourse knowledge apparently guided written production but not in a formulaic way.

Anderson (1985) points out that "discussion of forms is unpopular at present because of the movement in composition pedagogy . . . away from an approach that focuses on the characteristics of good writing to one that focuses on the processes by which good writing is created. As a result, discussion of the forms of writing tends to be scorned" (pp. 11-12). Anderson outlines several reasons why attention to "forms" is important: (a) the competent use of conventional forms in a job setting marks one as a "bona fide member of the culture of the workplace" (p. 12); (b) conventional forms help readers know what to expect as they read; and (c) knowledge of form probably operates as an integral part of the composing process, as strongly suggested by the example above.

Teachers of writing clearly need a theory of discourse that will enable them to think about the demands of various writing tasks. Unfortunately, which theory of discourse is most appropriate for teachers is not at all clear. Several competing theories are available. Probably the most useful current theories for teachers are those devised by Kinneavy (1971) and Moffett (1968). In addition, teachers will find knowledge about modern developments in the analysis of style and cohesion useful. Colomb and Williams (1985) provide an informative example.

Judging Writing

In addition, teachers need to be able to judge specific pieces of writing, diagnose problems in light of writers' purposes, and use that knowledge to guide their instructional planning and coaching. The question of what effective writing is cannot be answered in the abstract. What is effective for a narrative in a short story may not be effective as a narrative for *Time* magazine. An effective argument in a personal letter may not be effective in a court of law. The criteria for judging the effectiveness of writing vary with the purposes of the writer, the attitudes and knowledge of the intended audience, and the context in which the writing is received (e.g., read in private, listened to in public). Teachers need to understand how criteria vary within the range of purposes, audiences, and contexts. Being able to apply these criteria during the course of instruction is crucial to coaching individuals, to evaluating the effectiveness of instruction, and to revising instructional plans to meet the needs of individuals.

The following two pieces of unedited writing illustrate how criteria help guide instruction in general and the coaching of individual students. Both were written at the end of a sequence of instruction, the goal of which was to enable students to write personal narratives capable of arousing empathy in an audience. The first composition is the posttest for the sequence. The second, the revision, is a follow-up to the posttest. Most readers will recognize some difference between the two pieces. But what precisely is the difference?

THE SOCCER GAME [first draft]

Last weekend I was in a soccer game against Hammond. It was almost the end of the game when I scored for our team. Our Coach called me out of the game. He welcomed me to the side with a cheering smile. He yelled, "that's the way to do it" and he asked How I got the goal. I replied, "I got a pass from Charlie and I kicked the ball inches from the goalie and then it went in." My coach said, "that I'm improving at the game and that I will be fantastic in the years to come." As I sat down on the soggy grass, my dad came over and he commented on the great score I made. I said, "I just got lucky." My dad asked, "If I needed a ride at the end of the game" and I said, "yes, I need a ride." Then me and my family drove home from the thrilling soccer game.

* * * *

THE SOCCER GAME [revised draft]

There was a minute in the thrilling soccer game left. Our team, the vikings were tied with Hammond 1 to 1. I was dribbling the ball at a fast pace down the field. I could hear the other team's feet trembling against the hard, dry ground. The light-weighted soccer ball was gliding over the hard surface every time I gave it a soft tap. My heart starting pumping faster as I closed up on the other goalie. My teammate, Charlie was following me on my right side. My feet felt like two humming birds flying to their nests. The fullback on the other team was pushing my shoulder trying to lure the ball away. I passed the ball to Charlie who was just a few feet ahead of me. He dribbled the ball to the goalies box then he centered it to me. I started shaking like a leaf as I kicked the ball past the darting goalie and into the big goal net. I started jumping for joy as my teammates came around me to share my happiness.

The first composition is far more specific than the young man's earlier writing had been. It includes specifics about the game, the score, how the winning goal was scored, what the coach said afterwards, what the father said, and what the boy said. Encouraging writers to be more specific was one of the goals of instruction.

But there is something missing. The writer provides no sensory details that allow us to capture the specifics of the scene and action in our imaginations. Nor does he supply specifics that reveal his own personal feelings or state of mind during the event. We have to supply those details ourselves. The writer appears not to have considered audience response, but has used what Bereiter and Scardamalia (1982) call a what-next strategy. He adds one detail after another as he recalls the events. Curiously, although the intended center of the composition is scoring the goal, that particular event and the writer's immediate response to it have largely been ignored.

At the suggestion of the teacher, the writer focused the second piece on scoring the goal. The teacher's comment was simply, "This is a really good idea. When you revise, focus on scoring the goal and how you felt while you were doing it." In the revision, the student focuses on the immediate events, his reactions leading up to scoring the goal, and his reactions upon the score. His use of specific sensory details and metaphor allow the reader to identify more closely with the excitement the writer must have felt as he was engaged in the particular action.

This revision is a total revamping of the writing. Studies of student revision indicate that they tend to be minimal at best (e.g., Bridwell, 1980). This young man's teacher has provided discourse knowledge and knowledge about developing content through a variety of activities. As a result, the student clearly has the procedural knowledge to use his teacher's advice. He is able to focus on the experience, provide his readers with a good representation of his actions and responses, and create greater empathy in the readers.

Teachers who do not understand the qualities of good writing as they appear for particular purposes and audiences will be unable to provide insightful and incisive comments to help students improve their writing. Worse, the teachers may mislead students into ineffective writing. For example, had the teacher above not understood the importance of focusing to achieve impact, she might have suggested only that the student correct the punctuation of the dialogue. Such a suggestion might have resulted in correctly punctuated dialogue, but the impact of the writing would be no greater, and the student might have assumed that his lack of focus was good.

Where do prospective teachers learn about the characteristics of good writing? Once again, there are competing views of what makes a good argument, a good narrative, or a good analysis. Prospective teachers should probably become familiar with both criteria and the theoretical considerations underlying them. An excellent place to begin is Cooper and Odell's (1977)

Evaluating Writing: Describing, Measuring, Judging. More important, prospective teachers need to see the value of studying student writing for its own sake and for what can be learned about the writers and their conceptions.

Content and Inquiry

In addition to knowledge of discourse, writers require knowledge of procedures for developing the content of writing. In Figure 8.1, that element is labeled "content." (Bereiter, 1980, calls it the "content processor.") In a series of careful studies, Bereiter and Scardamalia (1982) show that when youngsters come to school, they have the schema for conversation. One conversational turn by one partner prompts a comment by the other. In writing there is no conversational partner to prompt the processing of additional content. Bereiter and Scardamalia (1982) point out that when young children are asked to write on a particular topic, they produce about as much as a normal conversational burst would include. When they are asked to say more, they produce about another conversational burst. Providing a series of "contentless prompts" indicates that children have far more content available for writing than they actually use. The process of recalling content for use in writing is probably one of the simplest of the content-processing strategies. But it is one that children apparently need to learn.

A number of studies involve students in more complex kinds of content-processing strategies and have shown a powerful impact on the quality of students' writing (reviewed in Hillocks, 1986). Practicing such strategies appears to help writers inquire more effectively into the data they have available for writing and to transform them more adequately into the content of their writing. For example, some studies involve students in observing carefully and transforming sensory perceptions into language for use in writing. These students show large gains in the effective use of detail in later, independent writing (Hillocks, 1979, 1982). Other studies involve students in analyzing data for use in developing arguments (claims, evidence, warrants, counter-arguments, and so forth). Students in these studies show large gains in developing arguments more fully and effectively (e.g., McCleary, 1979; Troyka, 1973).

All such studies strongly indicate the necessity of helping students learn and practice the strategies by which they may examine and transform data for particular writing tasks. A great deal of research and theory indicates that teaching knowledge of discourse structures alone is inadequate. Every secondary English teacher knows that students can study the conventional ideas about paragraph structure, learn to identify topic sentences and methods of development, but fail when it comes to generating interesting and adequate paragraphs of their own. This is the same problem that Janet Emig (1971) identifies in her complaints about the five-paragraph theme: It provides students a frame into which they can pour ideas; unfortunately, it allows the ideas to remain shallow. Successful and versatile writers need to know a variety of procedures for transforming data into the stuff of writing.

If that is true, then teachers of writing need systematically to incorporate into their curricula experiences in using such strategies. Increasingly, teachers realize, as did the participants in the English Coalition Conference, that students of writing need help "in mastering techniques for discovering and testing . . . information to develop ideas" (Lloyd-Jones & Lunsford, 1989, p. 21). *English for the '90s and Beyond*, the final report of the secondary strand of the English Coalition Conference (1987), puts the case even more strongly, stating that students must "learn to be inquirers, experimenters, and problem solvers" (p. 6) not only to become more effective writers and readers but to become fully participating citizens in a rapidly changing world.

Just what are the "techniques for discovering and testing . . . information"? What strategies are involved in the processes of inquiry—especially as they pertain to writing in various disciplines? Several models of inquiry are available, for example, Dewey (1910). Minimally, for teachers of writing, this writer believes that an adequate model of inquiry should include the strategies summarized in Figure 8.2.

Figure 8.2 suggests that any inquiry appears to begin with observing (collecting and noting new information) or with accessing prior knowledge. Whichever comes first, the process of inquiry appears to demand a continual interplay between new information and prior knowledge. The process of observing and using prior knowledge leads naturally to either comparing or contrasting phenomena. Comparing, on the one hand, leads to generalizations about what is observed or what is known. Contrasting (noting differences or dissonances), on the other hand, leads to the definition of distinctions and to refining generalizations.

Both generalizations and distinctions demand analyses and explanations through inference, interpretation, and hypotheses. Accompanying these strategies, on the one hand, is the creative impulse to question and imagine what might be. That impulse has a centrifugal force pulling the inquirer farther from the data, but permitting new perspectives on what is there. On the other hand, the need to test and evaluate at every juncture has a centripetal effect, pulling the inquirer back to the data to test and evaluate observations, generalizations, distinctions and definitions, explanations and hypotheses. Most current textbooks do not reflect a model of inquiry. We can infer from Applebee's (1981) study of the teaching of writing in secondary schools that most teachers do not see inquiry as an important part of writing. Nevertheless, a great deal of current research, theory, and carefully considered professional opinion strongly supports integrating strategies of inquiry with writing.

Many commonly assigned writing tasks demand the use of several of the strategies of inquiry outlined above. To write about a character in a literary work, for example, demands that the writer *observe* available evidence about the

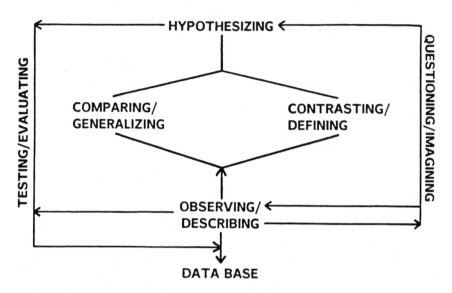

FIGURE 8.2: A model of inquiry (for developing content).

character; use *prior knowledge* in making sense of observations; *compare* the various bits of information in order to *generalize* about the character's behavior or values; *contrast* the same to find changes or anomalies; *question* the significance of what a character does; *imagine* what it might be like to be that character; *hypothesize* explanations of the character's behavior or significance; and *test* and *evaluate* all of these by examining new and old information. Even writing about a favorite place or person requires the strategies of *observation, comparison,* and *generalization.* Research projects and papers using primary source material (a practice increasingly recommended by state guidelines) demand the use of these strategies of inquiry.

THE EFFECTIVE TEACHING OF WRITING

Knowledge of discourse and strategies for inquiry, while necessary for the effective teaching of writing, are not sufficient. In addition, we need to ask what special pedagogical dispositions, understandings, and skills are necessary to help students learn strategies that will enable them to deal successfully with a variety of writing tasks in new contexts. Before proceeding to the specifics of teaching writing, it is imperative, I think, to comment on two dispositions that teachers must have to be successful. Although they are not exclusive to the teaching of writing, they are so important that I cannot ignore them here.

The first has to do with assumptions about the capabilities of students. A recent case study (Hillocks, 1989) examines the beliefs and instruction of two English teachers, one who believes her students have such extremely limited backgrounds that they are unable to deal with any but a text's most superficial meanings, and another who recognizes the difficulty his students encounter but assumes that with appropriate instruction they will be able to overcome it. The first teacher structures her classroom for the presentation of bits and pieces of information that she believes will develop students' background to the point where they will be able to comprehend what they read on their own. However, in her classroom, the comprehension required of students is minimal, focusing on literally stated main ideas and details, and ignoring implied meanings. In the first teacher's class, six students provide 85 % of all student response, and 67 % of all student responses consist of three or fewer words. In short, students have a minimal role in the production of meaning in that class.

The second teacher, who assumes that his students will be able to work out meanings for themselves, structures the class to help students understand the literary problems they encounter. The result is that all students contribute to the discussion. Only 14 % of student responses consist of three words or fewer. Indeed, 47 % of student responses are more than one line long. More important, students construct complex meanings for themselves and come to understand sophisticated literary concepts.

If we assume that students are unable to learn any more than the most simplistic material because they have very weak backgrounds, we will tend to adjust our teaching to that level. As Cohen (1988) points out, this attitude helps us confirm our success as teachers. If we assume, in contrast, that students can learn and if we adjust our materials and activities to prepare them for more complex concepts and tasks, we will find that they reach eagerly to deal with tasks that before were obscure.

The second assumption is closely related to the first. We have to assume that teaching is a deliberative activity, open to reflection, assessment, and revision. If we assume that teaching is deliberative, we assume that we can change it to help learners learn more. If, in contrast, we see teaching as formulaic (going through a set of predetermined activities without regard to their immediate effects), then we assume that what we do as teachers makes little difference to the learning of our students.

Given these two assumptions—that our students can learn more and that effective teaching involves deliberation—we can look more closely at the main business of teaching writing: to help students learn strategies that will enable them to deal with a variety of writing tasks in new contexts. Learning strategies for use in new contexts means learning procedural knowledge.

Teaching Procedural Knowledge

Psychologists discriminate between declarative knowledge and procedural knowledge, knowledge of *what* as opposed to knowledge of *how*. We may have declarative knowledge of Beethoven's "Pathetique Sonata" from having heard it many times. We may recognize it from as little as two or three successive bars. We may be able to describe its movements and tempos, but all this is declarative knowledge. The knowledge necessary for playing it is procedural and involves minute bits of information about how to press and hold piano keys, how to move from one chord to another, how much pressure to give keys for notes appearing in the melodic line, and so forth.

Most procedural knowledge is neither taught nor learned in verbal form. Rather, it is modeled by the teacher, approximated by the student, coached by the teacher, and developed in process over a period of time in a variety of simpler contexts. When teachers believe students are ready for the "Pathetique," they demonstrate, coach, break it down into manageable parts, focus on even as little as some portion of a single measure at a time, and then encourage synthesis of the whole.

The procedures involved in writing are even more complex, for the writers must invent their own scores. Just as we would not expect a pianist to learn a complex sonata simply as the result of hearing several outstanding performances (declarative knowledge), we cannot expect writers to learn from models or the rules invoked in teachers' comments. Procedural knowledge must be learned *in process*—but with the help of models, coaching, and the facilitation that comes from making tasks manageable and varying the contexts in which they are learned.

Figure 8.3 illustrates the effects of concentrating on certain kinds of declarative knowledge as opposed to procedural knowledge. This figure represents some of the findings of a meta-analysis of composition studies (Hillocks, 1986). The first two foci of instruction, grammar and models, both concentrate on declarative knowledge. In the case of grammar, the pertinent knowledge has to do with the names of parts of speech, parts of sentences, types of sentences, and so forth. In treatments focusing on model compositions, the declarative knowledge was of organizational structures in compositions, the nature of introductions and conclusions, the use of evidence, and so forth. Students read the writing of other writers to see how they had handled the problems confronting them. Declarative knowledge of the patterns observed was expected to act as a guide for student writing.

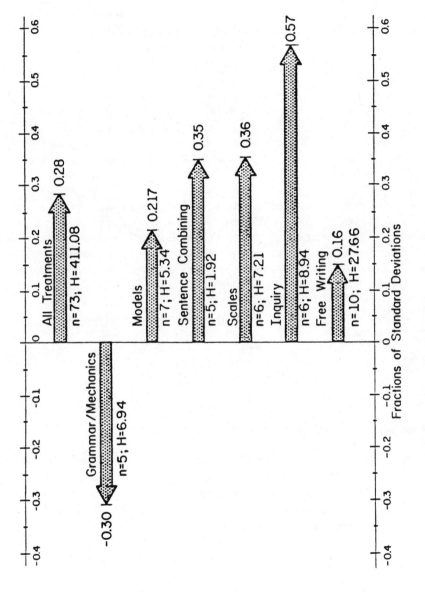

FIGURE 8.3: Focus of instruction—Experimental/control effects.

The remaining four treatments may be regarded as focusing on procedural knowledge. Sentence combining provides students with practice in manipulating a variety of syntactical structures in many different contexts. The "scales" treatments ask students to apply sets of criteria to various pieces of writing, make judgments about the strengths and weaknesses of that writing in terms of the criteria, generate ideas for improving weaknesses, and make revisions using the criteria and the ideas generated. The inquiry treatments focus on learning particular strategies for transforming raw data into the content of writing—the strategies of inquiry outlined earlier in this chapter.

The category of free writing incorporates most studies that made use of the general process of writing (prewriting, drafting, revising, receiving feedback, and editing). Figure 8.3 presents the effect sizes for these treatments (the difference between the experimental treatment and control treatments expressed as a portion of a standard deviation). Clearly, the two treatments that focus on declarative knowledge, grammar and models, do much less to enhance the quality of student writing than the three procedural treatments that focus on specific strategies. The fourth procedural treatment, free writing, which focuses on general process elements of writing, cannot in itself be expected to have a powerful impact on the quality of writing. Although it presents general processes that students surely need to be aware of, it does not provide specific information necessary to the successful operation of subprocesses demanded by particular writing tasks.

Undoubtedly each focus of attention makes some contribution to helping students become better writers. Even a knowledge of usage and the conventions of mechanics comes into play at lower levels of the composing process: the production of graphemic units and editing (see Figure 8.1). Successful teachers of writing do not use one of these foci of instruction exclusively. All or most are integrated.

Planning, Reflection, Assessment

Many highly successful treatments reflect careful selection of materials (both models and sets of data for analysis) and sequencing so that students use strategies in highly supported situations, moving to new contexts with less teacher and peer support (e.g., Faigley, 1979; Hillocks, 1979, 1982; McCleary, 1979; Sager, 1973; Troyka, 1973). All of these treatments allow students to concentrate on some part of a complex writing task before independently undertaking the task in all of its dimensions. In addition, when students undertake a new task, the instruction provides a high level of support in terms of modeling, teacher coaching, peer support, and so forth.

Sager's (1973) experimental treatment, for example, sets out to teach students a set of criteria (or scales) used to guide their own writing. Obviously, this is a complex task that includes learning what the criteria are, how to use them to make judgments, how to use the judgments to prompt better writing, how to generate the improvements, and how to synthesize them in writing. In Sager's treatment, students gradually undertake more of these tasks independently and in new contexts. At the beginning, teachers explain the criteria and lead students in applying them to selected compositions, discussing weaknesses and ideas for improvement. Next, students work in groups applying the criteria to selected pieces of writing and generating ideas for improvements. Then each student synthesizes the ideas generated by the group to revise the composition. Eventually students proceed with these tasks independently.

During the course of instruction, the tasks change from relatively simple to complex, students move from dependence to independence, and students have many opportunities to apply what they are learning in new contexts. At the same time students are working with whole pieces of discourse rather than with the isolated bits of discourse that appear in worksheets and that have little meaning for anyone. A large body of empirical evidence from cognitive psychology provides strong support for these ideas about learning transferable strategies and helps to explain how and why such instruction works (see, for example, Bereiter and Scardamalia, 1987, especially pp. 254-256, and Bransford, 1979, especially pp. 205-245).

Planning. As suggested above, one of the most important dimensions of planning—especially for complex writing tasks—is the careful analysis of the task to reveal its dimensions and problems. Such analysis permits treating complex tasks in manageable parts and leads to the selection of materials of various kinds intended to help students learn and practice the dimensions of the task. McCleary (1979) and Troyka (1973) base instruction on an analysis of argument. Focusing on ethical argument, McCleary's treatment systematically introduces students to the concepts of principles, exceptions, obligations, consequences, and so forth. Students then identify the obligations, consequences, and principles in certain ethical controversies. They next work at identifying and analyzing these concepts in a variety of ethical problems and developing appropriate arguments about them.

Troyka's (1973) instruction recognizes the importance of predicting opposing points of view and their attendant arguments in order to find a solution through compromise, to structure one's own position more clearly, or simply to counter the opposing points. Both McCleary (1979) and Troyka recognize that effective arguments are based on specific situations and particular sets of data. Accordingly, their instructional materials provide situations and sets of data for students to examine in developing arguments.

The analysis of a writing task will address questions related primarily to discourse as well as questions related primarily to substance. In other words, what will a writer have to know about discourse and about the processing of data or content to accomplish the writing task successfully? To write a fable, for example, a writer must know that a fable consists of a story plus a moral (and that sometimes the moral is implied), that the characters are often animals who talk and act as human beings, that at least one animal usually represents some human foible, that the plot often reveals the foible in the animal, and that the moral grows out of and comments upon the story. Knowing what a fable is, however, is a necessary but not a sufficient condition for writing one. Writers must also be able to generate appropriate ideas. Analysis suggests three possible directions for developing fable ideas: (a) begin with a moral, attempt to find a situation to illustrate it, think of animals to fit the situation, and so forth; (b) begin with a situation in which one character behaves foolishly, think of an animal to take the part of that character, and so forth; (c) begin with an annoying human quality, think of an animal that might symbolize that quality, generate ideas about how that animal might treat others, think of ways those actions might bring about the animal's own downfall or embarrassment, generate a moral.

This analysis suggests that teaching students to write fables will involve teaching not only what a fable is, but how to generate ideas for developing a fable, using one or more of the sets of ideas listed above. (Experience indicates that the third helps more students produce better fables more quickly.)

A second step in planning involves the selection of materials: models and data sets. Ordinarily, good models for use in instruction are those which clearly illustrate the salient features of the kind of writing in question. But they must be accessible and interesting to students. The other kind of material—what I call data sets—does not appear in most textbooks. However, in the meta-analysis alluded to above, instruction that uses data sets to help students learn strategies for coping with the substance of writing (inquiry) has greater impact than the other foci of instruction. In the case of argument, for example, both McCleary (1979) and Troyka (1973) present cases of controversial situations with relevant data. Students must learn to generalize about the data presented, analyze the situations, make predictions about the audience, select the data that will support generalizations appropriately, and so forth.

The teacher selects data that are likely to be of interest to students and that provide them with common material to analyze and discuss. Having common material allows students to develop and try arguments with their peers, who are equally knowledgeable about the situation. When students do not have a common knowledge base, they may be unable to formulate their own ideas from real information, support generalizations, predict opposing points of view, and so forth. They cannot experience delivering an argument to others who have comparable information but a different perspective and who can serve as a critical audience.

In addition to selecting materials, the teacher must also design effective activities in which the students can come to understand and actively use strategies required by the writing task. These include effective initial teacher-led discussions to introduce new strategies and information, small-group discussions in which students help each other to apply strategies to new problems, as well as group and individual activities for writing, revising, and feedback. The most effective of these activities focus attention on specific strategies, facilitate learning by allowing students to work with some part of a complex strategy, and vary the contexts for use. (For solid examples, see Kahn, Johannessen, and Walter, 1984, and Smagorinsky, McCann, and Kern, 1987.)

Finally, teachers must sequence the materials and attendant activities to move students from dependence on the teacher, when information and strategies are new, to independence as students gradually gain knowledge and experience. This sequence may first focus on producing certain parts of a complex writing task so that students can concentrate on one problem at a time when the task is relatively new. For example, students might focus on writing dialogues between characters in conflict before writing a full short story. The sequence may allow students to practice certain strategies of inquiry in a variety of supported contexts before requiring them to use the strategies independently in some new context. For example, in learning to generate criteria, students may begin by using supplied criteria to classify examples, then contrast supplied examples to generate criteria, and finally generate both examples and criteria independently, each of these in a new context. (For an extended discussion of such a sequence for teaching definition, see Johannessen, Kahn, and Walter, 1982.)

Assessment and reflection. The kind of planning suggested here is an art requiring assessments and judgments about students and their capabilities, about materials and the problems they may involve, about the strategies required in a writing task, and about how students interact with materials and activities to become independent. It is an art that requires considerable reflection at every stage of planning, teaching, and assessment. Even while teaching is in progress, teachers should be able to monitor the activity as it develops, watch for difficulties that students encounter, and make changes as necessary. Such teaching requires active use of the kinds of knowledge discussed earlier.

For example, one student teacher recently asked a group of low-achieving students in a Chicago public school to examine a set of data with an eye to selecting statements that supported one of two different arguments and to explain how particular data supported that proposition. She saw from student responses that they were unable to distance themselves from the data in order to make those deliberate judgments. Immediately, she changed the assignment, asking them to select the data that they believed would support their own personal point of view and to explain why. The activity went forward without further difficulty, maintaining the interest of the students at a relatively high level.

In teaching fables, one teacher noted that beginning with morals proved particularly difficult for seventh graders. He switched immediately to brainstorming for human frailties, qualities or behaviors that students resented in others. The students suggested such things as "talking about you behind your back," "telling secrets," "pretending to like a person that you really didn't like," and so forth. Reflection at this crucial moment in the teaching process enabled the students to go on to produce successful fables.

In other words, for assessment and reflection to be productive, they must be involved at every step of the teaching process, examining both the effect and the value of teaching. Teachers must ask not only whether students have learned to write effective fables, arguments, or narratives, but whether those learning experiences have had real value to the students as writers and as people. Only by asking such questions persistently can we expect to develop effective curricula in writing. And by asking them persistently, we can continue to develop our knowledge about the teaching of writing.

Teachers of writing, then, need to know what it feels like to be a writer. If they themselves write, they will know the process of developing a piece of writing from jotting notes to drafting and sometimes to interminable revising and proofreading. Teachers who know this will be predisposed to understand struggling students and will be able to guide them through the general writing processes.

However, more than mere knowledge of, and willingness to use, general writing processes is required for most writing tasks. Teachers must be guided by a theory of discourse that includes ideas not only about the modes and functions of discourse, but of the strategies entailed in particular treatments of content. They also need to know procedures for analyzing writing tasks, for inventing materials and activities, and for assessing the effectiveness of their own inventions both during teaching and following it. In this sense, the teaching of writing is an art, but one that is learnable and open to examination through a variety of analytical tools.

REFERENCES

Anderson, P. V. (1985). What survey research tells us about writing. In L. Odell & D. Goswami (Eds.), *Writing in nonacademic settings* (pp. 3-77). New York: Guilford Press.

Applebee, A. N. (1981). *Writing in the secondary school* (Research Report No. 21). Urbana, IL: National Council of Teachers of English.

Bereiter, C. (1980). Development in writing. In L. W. Gregg & E. R. Steinberg (Eds.), *Cognitive processes in writing* (pp. 73-93). Hillsdale, NJ: Erlbaum.

Bereiter, C., & Scardamalia, M. (1982). From conversation to composition: The role of instruction in a developmental process. In R. Glaser (Ed.), *Advances in instructional psychology* (Vol. 2, pp. 1-64). Hillsdale, NJ: Erlbaum.

Bereiter, C., & Scardamalia, M. (1987). *The psychology of written composition.* Hillsdale, NJ: Erlbaum.

Bransford, J. D. (1979). *Human cognition: Learning, understanding, and remembering.* Belmont, CA: Wadsworth.

Bridwell, L. S. (1980). Revising strategies in twelfth grade students' transactional writing. *Research in the Teaching of English, 14,* 197-222.

Calkins, L. M. (1983). *Lessons from a child: On the teaching and learning of writing.* Portsmouth, NH: Heinemann.

Church, G. T. (1989, February 6). The other arms race. *Time,* pp. 20-26.

Cohen, D. K. (1988). *Teaching practice: Plus ça change . . .* (Issue Paper 88-3). East Lansing: Michigan State University, National Center for Research on Teacher Education.

Colomb, G. G., & Williams, J. M. (1985). Perceiving structure in professional prose: A multiply determined experience. In L. Odell & D. Goswami (Eds.), *Writing in nonacademic settings* (pp. 87-128). New York: Guilford Press.

Cooper, C. R., & Odell, L. (Eds.). (1977). *Evaluating writing: Describing, measuring, judging.* Urbana, IL: National Council of Teachers of English.

Dewey, J. (1910). *How we think.* Boston: Heath.

Emig, J. (1971). *The composing process of twelfth graders* (Research Report No. 13). Urbana, IL: National Council of Teachers of English.

English Coalition Conference. (1987). *English for the 90's and beyond. Final report: Strand A-2, secondary.* Queenstown, MD: Aspen Institute for Humanistic Studies.

Faigley, L. L. (1979). The influence of generative rhetoric in the syntactic maturity and writing effectiveness of college freshmen. *Research in the Teaching of English, 13,* 197-206.

Graves, D. H. (1983). *Writing: Teachers and children at work.* Portsmouth, NH: Heinemann.

Hillocks, G., Jr. (1979). The effects of observational activities on student writing. *Research in the Teaching of English, 13,* 23-35.

Hillocks, G., Jr. (1982). The interaction of instruction, teacher comment, and revision in teaching the composing process. *Research in the Teaching of English, 13,* 261-278.

Hillocks, G., Jr. (1986). *Research on written composition: New directions for teaching.* Urbana, IL: ERIC Clearinghouse on Reading and Communication Skills.

Hillocks, G., Jr. (1989). Literary texts in the classroom. In P. W. Jackson & S. Haroutounian-Gordon (Eds.), *From Socrates to software: The teacher as text and the text as teacher* (pp. 135-157). Chicago: National Society for the Study of Education.

Housman, A. E. (1938). *The name and nature of poetry.* Cambridge: Cambridge University Press.

Johannessen, L., Kahn, E., & Walter, C. (1982). *Designing and sequencing prewriting activities.* Urbana, IL: National Council of Teachers of English.

Kahn, E., Johannessen, L., & Walter, C. (1984). *Writing about literature.* Urbana, IL: National Council of Teachers of English.

Kinneavy, J. L. (1971). *A theory of discourse.* Englewood Cliffs, NJ: Prentice-Hall.

Lloyd-Jones, R., & Lunsford, A. (1989). *The English Coalition Conference: Democracy through language.* Urbana, IL: National Council of Teachers of English.

McCann, T. (1989). Student argumentative writing knowledge and ability at three grade levels. *Research in the Teaching of English, 23*, 62-76.

McCleary, W. J. (1979). Teaching deductive logic: A test of the Toulmin and Aristotelian models for critical thinking and college composition. Unpublished doctoral dissertation, University of Texas, Austin.

Moffett, J. (1968). *Teaching the universe of discourse.* Boston: Houghton Mifflin.

Sager, C. (1973). *Improving the quality of written composition through pupil use of a rating scale.* Unpublished doctoral dissertation, Boston University.

Smagorinsky, P., McCann, T., & Kern, S. (1987). *Explorations: Introductory activities for literature and composition, 7-12.* Urbana, IL: National Council of Teachers of English.

Stein, N. L., & Glenn, C. G. (1979). An analysis of story comprehension in elementary school children. In R. O. Freedle (Ed.), *New directions in discourse processing* (Vol. 2, pp. 53-120). Norwood, NJ: Ablex.

Stein, N. L., & Miller, C. (1988, November). *Reasoning and thinking about writing arguments: A developmental study.* Paper presented at the meeting of the Psychonomics Society, Chicago.

Stein, N. L., & Trabasso, T. (1982). What's in a story: An approach to comprehension and instruction. In R. Glaser (Ed.), *Advances in instructional psychology* (Vol. 2, pp. 213-267). Hillsdale, NJ: Erlbaum.

Troyka, L. Q. (1973). A study of the effect of simulation-gaming on expository prose competence of college remedial English composition students. Unpublished doctoral dissertation, New York University.

9

Teaching/Writing in a Community
of Inquirers

JOHN T. GAGE

The question we are addressing—"What should teachers know about writing?"—may imply both that there is a stable body of knowledge "out there" and, if we could just say what it is, that all teachers need is to possess it. Such is not the case. The field of composition is so diverse at the present time, so cluttered with competing methods and ideologies, that it is impossible to claim or to practice a pedagogical approach to writing without at the same time assuming a part, whether actively or passively, in the energetic debate that characterizes the field. There is no consensus. Out there, among the composition theorists, there is considerable division and not a few axes to grind. Rather than knowledge of the sort that can simply be taken in and applied in practice, the field is in fact constituted by competing and incompatible claims for teachers' attention and allegiance (see, for example, Berlin, 1987; North, 1987). Some are alarmed by this state of affairs, claiming that without the possibility of hard knowledge and shared agreement about what we are teaching and how we are teaching it, students will suffer by being taught by whatever approach happens to be blowing in the wind. Others are more at peace with it, finding the strongly debated issues that characterize this field to be evidence of its health and of a pluralism that is finally desirable for a discipline that deals with central questions about learning and knowledge.

I will try not to use this occasion to defend my side of whatever issues I generally debate when I write and speak about teaching composition, though I will inevitably present parts of it to you. The question that we are all addressing cannot be answered by the proliferation of specific theories or pedagogies, but only by considering certain assumptions about our field that provide the only possible test of whether any theory or pedagogy, in the vast array of those available, makes sense. But assumptions are difficult to articulate because, like chemical and metabolic processes in the body, they are taken for granted, they derive from ideological or conceptual givens that are mostly unargued when scholars say what they think. Assumptions are what we think *with*, not what we think *about*. So, it is unlikely that I will succeed in identifying the actual assumptions that govern the views of writing that I will be discussing. What makes it most difficult is that the question of "what teachers should know" raises for me the even more perplexing question: What does it mean to *know* anything? In the face of this awesome question, you will find me coming around, eventually, to a plea for tolerance and pluralism. Even as I say this, however, I am haunted by the possibility that pluralism itself may go too far, as the poet J. V. Cunningham (1971) expressed in this epigram:

> This Humanist whom no beliefs constrained
> Grew so broad-minded he was scatter-brained. (p. 117)

Negotiating between the extremes of true belief in one method and not having any means to discriminate among methods is no easy task. The position I will defend, finally, is that what a writing teacher needs to know is how to live with the condition of uncertainty. And this, I also think, is what learning to write is all about.

"EITHER/OR THINKING"

My own work in the field of composition has been to promote methods of writing that develop habits of inquiry. I will say a bit more about this shortly. Reflecting on what this means in relation to the field of composition theory and pedagogy leads me to think that a significant impulse behind my work has been to try to negotiate between extreme views. Writing pedagogies are particularly susceptible to something I will call "either/or thinking." One method is proposed as an alternative to another, and the teacher is asked to choose. The word *alternative* appears so often in the advertising for writing textbooks that in order to distinguish a new book from the pack one would have to advertise it as "no alternative at all; just more of the same old stuff."

What are some of these alleged alternatives? I will write them large, risking little exaggeration, however. "Expression," for instance, is pitted against "competence" as two mutually exclusive aims of teaching writing, each of which will generate incompatible pedagogical practices. Teaching formal competence by direct means is often viewed as an obstacle to expression, for instance.

"Creativity," with its attendant stress on the values of imagination and personal narrative, may be pitted against "exposition" or "argumentation," with their attendant stress on formal models and logical formulae. Writing teachers may speak of a new emphasis on "process" as an alternative to a discarded view of writing as "product," as if it were possible to have one without the other.

And the most recent example of either/or thinking is found in the recent career of E. D. Hirsch, who in the 1970s advocated the teaching of imitable sentence patterns that might be abstracted entirely from any particular content. In the 1980s Hirsch repudiated that idea entirely and substituted for it a pedagogy focused exclusively on content: the cultural information, in the form of "facts," that literate readers and writers must have in common in order to communicate. *Either*, it seems, one teaches empty forms that constitute the technical competence of skilled writers, *or* one teaches the contextless information that Hirsch can organize into an alphabetical list and best-selling "dictionary."

CHOOSING SIDES LEADS TO DISTORTIONS

In the presence of such compelling dualisms, it seems necessary to make a choice. In practice, this tendency to have to choose sides leads, I believe, to distortion. It is the side that one does not choose that will be distorted to guarantee that one's own position will look good. Those who, for instance, are persuaded to become advocates of the new emphasis on "process"—although they too will disagree about what this means—have constructed a "straw man" and named him "product," a term that has come to signify radical intolerance of all errors in formal student writing as if they were transgressions of civil law. Similarly, those who are persuaded to become advocates of "expressive" writing are tempted to accept extreme characterizations of formal models or logical principles as impersonal and restrictive. One hears and reads phrases such as hegemonic, patriarchal, logocentric, life-killing.

In contrast, some who advocate argumentative writing have constructed a straw man out of "expression," and one hears or reads of him described as anti-intellectual, fuzzy-minded, undisciplined, and merely emotive. Choosing sides, then, becomes a potentially destructive activity, since it may blind one to the virtues of another's approach in the rush to discover its limits. Such debates can quickly degenerate into name-calling. I am a liberal-minded advocate of consensus and quality; you are an irrationalist. I am a feminist after recognition of difference and subjecthood for the powerless; you are an authoritarian grammarian in the service of prevailing power relationships. These are labels that shut off rather than encourage inquiry. And in the process of rejection, which goes along with strident advocacy of one or another extreme, any value that might be found in opposing viewpoints goes unacknowledged and undetected.

Process of Rejection

I once used a mixed metaphor to characterize this process of rejection. Actually I abused two clichés at once by combining them. I called it "throwing out the straw baby with the bathwater" (Gage, 1984). The occasion for my creation of this barbarous accretion was a review of a book about composition pedagogy that seemed to me, at the time, to illustrate the dangers of either/or thinking in this profession. The book was innocently titled *Rhetorical Traditions and the Teaching of Writing* (Knoblauch & Brannon, 1984), and in fact I agreed wholeheartedly with its conclusions about the teaching of writing. Here is the authors' summary of their conclusions:

> The basic features of a classroom predicated on assumptions of modern rhetoric are the following: (1) It's student centered rather than teacher centered; that is, its agenda is students' own writing and their development as writers, not a teacher's prescriptions about writing or a contrived time-table for that development. (2) It assumes that composing is a competence which develops through use, not a system of skills to be serially introduced through lecture/discussion and then practiced one-at-a-time in drills and exercises. (3) It is facilitative, not directive, and collaborative, not authoritarian; that is, teachers join in the process of making and responding to discourse in order to sustain students' composing by implicating themselves in the guesswork, exploration, and reformulation in which all writers engage. Rules and other absolutes disappear in favor of repeated acts of writing and continuous, collegial responding which assumes, in part, that other students' reactions can be as relevant as the teacher's and that *all* responses are valuable, useful, individual impressions to be weighed in rewriting while *none* are ultimatums for revision. (4) It reverses the ancient priorities of correctness, clarity, and fluency out of conviction that writers who have not learned to value their meanings by seeing how others value them have no reason to develop, indeed lack the basis for developing, any special expertise in their transmission. In light of these four basic features, the writing workshop is attitudinally distinct from the traditional classroom, and therefore irreconcilable with a traditional approach. It's an environment in which everyone, beginning with the teacher, is a writer and also a reader. The governing spirit of the writing workshop is the modern rhetorical perspective, where writing has heuristic value, where writers search for ways to organize experience as coherent assertions and patterns of assertions, where authentic purposes and intended readers guide the choices about what to say, as well as where and how to say it, where revising is perpetual in the search for meaning, and where individual creativity, the energy of personal statement within a community of interested readers, is more valuable than timid or enforced capitulation to hackneyed thought. (p. 104)

Labels Applied

This is indeed a noble enterprise, and one that teachers of writing would do well to understand and apply. I will in fact be advocating many of the same values later in this chapter. When I say I agree wholeheartedly with these conclusions, however, I mean that I agree with the positive side of what are always expressed as binomial choices. But I pause when I reflect just what it is that these authors require me to reject in order to join them in the choices we embrace together. Notice that the paragraph I have quoted is built on the rhetoric of antithesis: Its form is to assert "*this*, but not *that*." The form requires us to assent to certain values at the expense of other potential values. Of course the rejected values are presented in language that is loaded to make them unacceptable: "a *contrived* time-table for . . . development," "a *system* of skills . . . practiced *one-at-a-time* in *drills* and exercises," "not *directive* . . . not *authoritarian*," "rules and *other absolutes*," "*ultimatums* for revision," "*ancient* priorities," students "have *no reason* to develop," "*irreconcilable* with a *traditional* approach," and finally, "*timid or enforced capitulation to hackneyed thought*." Exactly what practices or pedagogies are being characterized by these labels? Whatever they are, the uncritical reader of this passage is invited simply to trash them, and they include nearly everything that may have constituted good and effective teaching of writing in the hands of good and effective teachers at one time or another. So the invitation here, on behalf of embracing a student-centered, collegial, supportive classroom in which students write meaningfully and responsibly, is in fact an exhortation to throw out any informed application of techniques from the past. While there is a lesson here for teachers who apply such techniques thoughtlessly, I pity the teacher who would read such a list and choose to remain ignorant of all the potential knowledge contained in what these authors call the "tradition" in favor of a so-called "modern" classroom in which there is nothing left for the teacher to teach and anything goes. Talk about absolutes! This passage is full of them.

Partial Readings of History

So, while I want to assent to the conclusions these authors reached in their book, I can do so only by reacting critically to the reasons they presented for them. I will paraphrase now the logic of their central argument: The traditional way of teaching writing (such as one finds in most textbooks) relies on categories and assumptions inherited from the ancient rhetoricians. Ancient rhetoric depends on an epistemology in which Truth (big *T)* exists apart from language and in which language serves to dress that truth up and make it palatable for an audience of dupes. But modern epistemology, since Kant, has situated truth (small *t*) *in* language, so that meaning is a construct of words and therefore subject to interpretation but not to verification outside language. So, if the traditional teaching of writing is based on an epistemology that has been rejected in the modern world, that way of teaching writing must be rejected in favor of one based on this new epistemology, in which students must be free to discover new meanings through language rather than being bound to pass on old meanings through language.

The authors have based their entire case on a reading of history that is partial and absolute. It is absolute because they see everything that was thought about language before, say, Kant as wrong, while seeing everything that has been thought about language since Kant as true. (I trust you catch the irony.) This watershed theory of the history of rhetoric is partial because it distributes into "ancient" and "modern" two views of language that in fact coexisted in ancient rhetoric just as they coexist in modern rhetoric. I can't give you a full demonstration of this here, but I can jump to the consequences.

To ignore the fact that the ancient rhetoricians debated exactly the same epistemological differences that these authors wish to see as marking the difference between ancient and modern thought, easily turns into an excuse to remain ignorant of the tradition of ancient rhetoric and all of the potential knowledge that it might contain. The roots for a modern epistemology of language derive from those ancient debates, even though *some* parts of ancient rhetoric are just as corny as these authors say they were. And to remain ignorant of the traditions that inform the controversies of one's own time is to deprive oneself of a means of thinking about similar controversies that are also present during one's own time. This is the consequence, I am afraid, of such a dualistic view of history, a reading of the history of rhetoric in which all real knowledge about language is called "modern" while the "tradition" represents nothing but lore and superstition and can only be accepted as "authoritarian," "directive," and a "capitulation to hackneyed thought." You must be either on the side of modern angels or in league with the traditional devil. My portmanteau cliché, "throwing the straw baby out with the bathwater," may not be eloquent but it is descriptive.

A CRITICAL ATTITUDE IS NEEDED

I suppose that this implies a lesson for the teacher of writing, and that is that one should know something about the history of one's own discipline. It is only by having some independent knowledge of Plato, Aristotle, Cicero, Quintilian, Locke, and Kant that one would be able to assess the accuracy of statements made about these same thinkers by the authors of the book I have been traducing. And it is only by knowing what the issues and arguments of these thinkers were that one can identify the same issues and arguments when they recur in contemporary controversies about teaching writing (see, for example, Gage, 1986). But I am not taking this position here, since the idea that every teacher of writing needs to be a scholar of the history of rhetoric is not only impossible and unrealistic, but unnecessary. While teachers of writing can only benefit from knowing about the history of rhetoric and composition, this knowledge alone is no guarantee of anything, any more than knowledge of all the contemporary rhetoricians who advocate different and contradictory positions can guarantee good teaching if teachers lack the critical ability to assess these positions for themselves.

All that is needed to see through the arguments of the book I have discussed is the knowledge that they *are* arguments. To read such a book critically, one does not need to assent to its invitation to think in an either/or mode. One can reserve for oneself the ability to say "yes, but . . . ." As much as I respect Tom Romano's idea of the teacher-writer expressed earlier in this volume, I would like to advocate the idea of the teacher-*inquirer*, not as an alternative but as a prerequisite.

So, rather than saying that there is any particular piece of knowledge about the history of rhetoric or about modern pedagogy that a teacher must have, I am saying that a critical *attitude* is what is most needed. I will say some more about this attitude and how I think it can be learned and try to apply it to the teaching of writing.

Where Critical Judgment Comes from

There is an essay I particularly admire and that, if it were in my power, I would have every teacher of writing—of *anything*—read. It was written by Wayne C. Booth (1970), and it is called "The Uncritical American, or, Nobody's from Missouri Any More." Of course this is not the only essay that might present teachers with the issue of where critical judgment comes from, and others may want to think instead about the same issue in the context of some favorite piece by Dewey or Bruner or William James or Peter Elbow or Hannah Arendt. In any event, Booth defines critical judgment as the act of assessing "the adequacy of the *case made* to the *conclusions*" (p. 65) or knowing "how to match the degree of [one's] convictions to the quality of [the] reasons" (p. 73). I wish now to make several observations about this definition.

First, as Booth points out, the necessity of making this kind of judgment is our "common lot." All of us, teachers or students, females or males, romantics or rationalists, poets or scientists, are constantly engaged in the activity of judging reasons, whether they are the reasons of others or our own. Even if we cannot give a definition of what makes a good reason—and I think most of us can't—we nevertheless apply criteria implicitly whenever we accept or reject a reason, whether it is one we hear or one we might choose to offer.

Second, we all understand somehow that it is possible to judge reasons well or to judge them poorly and that we are all equally guilty of doing both on occasion, depending, for one thing, on the degree to which we *want* to accept a conclusion. We all know, then, that since we have been wrong about such judgments in the past, the possibility of being wrong about them again is ever present.

Third, we have learned whatever we know about this process by doing it. We do not apply a memorized rule each time we make such a judgment. We apply instead a set of tacit standards that are in fact very complex and that we have learned just as we have learned the so-called rules of grammar: by active participation in the activity of making sense of our own and others' arguments.

Fourth, this definition implies a standard for assent that denies the possibility of closure in the discussion of any issue. What I mean is this: If we are obligated to measure the *degree* of our convictions against the *quality* of the reasons offered for them, then we have defined conviction as subject to degree. Many are accustomed to thinking of conviction as if it were a light switch having an "off" position and an "on" position: Either I hold a conviction or I do not. But this shift toward judging the adequacy and quality of reasons makes that analogy inappropriate. Having convictions, according to this way of thinking, resembles a rheostat more than a switch. Assent is possible *up to a point*, or *insofar as* the reasons are adequate. This attitude yields judgments that are real, but nevertheless subject to change (in either direction) if better reasons come along. It assumes that new reasons with the potential to change the degree of our convictions are always possible. And so it is this attitude that enables us to *consider* the reasons of others when they are offered to us, that justifies our willingness to inquire further into issues on which we already have convictions, and that promotes the free and tolerant exchange of ideas and reasons between people who hold different convictions.

Fifth, and finally, this definition of critical judgment reorients us to the idea of knowing and what it means. We are accustomed to think of knowledge in absolutist terms (and I do not reject the possibility of such knowledge in some areas), as a *commodity*, something that can be packaged and traded and remain essentially stable in the interchange of minds. But what I have been describing seems to me to transform our understanding of knowledge from a commodity to an *activity*. That is, something that we *do*, rather than something we *possess*, and that we do together, in discourse, when we reason. The kinds of reasons we create and the degrees to which we accept them, in other words, are not conditioned solely by rules and private understandings but are subject to the convictions, reasons, experience, and values of those other members of the inquiring community in which we interact. So that what we are able to believe is a result of the thinking that we have done together. It is a performance, a drama, that we enact together.

The Poet's Version: The Metaphorical Process

Lest you think that the process I am describing is based on logic, because I have emphasized the term "reasons," let me turn from the definitions of a rhetorician to the testimony of a poet. Another essay that I would have all teachers read, were it in my power to command, is by Robert Frost (1966), called "Education by Poetry." In it, Frost says he wishes to "go further and further into making metaphor the whole of thinking" (p. 37), and he illustrates how ideas that we take for granted originate in metaphors, a process of implying that one thing is somehow like another. Thinking is relational in this way. This means, of course, that such thinking seems valid only to the extent that we recognize the limits of such relationships, so that, as Frost says,

> unless you are at home in the metaphor, unless you have had your proper poetical education in the metaphor, you are not safe anywhere. Because you are not at ease with figurative values: you don't know the metaphor in its strength and weakness. You don't know how far you may expect to ride it and when it may break down on you. (p. 39)

He illustrates this process of a metaphor breaking down as follows:

> Somebody said to me a little while ago, "It is easy enough for me to think of the universe as a machine, as a mechanism."
> I said, "You mean the universe is like a machine?"
> He said, "No, I think it is one . . ."
> I asked him, "Did you ever see a machine without a pedal for the foot, or a lever for the hand, or a button for the finger?"
> He said, "No—no."
> I said, "All right. Is the universe like that?"
> And he said, "No, I mean it is like a machine, only . . ."
> "It is different from a machine," I said. (p. 40)

So if thinking is like a metaphorical process, creating relationships between one thing and another, what one learns by studying metaphor, Frost says, is that one has to know when it breaks down, a matter of judging the adequacy of relationships. And, like Booth's idea of critical inquiry, Frost's is meant to be a process that opens up possibilities rather than shuts them down.

> We ask [students] in college to think [he says], . . . but we seldom tell them what thinking means; we seldom tell them it is just putting this and that together; it is just saying one thing in terms of another. To tell them that is to set their feet on the first rung of a ladder the top of which sticks through the sky. (Frost, 1966, p. 41)

I could draw from Frost's statements about thinking as metaphor the same consequences that I itemized in the case of Booth's definition. Let me merely add one more, however, that will return me to my theme of either/or thinking. Such a view of the process of creating ideas, and of recognizing their potential limits at the same time as we recognize their potential strengths, destroys the neat dichotomy between "creativity" and "rhetoric" that characterizes much talk about composition; that is, it suggests that all thought is creative thought—even that which is bound by the constraints of form—and at the same time acknowledges that conditions of judgment pertain to all arguments, whether overt or implicit in the form of expressive or metaphorical writing. Writers must create, and they must subject their creations to judgments based on conditions of communal assent. The choice between creative or expository writing, to bring the matter down to curricular earth, is a false choice, since each is necessarily present in the other. Each can, and should, learn from the other, but if they are seen as mutually exclusive alternatives this is not likely to happen.

Having reinvented Aristotle's Golden Mean, I suppose, I could go on to show that this process of struggling creatively within conditions of constraint, and its relation to knowledge as a performed activity that is contingent on communal acts of judgment, is present in even the earliest treatises of the ancient rhetoricians and is more or less present in all but the most practical and reductive theories of composition today. But I will forgo this analysis and turn instead to the original question, What should a teacher of writing know?

WHAT SHOULD A TEACHER OF WRITING KNOW?

I was addressing a group of high school teachers once and arguing, as I have been doing indirectly here, that students of writing must see themselves as part of an inquiring community; that they must write about ideas that are their own, in response to genuine issues subject to different positions; and that they must find reasons that acknowledge the possible reactions of those other members of the community of inquiring minds in which they participate as they compose. I cautioned that the students would find this process difficult because it requires that they think for themselves when they encounter issues that have no obvious answers. One of the teachers in the audience became very excited because what I was saying reminded her of her first experience in a college-level composition course:

> My professor had us read *Hamlet* and then assigned us to write on the question of whether Hamlet is an Aristotelian tragic hero. I panicked and went back to my room and cried because I couldn't think of anything to say. So I went back to the professor and told him that I couldn't write the paper. He asked me if I had read the passage from Aristotle's *Poetics* that he had also assigned, and I confessed that I hadn't. He told me to read it and then

see if I could answer the question. I read the *Poetics* and found the answer and got the paper done.

I thought this was a wonderful story, so I asked her what difference this experience had made to her, how it affected her teaching of English to high school students. And then, very sincerely and emphatically, she replied: "No student of mine ever leaves my class without knowing the definition of an Aristotelian tragic hero!"

Here in this anecdote is, I believe, the core of our problem. Here is a teacher, at least in this response, who values easy answers over hard questions and who seems so uncomfortable with the struggle with uncertain ideas that she would protect her students from it. Yes, we can teach students such definitions, just as we can give them formal models of essays to imitate, but we may do so at the cost of teaching students to take less responsibility for their own thinking. Students take more responsibility for their own thinking if they are asked to respond, with what they know and can find out, to issues that do not have obvious and absolute answers, for this process requires them to think about reasons and to judge them critically against the convictions and reasons of others. Only such a communal process can produce the sense of responsibility, for what one says and for the reasons that one offers, that will produce genuine inquiry in the writing and reading that students will do after the composition class is over. Lest I be accused of either/or thinking myself in this statement, however, let me add that this process, which is open-ended and unpredictable, may be *guided*, if not *governed*, by principles of form and rationality that may be taught and learned in the process of using them.

Teachers Should Engage in Active Inquiry

The issues that are being debated in composition pedagogy today are issues that have no obvious or absolute answers. This situation, rather than being a problem, constitutes an opportunity for teachers to engage in the kind of critical inquiry that they should be encouraging in their writing students. For teachers to encourage this kind of active inquiry, they must themselves be engaged in performing it. They learn to do it, after all, in exactly the same way that students do. Just as students do not learn this process by reading about it in a textbook but must become actively engaged in inquiry along with other members of a discourse community, teachers will not learn it by reading hortatory writing such as this or by being told what pedagogical theory they must apply. They must also function as a discourse community, actively engaging in debate about methodology and pedagogy with their peers and with scholars, asserting what they know from their experience and allowing those assertions to be tested according to the adequacy of the reasons they are able to create in their defense.

In the current environment, where many ideas about the teaching of writing are available, many of which are ideologically and methodologically incompatible and all of which have strenuous advocates demanding assent, teachers can easily think it necessary to take sides and to ally themselves with one or another of the prevailing ideologies. I would hope that such an uncritical demand of teachers could be exchanged for one in which they themselves become part of the debate, by being advocates and by being a critical audience, so that the issues are kept alive and the investment in knowing how to teach is vital and continuous. But the cost of this enterprise, as I have suggested, is to give up the idea that all the good reasons will be found on one side and that that side represents the truth about teaching writing. As Robert Floden and Christopher Clark (1988) have put it, in advocating increased opportunities for professional dialogue among teachers, "talking can remind teachers that uncertainty is an essential, important part of teaching, not merely a worry and a trouble" (p. 519).

Teachers Must Know How to Live with Ambiguity

Our knowledge of this art—of teaching as well as writing—is not of the sort that enables convictions of the light switch variety: either true or not true. What we know about teaching writing is subject to the tentative agreements that are forged in controversy and communal discussion, and it is therefore knowledge that we can only claim to possess *up to a point*. That any method of teaching writing, when it is held to be the true one, will break down, is, I believe, the result of the nature of the enterprise. That is because writing is not one thing, it is a messy combination of many processes—some fixed, some variable, some known, some unknowable—and any theory or method of teaching writing will be a metaphor—powerful but necessarily limited—of this process. Any way of teaching writing, then, is also a way of not teaching writing.

Our problem is not to decide which particular fact about writing is indispensable. Our knowledge of writing is not of the factual sort. What teachers must know is *how* to get along without such knowledge, how to live with ambiguity, how to muddle through in the face of informed but conflicting viewpoints. Responsible muddling through, if you will accept the possible contradiction in terms, is a matter of working out ways of teaching for oneself, in the thick of the debate about many such ways, knowing that one is responsible to apply the best reasons one can, and that those reasons will always be subject to being tested against the best reasons of others—just as students who learn to write responsibly must also do.

In order for teachers to do this, they must be part of an active community of inquirers, one in which disagreement is tolerated, ideas are listened to, and critical judgment is practiced. The necessary conditions for such a community to thrive are few: Teachers must have access to the debates; they must know the issues that various advocates are addressing. In addition to access to controversies, they must have a forum for discussing them, a collegial setting in which they enter the dialogue by becoming active advocates and a critical audience. As teachers are given the resources and are enfranchised to carry on this inquiry among themselves, and if different voices are seriously credited in the process, the outcome can only be that the reasons will get better and the knowledge of the community of teachers will become more adequate to their own situations. In the end, it is teachers who should be telling each other, not us telling them, what teachers need to know about writing.

REFERENCES

Berlin, J. (1987). *Rhetoric and reality: Writing instruction in American colleges, 1900-1985.* Carbondale: Southern Illinois University Press.

Booth, W. C. (1970). The uncritical American, or, nobody's from Missouri any more. In *Now don't try to reason with me: Essays and ironies for a credulous age* (pp. 63-75). Chicago: University of Chicago Press.

Cunningham, J. V. (1971). *The collected poems and epigrams of J. V. Cunningham.* Chicago: Swallow Press.

Floden, R. E., & Clark, C. M. (1988). Preparing teachers for uncertainty. *Teachers College Record, 89,* 505-524.

Frost, R. (1966). Education by poetry. In H. Cox & E. C. Lathem (Eds.), *Selected prose of Robert Frost* (pp. 33-46). New York: Holt, Rinehart and Winston.

Gage, J. T. (1984). The 2000 year-old straw man. *Rhetoric Review 3,*(3), 100-105.

Gage, J. T. (1986). Why write? In D. Bartholomae & A. Petrosky (Eds.), *The teaching of writing* (85th yearbook of the National Society for the Study of Education, pp. 8-29). Chicago: University of Chicago Press.

Knoblauch, C. H., & Brannon, L. (1984). *Rhetorical traditions and the teaching of writing.* Upper Montclair, NJ: Boynton/Cook.

North, S. M. (1987). *The making of meaning: Portrait of an emerging field.* Upper Montclair, NJ: Boynton/Cook.

Part II

. . . TO DIVERSE LEARNERS

Student Learning and Cognition

The previous several chapters of this book have examined the most common school subjects. The chapters we now turn to examine the other side of the equation: the students who are to learn these subjects. In the past, questions about students have been the province of educational psychologists, but recently sociologists and anthropologists have entered the fray as well, each with their own views about what aspects of students are most important for teachers to understand. The result comes close to a Tower of Babel, for the psychologists had never developed an agreed-upon stand, even before they were joined by others.

We begin by hearing from the psychologists. I include three chapters in this section, each of which represents a distinct position on the matter of relevant knowledge about students. The first, by Robert Floden, argues that student knowledge is held in the form of schemata, so that ensuring that students hold the right schema for a particular topic is a central goal of teaching that topic. Yet, because students are continually forming and reforming these schemata, and because they are likely to interpret a new idea by tying it to an already existing schema, teachers must know something about how schemata are formed, how they influence students' understanding of new material, and how teachers can learn, through their conversations with students, more about students' schemata. In the second chapter, Alonzo Anderson criticizes Floden for taking a static view of knowledge. He adopts Vygotskian theory to respond to Floden, and emphasizes the social and interactive side of learning more than its internal, cognitive side. For Anderson, the processes of teaching and learning exist only in response to one another; both the processes and the participants' understanding of them are more fluid than Floden envisions them. Finally, Siegfried Engelmann questions schema theory on the grounds that it displaces the issues from what is in the student's mind to how to put the appropriate stuff there. According to Engelmann, the question is one of designing instruction so that it clearly conveys the desired schemata. Engelmann doesn't believe that teachers have either the training or the time to do this adequately.

Both Engelmann and Floden illustrate their points using substantive topics—photosynthesis and fractions—that have come up before, when the subjects of science and mathematics were being considered. The contrast between their views and the views of the subject matter specialists offers us additional perspectives on the relationship among teaching, learning, and subject matter.

10

What Teachers Need to Know About Learning

ROBERT E. FLODEN

A year ago I was leading a class of about 20 students preparing to teach. Their program was organized so that I was working with a group that had indicated a special affinity for mathematics. Either they were mathematics majors planning to teach math in high school, or they were elementary education majors who saw mathematics as one of their favorite academic subjects. Somewhere in the discussion I asked them to think back to their own experiences in mathematics, either in secondary or elementary school. When I asked whether they had found mathematics difficult, most of them said "no," though perhaps they really had to do a lot of work. This was no surprise—these students were in this group because they liked mathematics. Then I asked them whether the *other* pupils in their elementary and secondary classes had found math hard. They didn't think so.

That *is* surprising. Many elementary and secondary school pupils do find mathematics difficult, puzzling, even mysterious. Though it might be possible that these students all had such outstanding teachers that their entire classes found mathematics easy, it is more likely that these students were wrong about how difficult other students found mathematics. That error in perception was of little moment while these students were themselves pupils. But when they become teachers, a similar misperception about their students can lead to the awful, but all-too-common, situation in which the teacher explains the concept accurately, then can't understand why many pupils don't get it.

Often, these teachers will attribute the lack of learning to insufficient student attention or motivation. If the problem persists, the teacher may learn that some pupils won't learn from their teaching, but attribute this to innate differences among pupils. "Some people just aren't good at math. It doesn't matter how many times you go over it. They just don't get it." If extreme advocates of subject matter knowledge for teachers observed the class, they might reach the same conclusion. The explanation was clear (to the observer), so any failure to learn must be the pupil's fault.

This scenario, repeated in teacher education programs across the country, contributes to the problems of schools where little learning takes place, even when the teachers are devoting time and energy to their instruction. One root of this problem is that these teachers have difficulty imagining how their instruction looks to their pupils, how the pupils perceive what they are studying and what they are supposed to do, or how they learn content that is in some ways new or foreign to them. If teacher education could turn this situation around, teachers might begin to realize that success in teaching depends on having the content make sense to the pupils. Having it make sense to oneself or to a colleague is important, but insufficient.

The bulk of this chapter will argue that teachers should understand how pupils use their existing knowledge to make sense of what is going on in their classroom. Teachers who understand this idea, even in a general way, will more likely be aware of ways in which pupils might misunderstand content that seems clear (even obvious) to the teacher, and will more likely make the effort required to determine whether pupils *understand* what they are studying.

In later parts of the chapter, I will show how teachers could generalize from this knowledge about *pupils* to get a better appreciation of how *teachers* themselves learn, and about how *scholars* in the disciplines develop new knowledge.

SCHEMA THEORY

When pupils engage in the tasks of schooling, they try to fit what they are experiencing into their current knowledge and understanding; that is, pupils make sense of instruction in ways that depend on what is already in their minds. Because pupils know different things than teachers do, pupils' interpretations of instruction may differ from what their teachers intend. Psychologists use the concept of "schema" to organize what they know about human perception, learning, and memory (see, e.g., Alba & Hasher, 1983; Anderson, 1977, 1984; Thorndike & Yekovich, 1980). Schemata (i.e., more than one schema) are organized, general descriptions or rules for how to act in particular situations. They can be thought of as prototypes of things or things to do, outlines for which the specifics can be filled in.

Associated with each schema are various particular characteristics or qualities that provide specific instances of the general schema. For example, a pupil may have a schema for "worksheet" that indicates that worksheets have writing on them, include tasks that the pupil must do, are printed on ditto paper, and so forth. The pupil's knowledge about specific worksheets is organized around this general description. Or the pupil may have a schema that governs what to do when the teacher leaves the room. This might include checking for the presence of other adults and doing different things depending on whether or not other adults are present.

Pupils' knowledge of the various school subjects, like mathematics or social studies, is structured around schemata. In mathematics, the pupil might have a schema for arithmetic operations that involve two numbers. The schema would indicate that an operation takes a pair of numbers and gives a third number as a result. As pupils become more sophisticated, the schema might become elaborated to include the idea that the order of the two numbers may or may not make a difference (e.g., $2 + 3 = 3 + 2$, but $2 - 3 \neq 3 - 2$) or that some pairs of numbers may not correspond to any third number (e.g., $7 \div 0$ is undefined). Schemata are important because of the role they play in comprehension and recall. When pupils encounter something new, they attempt to interpret it by means of their existing schemata. Once a likely match is found with a schema, the pupil will attempt to fit all aspects of the new information into the structure of this schema.

Pupils who begin to study division, for example, may try to fit it into their schema for a binary mathematical operation (Davis, 1984). This seems a promising framework for interpretation, since division involves two numbers and yields a third number as a result. It appears easy to make sense of this new concept to be learned. "It is just like the things we already studied." The particularly sophisticated pupil will wonder whether order makes a difference or not, and perhaps whether any number keeps things the same, in the way that zero functions for addition (any number plus zero is that same number) and 1 for multiplication (any number times 1 is that same number).

In the absence of some schema that provides the framework for incorporating new information, comprehension is difficult, if not impossible. Let me demonstrate this by asking you to consider the following passage:

> If the balloons popped the sound wouldn't be able to carry since everything would be too far away from the correct floor. A closed window would also prevent the sound from carrying, since most buildings tend to be well insulated. Since the whole operation depends on a steady flow of electricity, a break in the middle of the wire would also cause problems. Of course, the fellow could shout, but the human voice is not loud enough to carry that far. An additional problem is that a string could break on the instrument. Then there could be no accompaniment to the message. It is clear that the best situation would involve less distance. Then

there would be fewer potential problems. With face to face contact, the least number of things could go wrong. (Bransford & Johnson, 1972, p. 719)

Most people find this passage confusing. The individual sentences all make sense, but they seem to be sentences from a variety of different stories. Just when it seems that it is starting to make sense, the next sentence seems to go off in a new direction. This illustrates how instruction in a new area might seem to a child with no framework that can serve to organize and interpret what is going on.

Now look at Figure 10.1 showing a modern Romeo, using helium balloons to lift the speaker for his voice and guitar playing to the level of his Juliet's apartment window. Suddenly, words like "wire" and "instrument," which seemed to refer to some scientific apparatus, take on new meaning. The passage above, read with this illustration to give an overall framework, suddenly makes complete sense.

Although comprehension is difficult without a schema, it may still be possible for pupils to cope with some of the exercises teachers could pose for them. Consider the following passage (for which Judy Lanier gets credit):

It is very important that you learn about traxoline. Traxoline is a new form of zionter. It is montilled in Ceristanna. The Ceristannians gristerlate large amounts of fevon and then bracter it to quasel traxoline. Traxoline may well be one of our most lukized snezlaus in the future because of our zionter lescelidge.

No student could make sense of this passage, though the sentences all seem to be written in English.

Now consider the following worksheet questions:

Directions: Answer the following questions in complete sentences. Be sure to use your best handwriting.

1. What is traxoline?
2. Where is traxoline montilled?
3. How is traxoline quaselled?
4. Why is it important to know about traxoline?

Students could perform well on this worksheet without understanding the content. If they did perform well, the teacher could have no way of knowing whether the students had schemata that enabled them to fit the content into some framework of meaning, or merely a schema for completing exercises like these. While this example is nonsense, the same pattern—lack of understanding,

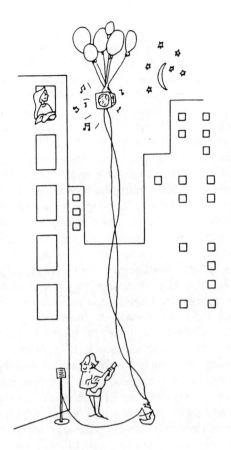

FIGURE 10.1   **A modern day Romeo scene.** Reprinted with permission from Bransford and Johnson (1972), p. 718.

"adequate" performance on assignments, lack of clear signals that something has gone wrong—might well occur if the initial paragraph had been about real concepts such as photosynthesis, metabolism, and oxygen-carbon dioxide cycles.

These examples illustrate the role that schemata play in initial comprehension. They provide the structure that is used to give sense to information and events. Let me now show how schemata have a more extended role. Consider the following story:

> Susan welcomed her friends. She was smiling as she opened the packages. After she blew out the candles, they all ate ice cream and cake. They played some games before they had to go home.

When children are asked what is going on in this story, they usually say that it is about a birthday party. Many of you probably have the same impression. If you look back at the story, however, you will notice that the story never says this. What the children have done is to fit the information that is there into their schema for birthday party, then used that schema to elaborate what they actually read so as to complete the structure they were using for interpretation. This illustrates how schemata provide not only a way of organizing new information, but also a way of elaborating, of adding to, that information according to the sense assigned to it. Further examples from reading comprehension are easy to construct. Anyone reading with reasonable speed does a lot of filling out of information at the levels of letter recognition, word recognition, and sentence comprehension. The same is true for listening to the teacher or to another pupil.

Interpretation and elaboration take place as information is recalled, not just as it is incorporated initially. Research going back to the 1930s (Anderson & Bower, 1973; Bartlett, 1932; Black, 1984; Schank & Abelson, 1977) has demonstrated that as people recall stories, they arrange and elaborate them so that the stories make more sense than when they were first heard. Details that do not seem to fit are forgotten. Other details are added to complete the overall structure. Discrepant events are revised or omitted. In school instruction, this means that pupils' schemata continue to play an active role in their understanding, even after initial instruction is completed. When trying to remember things about topics studied earlier, pupils recall the information not as it was seen then or even as they made sense of it then, but as it now makes sense in terms of current ways of organizing facts and concepts. So pupils who now have an active schema about the way geography affects life in a region, will seem to remember relationships among geography and life in Africa, even though that schema may not have been used to make sense when they were doing the social studies unit on Africa.

What difference would it make for teachers to know the importance of schemata for comprehension, elaboration, and recall? From what I have described so far, the most likely difference would be that teachers who appreciated the importance of schemata would recognize that pupils will be able to understand and remember things that go on in their class only if they have some framework that organizes or connects the bits and pieces of information. Teachers would probably ask themselves whether their pupils had an appropriate framework for interpreting the work at hand, and if not, would provide them with one.

This would be consistent with the admonition, incorporated into many teacher evaluation systems, that the teacher should provide an advance organizer. Indeed, the research basis (e.g., Ausubel, 1968; Mayer, 1979) for that requirement is of a piece with the research supporting my claim. But understanding the point of providing an advance organizer (rather than just learning the rule that the teacher should always provide one) allows the teacher to judge what sort of organizer would be helpful, or whether one is necessary at all. If pupils already have an appropriate schema available, the teacher need not spend time elaborating a framework.

So far, I have assumed that pupils either use an appropriate schema or have difficulty because they lack a schema. A frequently occurring third possibility is that the pupil uses an inaccurate or misleading schema. Pupils do not enter the classroom with empty heads, or even with open minds. They already have many schemata that have been elaborated as they tried to make sense inside and outside school. Some of these schemata incorporate patterns or relationships that distort or contradict the beliefs that the teacher hopes the pupils will learn. A common, though not trivial, example is that most young pupils probably believe the Earth is flat; teachers and geography books give a different message. Or pupils may think that what makes a poem good is whether it rhymes.

Common sense indicates that instruction ought to dispel these ideas. Schema theory adds the insight that, as long as these beliefs persist, pupils will use them to make sense of new information they encounter in class, with resulting distortions. Pupils tend to interpret instruction to fit what they already know, rather than trying to modify their existing knowledge or to create new schemata. (For examples in science teaching, see Driver, Guesne, & Tiberghien, 1985; for examples in mathematics teaching, see Davis, 1984.) Thus, for instance, pupils hearing about the U.S. presidential system will tend to assimilate the relationship between the president and Congress into the set of relationships for which they have schemata, for example, parent and child, teacher and pupil, or boss and worker. But none of these prototypes appropriately represents the U.S. system of checks and balances. Hence any successful assimilation into one of these schemata will require distortion.

The danger of distortion provides an important reason for teachers to attend to pupils' schemata. To avoid such distortion, teachers must either see that pupils make a good selection of a schema, or create situations that will bring pupils to alter their schemata. Let me describe an extreme case of such distortion, a case that usually makes a strong impression on the undergraduates I teach.

Benny was a fifth-grade mathematics student nominated by his teacher as someone who was doing well in mathematics (Erlwanger, 1973). The teacher's assessment was based on Benny's strong performance on the examinations provided with the individualized mathematics curriculum Benny had been using for several years. A researcher interviewing Benny was surprised when Benny claimed that 1.2 was the same as ½. When asked to explain this, Benny talked about his understanding of mathematics and of the testing process. Answers on the test, he said, would be counted correct only if they matched the answer key. Thus, if the key said ²⁄₄ but you wrote ½, you would get it wrong, even though you knew that the two answers were equivalent. In the same way, 1.2 might be counted wrong if the key said ½, though the two were equivalent. Mathematics, said Benny, was just a collection of unrelated rules, one rule for every test. Once you figured out the rule for a particular test, you could do those problems. But you had to start from scratch again for the next test.

Benny was unusual. His case suggests what is possible, but is more extreme than what teachers typically experience. But teachers regularly encounter the problem that pupils' inappropriate schemata—sometimes called subject matter misconceptions—create problems in their interpretation of instruction. Teachers with little understanding of schema theory may not realize that the problems exist.

For an everyday educational example, let me return to pupils' initial belief that the Earth is flat. Teachers need nothing more than common sense and a bit of experience to realize that pupils may often enter with this belief. An understandable teacher response would be to give the pupils a more accurate belief, backed with some rationale. So a fifth-grade teacher might have the pupils read about Columbus's voyage or might tell them about how the Earth looked to astronauts out in space. On a quiz, the pupils might then indicate that they now believed that the Earth was round.

But this apparent instructional success could be deceptive. In a study of 2 second-grade classes, Nussbaum and Novak (1976) interviewed pupils who had been through a sequence of instruction on the Earth's shape. Many children interviewed began by saying that the Earth was round like a ball, but as the interview continued it became clear that it would be more accurate to say that they believed the Earth was flat.

> It would be a mistake, however, to infer that their answers are meaningless to them. Each child hears about the Earth's spherical shape from different sources. Failing to understand its real meaning, the child attempts to make some sense of it for himself. . . . Some examples of this sort are the following.
>
> (a)   Daryl . . . was asked, "Why do people say that the Earth is round like a ball?" His answer was, "Because sometimes roads go in circles around trees in parks."
>
> (b)   Chris . . . answered the same question as follows: "Because the Earth is round on hills and mountains."
>
> (c)   Other children answered the question, "Which way do we have to look to see the Earth?" by saying, "We have to look up to the sky." Further probing revealed that they believed that there are two Earths. The one they live on is flat, and the other, which is round like a ball, is a kind of planet in the sky. (Nussbaum & Novak, 1976, p. 542)

In summary, it is important for teachers to understand that pupils actively impose sense, both on their current environment and on their own memories. Because pupils' schemata are not those of the teacher, they may make different sense of instruction than that intended by the teacher, and they may put things they have learned together in ways the teacher finds misleading or even mistaken. If teachers understand this principle, they will be more likely (a) not to assume that satisfied pupil faces mean that pupils have learned what the teacher hoped they would learn, (b) consequently to do more to probe the understanding of at least a sample of pupils (more about this below), (c) to attempt to take pupils' current knowledge into account in planning instruction, and (d) to assume that, because students may have different schemata, they will have to represent the subject matter in more than one way.

Learning and Schemata

Knowing that schemata affect understanding and recall is important. Even more important for teachers is understanding learning. Three things need to be understood: (a) how to help students draw on appropriate schemata; (b) how to lead students to exchange inappropriate schemata for better ones; and (c) how to assess students' understanding and then identify schemata they are using. In the first case, the teacher who understands how having access to an appropriate schema enhances proper understanding and recall, will construct lessons and tasks to increase the chances that pupils will make an appropriate selection from among their current schema. In the second case, teachers who appreciate the difficulty of altering schemata will use procedures for conceptual change teaching (term defined on p. 285), such as confronting pupils with ways in which their schemata do not adequately represent the world, helping pupils see that other schemata might overcome this problem, and providing support that may be needed as the shift is made. In the third case, teachers who recognize the role that schemata play in constructing responses to novel situations will use assessment methods that require pupils to demonstrate their understanding, rather than using tests that rely only on recall and recognition.

Linking Instruction to Existing Schemata

In many cases, pupils come into a teacher's class with knowledge of concepts and their relationships that are reasonably accurate. Whether gained through instruction in a previous school year, through interactions with parents and other adults, through personal experience, or through independent reading, the pupils begin instruction with some reasonably accurate general framework for understanding; that is, the schemata that they bring to the classroom are appropriate enough to serve as the basis for further learning of the subject. In this case, the teacher's job is to help the students activate those schemata so that they can be used to interpret and elaborate new information provided during instruction. Possession of an appropriate schema is of little use if the pupil does not use it when the occasion arises. The pupil might even use a different, less appropriate, schema, rather than the one that the teacher sees as the proper framework for understanding the lesson at hand.

The actions that the teacher should take to activate the proper schemata are consistent with common sense. They include beginning instruction with a framing statement or example, drawing explicit links back to prior instruction (where the schema was originally learned or used), and asking the students to state what they see as the "big ideas" in what they are studying. In each of these cases, the intent is the same—to help the students retrieve the appropriate schema from memory. In many cases this will be easy, because the current learning context is similar to ones in which the schema was previously used.

In other cases students will have difficulty recalling the proper schema or deciding which of several possible frameworks is the one they should use. That would likely be the case if the schema had been learned in a context quite different from that of current instruction. For example, a student might have schemata about habitat that had been learned in science. Those schemata might be appropriate for thinking about the physical environment of a country considered in social studies. But, without the teacher's help, the student might not bring the schemata to bear, because the context of studying science seems so different from that of studying social studies.

What is important for the teacher to know in such situations is that students will understand and remember better if they use the appropriate organizing principles they have already mastered to make sense of what they are learning. This requires subject matter knowledge of appropriate ways of organizing and interpreting content. These have been discussed in other chapters of this volume. Here we are concerned with what teachers need to know about *student learning* in order to help the students use those schemata. Teachers need not know that these organizing ideas are called "schemata," but they do need to know that students need guidance in figuring out which organizing principles are appropriate.

An example will illustrate how teachers should translate this knowledge into classroom action. Imagine a teacher about to begin teaching her sixth graders a unit on photosynthesis. (For a more detailed discussion of teaching photosynthesis for conceptual change, see Roth, 1985, and C. Anderson's chapter in this volume.) One of the organizing principles for the unit might be that plants, like animals, need food to provide energy for growth and the operation of the systems of the organism. Some especially important ideas are that food gets transformed to waste material, that it may need to be processed by the organism, that the organism may store food for later use, and so on.

Many pupils may enter the class with a reasonably accurate schema for food, learned in the context of studying about animals. But the pupils may not think to try to use this schema to interpret what they are learning about photosynthesis in *plants*. If they do use the schema, they will be looking for substances that the plant uses for energy, may store, will convert into waste material, and so on. But it will not be easy for pupils to see that this schema learned in the context of studying animals is appropriate for plants as well. In fact, pupils typically will instead use the everyday schema that food is anything that a living thing takes in. This everyday schema is problematic because it does not allow pupils to distinguish between the carbon dioxide the plant takes in (which is *not* food) from the starch stored in roots or seeds (which *is* food).

The teacher with no understanding of the importance of activating students' proper schemata might begin instruction by describing the different activities the pupils would be doing or how much they will enjoy the work with plants. This might give students an idea of what things they will be doing and might provide some motivation to participate in the instruction. But it will not make it any more likely that the pupils will recall the previous framework they had for thinking about food. The danger is that the pupils either will have little means of organizing what they are learning or that they will use some organizing principles that do not support what they should be learning about photosynthesis.

The teacher who understands the importance of using the right schema, on the other hand, will begin the instruction in some way that will remind pupils of the frameworks they already have and that will indicate which frameworks will be best to use in the instruction to follow. For example, the teacher might begin by reminding the pupils of their study of animals and of what they had learned about food for animals. This might be done by the teacher recalling what the pupils had done, or by asking pupils what they remembered about food for animals. Why do animals need food? How does it help them? Do they use all the food they eat right away? What happens to the food as it is used?

The teacher might continue by saying that the unit coming up will help them to understand how the ways plants get, store, and use food are similar to or different from those for animals. They will see that plants get their food in a different way, but that the ways they store and use it are similar. The teacher might also suggest that pupils think about how what they learned about food does or does not fit the case of plants.

I have made this a bit heavy-handed to get across the idea that there are many things teachers can do to help students recall schemata that they already have and to decide whether or not to try to use a particular schema to make sense of instruction. What an expert teacher would actually do might be more subtle, for there are motivational advantages to leaving things unsaid as a unit begins. What I have described may recall the use of "advance organizers" (Ausubel, 1968). Properly used, advance organizers will typically serve to activate appropriate schemata. It is important to note, however, that not all introductory statements about a lesson to follow will serve to activate the proper schemata, though someone observing the teacher might count them as advance organizers.

It is not enough, for example, simply to list the topics that will be covered during the lesson or unit. A list may help pupils to keep track of what topic they are supposed to be working on, but the list may not have the structure that would be best for understanding, recalling, or applying the content. For example, the teacher might begin the unit on photosynthesis by mentioning the different activities that will be part of the unit: growing plants in the dark and in the light, learning about the cycle by which plants make starch from water and air, and learning what makes plants green. This is informative, but will not call up the principles learned when studying animals.

How Schemata Change

Teachers have it relatively easy when pupils come with the right schemata. Teaching is much more difficult if pupils come with schemata that are inappropriate for interpreting the upcoming instruction. In this case, the teacher must somehow get pupils to change their schemata, a task much more difficult than merely reminding pupils to use the frameworks they have. The great human ability to make sense of new information creates the obstacles to changing schemata. Pupils are good at reconciling what they see or hear with what they initially believe, but the reconciliation often grossly distorts the new information.

Recall the previous example about learning the shape of the Earth. The example is striking because the pupils were able to sit through instruction designed to change their view about the shape, without making any fundamental shift in their initial beliefs. Each of the pieces of evidence intended to change their views was reinterpreted in a way that preserved those views. Moreover, the pupils were able to make these changes in ways that hid their persistent flat-earth views from the teacher, thus making it even more likely that they would continue to be able to hold them.

To change pupil's schemata, it is helpful if teachers know something about current thinking on the conditions under which such change is likely. It is usually not enough to describe the appropriate schemata or to do work designed to gradually build up the proper understanding; something more dramatic is required. The term "conceptual change teaching" is used to describe an approach designed to confront directly the problem of how to get pupils to revise their initial basic conceptions of a subject area. The inspiration for this method comes both from Piaget's description of the importance of cognitive conflict for conceptual reorganization (e.g., Piaget, 1971, uses the term "accommodation") and from the historical and philosophical literature on how basic conceptions ("paradigms") changed over the history of science (e.g., Kuhn, 1970).

According to Posner and his colleagues (Posner, Strike, Hewson, & Gertzog, 1982), getting pupils to make a fundamental change in their schemata requires (a) that they be dissatisfied with the current schema, (b) that they are able to understand an alternative schema, (c) that the alternative seems initially plausible, and (d) that it seems like it might be fruitful to try to apply the alternative to new situations. Creating dissatisfaction means that the teacher must bring to pupils' attention some of the ways in which their current schemata do not fit either with other things they already know or with things they are experiencing or learning about in class. Thus, for example, pupils' idea that poetry is something that rhymes might be called into question by having students look at nonrhymed verse in a poetry anthology. Though this experience alone will not be enough to get pupils to shift to a different schema for thinking about poetry, it might be enough to create some dissatisfaction with the current schema. Dissatisfaction is more likely if the teacher explicitly draws pupils' attention to the discrepancy between what they believed about poetry (i.e., that it rhymes) and the information that doesn't fit this belief (i.e., that this piece is in a book of poetry, but doesn't rhyme).

In trying to create this dissatisfaction, it is especially important that teachers know how to figure out what students currently believe and how to keep track of their attempts to reconcile current beliefs with new evidence. In the example of the shape of the Earth, the teacher may well have expected that learning about Columbus's voyage and the flights of the astronauts would have been enough to bring about dissatisfaction with a flat-earth theory. But the pupils' creative strategies for reinterpretation probably removed their discomfort. To counter this tendency, the teacher would have needed to figure out what beliefs the children adopted, so that the problems with those beliefs could be brought out. Dissatisfaction with initial schemata is insufficient, however. Unless the pupils have some reason for adopting the schema that the teacher thinks appropriate, they will either cling to their initial beliefs or come up with their own—possibly inappropriate—new schemata. To get pupils to switch to the appropriate organizing framework, the teacher must make this seem attractive.

At the most basic level, the teacher must help the students understand the schema. If they do not understand it, they can hardly be expected to adopt it. Once they understand it, pupils must have some reason for thinking that it will be worthwhile. From the pupil's perspective, being worthwhile means being something that helps to remove the dissatisfaction produced by the current schema, as well as being something that seems likely to be useful for further learning. Thus the teacher needs to know the importance not only of getting pupils to understand the appropriate schema, but also of helping them see the comparative advantages of this schema, both in resolving current difficulties and in learning about other topics. Again, the abilities to give this explanation and to show comparative advantage depend on knowledge of the subject being taught. Knowledge of schema theory makes teachers realize what sort of explanations are required, especially that simply presenting students with the schema to be learned is unlikely to be effective.

To return to the example of teaching photosynthesis to sixth graders, many pupils may think that water and soil are food for plants. The teacher who is knowledgeable about schema theory recognizes that this framework for thinking about plants will interfere with students' understanding of the need for photosynthesis to *make* food. If the plant can simply absorb food from the soil, it has to need to make it and hence no need for light. The teacher with no understanding of how schemata change might simply explain the process of photosynthesis to the students, perhaps using experiments to make the need for light vivid. The teacher with an understanding of how schemata change, however, will begin by finding out what pupils believe. If they believe that water and soil are food for plants, the teacher might do an experiment that demonstrates that plants grown in the dark soon die. The teacher would then try to create discomfort with the initial beliefs by pointing out to the pupils that the plants had plenty of water and soil, yet died.

This latter teacher would also introduce the theory of photosynthesis as an alternative way of thinking about how plants get their food—plants manufacture their food from water and carbon dioxide, using light as the source of energy. The teacher would show the comparative advantage of this theory by helping the pupils to recognize that this alternative explains why plants in the dark die. Furthermore, the teacher might show how this explains other things, like where the energy that all living things need gets into the food chain in the first place. Or the teacher might simply tell the pupils that thinking about food for plants in this way will be helpful in their later study of plants. Understanding how schemata change leads the teacher to go beyond simply giving a clear explanation, to giving the students good reasons for changing their beliefs.

Determining Pupils' Schemata

A theme that should be clear from the preceding sections is that teachers' knowledge about schema theory will lead them to address their instruction in part to the conceptions that pupils bring with them to instruction. Recognizing that schemata will affect the interpretation of instruction or that teachers must make pupils dissatisfied with misconceptions will be of little moment unless the teacher has some way of determining the substance of pupils' schemata. The great attraction of everyday beliefs about teaching and learning is that they do *not* require much initial assessment, except to avoid redundant instruction. They assume that if teachers explain a concept clearly, pupils will learn it; that if teachers have pupils practice a skill, the skill will be mastered. Schema theory is more challenging because it suggests that instruction may fail if the teacher has not taken account of how pupils might misinterpret it.

Learning about a pupil's understanding. The solution to this problem of initial assessment probably seems obvious: Give a test. Over the last half-century, schools and teachers have increasingly relied on pencil-and-paper "objective" tests as an efficient method of determining what schoolchildren know. The problem of how to decide what pupils know seems to be one of selecting from the rich array of available tests. Test developers have, however, been successful mostly at writing items that assess recall of facts and proficiency in simple skills. Testing pupils' understanding of central concepts has proven difficult, and the selection of tests reflects the relative difficulty of testing in these different domains (Fredericksen, 1984). Tests that would go beyond giving a simple "yes" or "no" answer to whether a student understands a concept are rare. Yet determining pupils' schemata requires knowing more than whether the pupils have already mastered an area; it requires knowing *how* pupils *currently think*.

It is no accident that most educational tests concentrate on a child's knowledge of facts and skills, rather than on the organization of knowledge. Asking the child to name the capital of New Mexico is a reasonably good way to find out whether that information can be recalled. No similarly straightforward question will get at the way the child sees the concept of "food" in a constellation of other knowledge and beliefs. Asking children to describe their own organization of knowledge will not work, because people know many things without being able to give an analytical description of their knowledge.

Kenneth Strike (1977) put it eloquently when he said that trying to determine the structure of children's minds from talking with them is like trying to describe the economy of Manhattan on the basis of the traffic going over the bridges and through the tunnels. It is clear, however, that one learns more from in-depth interviews with children about a topic than from looking at their performance on a multiple-choice test. Think again about the Earth example. Those pupils would respond on a multiple-choice test that the Earth is round, yet the in-depth interviews showed that "round" has various nonstandard interpretations.

Two examples should give some idea of the problems with having teachers rely on commonly available tests to assess pupil understanding. In a test of simple reading skills, many pupils in southern California were shown pictures of objects and asked what sound the name of the object started with. One item showed a picture of a castle. A researcher interviewing some of the children who gave the incorrect response, "D," found that the children thought the picture represented Disneyland.

The case of Benny (Erlwanger, 1973), discussed earlier, is a striking example of how a teacher might drastically misread a student's understanding if a readily available test is used as the means of assessment. Recall that, on the basis of his test performance, Benny had been recommended as someone who was doing *particularly well* in math. Yet Benny had ideas about mathematics—both conceptual understanding and computation—that were wildly off base. Such tests are an efficient way of getting some information about student performance, but they are typically of limited use for deciding what schemata pupils enter with. They are especially weak in providing information that goes beyond whether or not the pupils seem to have already learned a particular concept.

Researchers who carry out inquiries on the operation of pupil schemata have relied on clinical interviews to assess pupils. By posing several problems to a pupil, then asking for explanations, elaborations, and illustrations, the investigator is often able to get beyond whether or not the child is able to produce the set of key words associated with a topic of instruction. Is this interview technique a device teachers might also use? Unfortunately, clinical interviewing is prohibitively time-consuming for a teacher who must work with classes of 20, 25, or more. As a conservative estimate, it might take a teacher 15 minutes to interview a child on a single concept. Interviewing every child on a single mathematics concept might then take two weeks of the time regularly set aside for math instruction. Knowledge of schemata would be of little use if the teacher had no time for instruction.

Knowledge of common preconceptions. One way out of this dilemma is to recognize that, though individual pupils may have some idiosyncratic beliefs, particular schemata are widely shared, at least in broad outline. The belief that the Earth is flat, for example, is common among fourth graders. It is common enough, in fact, that the teacher would not go far wrong to plan instruction on the assumption that most children shared this belief. This simple example illustrates one way of solving the problem of needing to have some idea of pupils' conceptions, but not having time to probe for them. If teachers learn some of the common conceptions that students bring with them to school, the teachers can (tentatively) assume that many pupils in class share these conceptions. Experienced teachers sometimes learn such common conceptions over their years of experience with different classes.

Note that the common conceptions indicated here are not Piaget's stages of cognitive development, though those stages are similar in being an indication of ways in which many children of a certain age may think. Piaget's stages are probably among the most widely taught principles of educational psychology. But these stages are too general to be of much use in teaching elementary school children. If teachers are aware of the specific conceptions pupils bring to the study of a given topic, they have little need for additional knowledge of the Piagetian stage the child is likely to occupy.

Learning to probe student responses. Another strategy for learning about the schemata pupils are currently using is to probe the understanding of a few pupils, assuming that they represent the class as a whole. It resembles the previous approach in trying to orient instruction toward commonly shared conceptions, rather than taking into account the conceptions of every child or even the details that may differ among children who share a general conception. It goes beyond that approach, however, in trying to determine the conceptions held by *this particular* class, rather than assuming that this class is like every other class at the same grade level. It also has the advantage of not requiring the teacher to remember the common schemata for every topic taught and of not forcing the teacher to wait until research has documented commonly held schemata for a wide variety of topics. Current research has seldom gone beyond a few topics in science taught in the upper grades. Knowing some of the schemata that are likely to be held would still be an advantage, however, because it would make it easier for a teacher to draw inferences from brief interactions with a pupil.

One fairly easy way to probe for pupil understanding is to ask pupils occasionally to explain the answers they give. It is surprising and sometimes dismaying how often pupils will reveal their idiosyncratic interpretations when they try to give an explanation that goes beyond repeating the text. Asking, "Could you explain that to the rest of the class?" is likely to get beneath the surface of a student's response.

Instructional problems with probing student responses come not so much from difficulty in posing questions as from the difficulties that arise as a result of posing them. Asking students to explain something tends to slow the pace of interaction, especially when pupils are not familiar with such questions as a part of instruction. A reduced pace can create management problems if other pupils begin to let their attention wander as their classmate works to formulate an answer.

Probing for understanding also makes the course of instruction for the day less predictable for the teacher. The direction in which to move the class depends on what schemata pupils seem to have adopted. If a schema is inappropriate, the teacher must plan how to show its inadequacies, without the luxury of a few minutes of quiet thought to plan the next move. So being able to probe for pupil understanding requires knowing how to cope with the uncertainty that comes with confronting what pupils actually do understand.

SOME SIDE BENEFITS OF UNDERSTANDING SCHEMA THEORY

Teachers' primary benefit from understanding schema theory is that they will be better able to help pupils learn subject matter. But understanding how schemata affect thought and how schemata change also transfers to other areas of teachers' work, especially to their own knowledge about teaching and their understanding of the disciplines they teach. The transfer to these areas may not be of enough importance *in itself* to warrant teaching teachers about schema theory, but it is a valuable extra benefit.

Learning to Teach

Because schema theory applies to all human learning, it applies to teachers as they learn how to teach. In particular, teachers enter their teacher preparation with firmly entrenched schemata about teaching. Lortie (1975) has pointed out that teachers have spent 12 or more years in classrooms observing teachers and teaching. That extended apprenticeship of observation builds firm ideas about the purposes and methods of teaching. These schemata about teaching will then be used by teacher education students to interpret their teacher preparation experiences. Like the firmly held naive conceptions of children, teachers will be more likely to reshape their experiences to fit their preconceptions than to abandon their ideas.

Like naive conceptions in other subjects, however, many of teachers' initial conceptions do not correspond to what research studies have documented about classroom processes. As I mentioned at the beginning of this chapter, my own teacher education students enter their program believing that all students have been and will be more or less like they were. They will find the same content easy or difficult and will have the same learning habits and motivations. That egocentric view will be difficult to change without teacher education experiences that highlight conflict with evidence from the classroom and make an alternative view more attractive.

Teacher educators will benefit by recognizing such a role for schemata in learning to teach. But how will such knowledge help teachers? It helps by providing an impetus for them to reflect on how they are learning to teach. Teachers have an advantage over their pupils in having a degree of intellectual development and maturity that makes it easier to consider reflectively how they learn and consequently to plan ways to improve their learning. If teachers recognize that they probably have preconceptions about teaching that interfere with their ability to see other possible interpretations, they can begin to search for evidence that might suggest problems with those preconceptions or even begin to imagine how events might be interpreted differently from a different perspective. If teachers realize that changes in their schemata will be difficult, and achieved only by confronting contradictory evidence, they can make a mental effort to take potential discrepancies seriously, to entertain the possibility that other perspectives on teaching might have advantages. Thus, teachers who understand schema theory can profit by applying the theory to their own learning. This self-referential application can also make vivid the ways in which schemata operate in the lives of their pupils.

Scholars' Schemata

Schema theory is not merely a theory of learning; it is also a theory of knowledge. It addresses issues of the connections among an individual's beliefs and between beliefs and the experiences that provide support for those beliefs. As a theory of knowledge, it can shed light on the ways in which the content of school subjects is supported through the work of scholars in the parent disciplines. Other chapters in this volume have emphasized the importance of having teachers understand the bases of knowledge or the methods of inquiry in the subjects being taught. Knowledge of schema theory can help teachers appreciate that disciplinary knowledge does not grow simply by slowly excavating facts and piling them on the mountain of knowledge. Scholars, like everyone else, are guided by the schemata they use to make sense of new evidence. For scholars, like pupils, learning things by fitting them into the existing schemata is easier and more common than changing the schemata themselves.

Students entering teacher education, like most young adults, think of the content of school subjects as the conclusions that have been "established," rather than as an active field of inquiry that scholars play an active role in constructing. Unless teachers themselves come to appreciate that knowledge is a human construction, they are likely to teach their subjects as a rhetoric of conclusions. Understanding how schemata operate in the learning of their pupils can help teachers see how schemata might affect the scholarly activities of mathematicians, scientists, and literary critics.

Take, for example, the idea that schemata shape the interpretation of evidence. The everyday view of the work of scholars is one of gathering evidence and observing the facts in order to draw generalizations. But "facts," in the sense of things unambiguously given in the world, do not exist. Scholars must use their existing mental frameworks to make sense of experience. Stanley Fish (1980) provides a graphic example from literary criticism. One year he was teaching two classes, one in linguistics and literary criticism and one in seventeenth-century English religious poetry. At the end of the first class one day, he wrote on the board a list of noted figures in linguistics as part of an upcoming reading assignment.

Jacobs-Rosenbaum

Levin

Thorne

Hayes

Ohman (?)

The question mark indicated that Fish wasn't sure of the spelling of this name.

Before the next class came in, Fish drew a box around the list of names and added a page number at the top, thus hinting that this list might have been taken from a book. When the students entered, Fish told them that the list was a poem like those they had been studying and asked for an interpretation. Using the schemata they had for analyzing poetry, the students saw this list of names not as a list at all, but as a poem.

> The first student to speak pointed out that the poem was probably a hieroglyph, although he was not sure whether it was in the shape of a cross or an altar. This question was set aside as the other students, following his lead, began to concentrate on individual words, interrupting each other with suggestions that came so quickly that they seemed spontaneous. The first line of the poem (the very order of events assumed the already constituted status of the object) received the most attention: Jacobs was explicated as a reference to Jacob's ladder, traditionally allegorized as a figure for the Christian ascent to heaven. In this poem, however, or so my students told me, the means of ascent is not a ladder but a tree, a rose tree or rosenbaum . . . an obvious reference to the Virgin Mary. . . . Levin [was seen] as a double reference, first to the tribe of Levi . . . and second to the unleavened bread carried by the children of Israel on their exodus from Egypt. . . . The final word of the poem was given at least three complementary readings: it could be "omen," especially since so much of the poem is concerned with foreshadowing and prophecy; it could be Oh Man, since it is man's story as it intersects with the divine plan . . .; and it could, of course, be simple "amen."
>
> In addition to specifying significances for the words of the poem and relating those significances to one another, the students began to discern larger structural patterns. It was noted that of the six names in the poem three—Jacobs, Rosenbaum, and Levin—are Hebrew, two—Thorne and Hayes—are Christian, and one—Ohman—is ambiguous, the ambiguity being marked in the poem itself (as the phrase goes) by the question mark in parentheses. . . . The structure of the poem, my students concluded, is therefore a double one, establishing and undermining its basic pattern (Hebrew vs. Christian) at the same time. (Fish, 1980, pp. 324-325)

Thus (budding) scholars in a field, like pupils, will bring schemata to bear in trying to make sense out of new information placed before them. (For discussion of the parallels between pupil learning and the growth of scholarly knowledge, see Gibson, 1985; Petrie, 1981.) Like pupils they, too, play an active role in establishing new beliefs. The image that scholarship is the mere accumulation of new "facts," which were always there to be found, is no more accurate than the image that school learning is the mere absorption of the knowledge laid out by the teacher or in the textbook. A more accurate picture makes the process one in which the current state of knowledge or belief plays a central, dynamic role in the continuing process of change. Scholars, like students, need to understand and internalize the methods and standards of inquiry in a field in order to channel their interpretations in productive directions.

CONCLUSION

I have argued that teachers should understand how pupils use their existing knowledge to make sense of what is going on in their classroom. Teachers who understand this idea, even in a general way, will more likely be aware of ways in which pupils might misunderstand content that seems clear (even obvious) to the teacher, and will more likely make the effort required to see whether pupils *understand* what they are studying. Knowledge of how the current set of mental schemata influence what is learned, and knowledge of conditions under which schemata are likely to change, can also be applied to interpreting the ways people other than pupils learn. Two sorts of nonpupils professionally important to teachers are scholars in the subject field and the teachers themselves.

Schema theory may seem so commonsensical and obvious that it hardly seems worth spending time on the topic in teacher education. Many teacher education students would probably give verbal assent to these principles. But many teachers continue to give lectures that make proper sense only to pupils who already know as much as the lecturer, and to limit checks for understanding to a cursory, "Any questions?" Perhaps what teachers need is the disposition and skill required to act on their knowledge of schema theory. I suspect that many teachers, however, do not really believe that pupils could misinterpret what goes on in class, except through lack of effort or attention.

REFERENCES

Alba, J. W., & Hasher, L. (1983). Is memory schematic? *Psychological Bulletin, 93*, 203-231.

Anderson, R. C. (1977). The notion of schemata and the educational enterprise: General discussion of the conference. In R. C. Anderson, R. J. Spiro, & W. E. Montague (Eds.), *Schooling and the acquisition of knowledge* (pp. 415-431). Hillsdale, NJ: Erlbaum.

Anderson, J. R., & Bower, G. H. (1973). *Human associative memory*. Washington, DC: Winston.

Ausubel, D. P. (1968). *Educational psychology: A cognitive view*. New York: Holt, Rinehart and Winston.

Bartlett, F. C. (1932). *Remembering*. Cambridge: Cambridge University Press.

Black, J. B. (1984). Understanding and remembering stories. In J. R. Anderson & S. M. Kosslyn (Eds.), *Tutorials in learning and memory: Essays in honor of Gordon Bower* (pp. 235-255). San Francisco: W. H. Freeman.

Bransford, J. D., & Johnson, M. K. (1972). Contextual prerequisites for understanding: Some investigations of comprehension and recall. *Journal of Verbal Learning and Verbal Behavior, 61*, 717-726.

Davis, R. B. (1984). *Learning mathematics*. Norwood, NJ: Ablex.

Driver, R., Guesne, E., & Tiberghien, A. (1985). *Children's ideas in science.* Philadelphia: Open University Press.

Erlwanger, S. H. (1973). Benny's conception of rules and answers in mathematics. *Journal of Children's Mathematical Behavior, 1*(2), 7-26.

Fish, S. (1980). *Is there a text in this class?: The authority of interpretive communities.* Cambridge, MA: Harvard University Press.

Fredericksen, N. (1984). The real test bias: Influences of testing on teaching and learning. *American Psychologist, 39*, 193-202.

Gibson, B. S. (1985). The convergence of Kuhn and cognitive psychology. *New Ideas in Psychology, 2*, 211-221.

Kuhn, T. S. (1970). *The structure of scientific revolutions* (2nd ed.). Chicago: University of Chicago Press.

Lortie, D. C. (1975). *Schoolteacher: A sociological study.* Chicago: University of Chicago Press.

Mayer, R. E. (1979). Twenty years of research on advance organizers: Assimilation theory is still the best predictor of results. *Instructional Science, 8*, 133-167.

Nussbaum, J., & Novak, J. D. (1976). An assessment of children's concepts of the Earth utilizing structured interviews. *Science Education, 60*, 535-550.

Petrie, H. G. (1981). *The dilemma of enquiry and learning.* Chicago: University of Chicago Press.

Piaget, J. (1971). *Biology and knowledge: An essay on the relations between organic regulations and cognitive processes.* Chicago: University of Chicago Press.

Posner, G. J., Strike, K. A., Hewson, P. W., & Gertzog, W. A. (1982). Accommodation of a scientific conception: Toward a theory of conceptual change. *Science Education, 66*, 211-227.

Roth, K. J. (1985). *Conceptual-change learning and student processing of science texts for plants.* Unpublished doctoral dissertation, Michigan State University, East Lansing.

Schank, R. C., & Abelson, R. P. (1977). *Scripts, plans, goals, and understanding.* Hillsdale, NJ: Erlbaum.

Strike, K. A. (1977). Cognitive structure: Nature and measurement. In G. J. Posner & the Cognitive Structure Group (Eds.), *The assessment of cognitive structure* (Curriculum Series Report No. 5). Ithaca, NY: Cornell University, Department of Education.

Thorndike, P. W., & Yekovich, F. R. (1980). A critique of schema-based theories of human story memory. *Poetics, 9*, 23-49.

11

Teaching Children: What Teachers Should Know

ALONZO B. ANDERSON

While preparing my response to Robert Floden's chapter about schema theory, I had two recurring thoughts. The first was related to the question that organized this volume: "What do teachers need to know about student learning and prior knowledge of school subjects?" My thought was that no one really knows this in advance. Rather, teachers must *discover* what their students bring with them to the classroom. More important, teachers must have the particular skills and knowledge that will enable them to simultaneously discover and elaborate student knowledge.

My second thought was that, while Floden presents a theory about student learning and knowledge that is different from the theory that I find most useful in assisting students in their learning process, there is much that I agree with in his discussion. For example, I agree with his theoretical assertion that students store and retrieve their past experiences. I also agree that students and teachers typically enter the teaching/learning interaction with different conceptions of the educational task to be performed as well as their respective roles in that interaction. Finally, I agree that probing plays an important role in the process of teaching and learning.

LEARNER AS EXTERNALLY ORIENTED

However, we diverge on the critical question of the dynamics of the students' information processing during the teaching/learning interaction. Floden presents a conception of the learner as being internally oriented; selecting appropriate responses from a structure that resembles a filing system. In contrast, I conceptualize the learner as being externally oriented. I view the learner as one who is active and assertive in the situation. Instead of comparing new information with existing information, or organizing and reorganizing rules of appropriate responses, I see the learner constructing meaning. I see students making meaning in the process of constructing a theory of their world and their roles in it.

Indeed, these thoughts, questions, and perspectives all grow out of my preference for thinking about teaching and learning in relationship to a zone of proximal development (ZPD). The notion of a ZPD is from the work of L. S. Vygotsky, based on a sociohistorical theory of development (Vygotsky, 1962, 1978). In essence, a ZPD focuses on an individual's potential growth within a specific domain rather than on his or her prior experience. This conception of teaching and learning provides a chance for teachers to examine "change in progress" without being overwhelmed by differential past experiences among the learners.

The unit of concern in a zone of proximal development is neither the process of teaching nor the product of teaching. In this approach, teaching and learning are interdependent and are considered as a whole. The unit of analysis is the change over time in the way the task is achieved as the student and the teacher interact with dual motives: doing the task and promoting the child's achievement with respect to the task. Before commenting more fully on the zone of proximal development, I would like to comment on an old idea regarding the relationship between home and school and then to allow that idea to suggest what I think teachers should know about student knowledge and learning.

BRINGING HOME INTO SCHOOL

An old idea can be resurrected to represent my view of what teachers should know about students' knowledge and learning. The phrase "in locus parentis" sums up the view. According to the old idea, schools were expected to act "in the place of parents," albeit the old interpretation concerned mostly the education of the moral character of the child. My view is that the school should act in the place of the parents, providing continuity with the educational events that involve the world around the child—those furnished by parents, family members, and the child's community—and preparing the child to return to that world with a better theory of it and prepared to act within it.

This notion is not equivalent to "start where the child is," as some constructivist views would suggest that we do; rather, like John Dewey, it calls for starting where the out-of-school environment leaves off and for preparing to send the child back from school the better for being educated. The school is a special environment in our own and many other societies—time and place are set aside (Cole & Griffin, 1987). We make jokes about ivory towers and theorists. But in industrialized nations, schools are where educational activities designed to help a child carry out the process of constructing a useful theory of the world (and being effective in that world) are supposed to take place. As educators, I think it is important that we not lose sight of this fact. We bring students from home and community settings (where they spend the majority of their time) to the school so that we can help prepare them eventually to make their own home in the world community.

This perspective suggests that what teachers need to know about student learning and student knowledge about school subjects is the manner by which students learn and acquire this knowledge when they are not in school: What math concepts do they use and how do they use them? When and how do they practice literacy? Is there such a thing as "everyday chemistry"? And if there is, how does it relate to school chemistry? I would, therefore, like you to keep this notion of bringing the home into the classroom in mind while I focus the remainder of this chapter on what I consider to be the essential theme of Floden's comments—that *teaching effectiveness is based on teachers' knowledge of their students*.

In particular, I wish to comment in more detail upon Vygotsky's theory and what he says about the intrapsychological processes of students—what Floden might refer to as schemata. It is interesting to note that most schema theorists, and other theorists as well, hold that background knowledge has a very important impact on student knowledge and learning. Therefore, in the process of discussing ZPD theory, I will also comment, using a sociohistorical perspective, on just how "background knowledge," or culture, might influence what pupils learn and how they learn. In this connection an important question is, "How much do teachers need to know about the background knowledge students bring with them to class?" Finally, I will comment on the things teachers need to know in order to carry out effective teaching/learning interactions.

THEORETICAL BACKGROUND

Vygotsky's Zone of Proximal Development

The sociohistorical school of psychology based on Vygotsky's work offers a way of understanding the development of student knowledge and skills. Vygotsky viewed the development of all higher psychological processes (what we now call *cognition*) as being fundamentally social in nature. From this perspective, the structure of the developmental process is intimately linked to the structure of social interaction. Vygotsky proposed that, developmentally, any higher psychological function appears twice, on two planes. First it appears on the social plane, in the context of social interactions, and then it appears within the individual child, transformed into a cognitive process. Thus, culture or "background knowledge" plays a very important role in cognitive development, because it shapes the child's experiences and forms of social interactions.

Vygotsky was interested in how children come to be able to guide and direct their own actions when solving a problem or completing a task. He believed that the development of this control was not simply a function of age, maturation, or direct instruction, but rather that skills, strategies, and forms of thought are acquired as children interact with adults and peers in specific problem-solving situations. Vygotsky argued that children arrive at a point where they can solve problems (e.g., math, science, and literacy) independently because they have in the past solved those problems, or similar ones, with help and guidance from others. The social organization of experience, or culture, creates a medium for development.

The social context in which new skills are learned can be organized in the form of a zone of proximal development. The zone is a metaphor for the range between what a child can do independently and what a child can do with help from others. The zone is the link between the two planes, interpsychological and intrapsychological. It is generally accepted in education that assessing students' initial level of knowledge is important so that instruction can be aimed at a slightly more advanced level. If instruction is aimed at the students' current level, the work is too easy and the children do not learn. If instruction is aimed at a level that is too advanced, frustration ensues and the children do not learn.

Rather, instruction should be aimed at the intermediate "soft spot," where learning can be maximized. In this way, education *leads* development. The zone is adjusted "upward" as the learner develops so that the learner can move toward independent functioning by internalizing the means by which the teacher regulates the learner's behavior. The learner internalizes the *kind of help* that has been provided by others and uses the same means of guidance to direct him- or herself. Culturally elaborated skills, that is, those that are valued and arranged for by a culture, have social origins in two senses. One is that the actual *procedures*, such as how to divide one number by another, decode a string of alphabetic symbols, or mix a chemical compound, are learned through social interaction. In addition, the *motivation* for the use of these skills is social in origin (for a further discussion see McNamee, 1987).

In Vygotsky's view, educational activity takes place within a zone of proximal development created by the teacher and the learner. Vygotsky used the ZPD to assess not only the cognitive potential of individual children but also educational practices. Like clinical teaching, the ZPD allows for the assessment of intrapsychological functioning within the interpsychological realm of activity in which cognitive growth occurs (Wertsch, 1985). The ZPD as an educational context is ideal for the assessment of students' knowledge and their approach to learning because interpsychological functioning is an essential requirement for educational activity.

The Zone of Proximal Development in a Nonschool Setting

Based on this perspective, I can suggest that one of the things teachers need to know about student knowledge and learning is *how* students have been successful in learning activities that occurred outside of school. Earlier, I suggested that we may learn how to act in place of parents by developing a better understanding of the educational events that occur in nonschool settings involving family and community members. I have drawn one such example from a large corpus of data collected during my ethnographic study of literacy development among low-income families in San Diego, California. However, before I describe the event itself, I would like to describe the context of the event, including the setting, the educational materials (a chemistry set) involved, and the participant structure of the event.

Overview of the setting. The example is taken from observations of a black family participating in the literacy study mentioned earlier. We were studying the middle child in the house, Elliot (age 9), who lives with his mother and two brothers, David and Tyrone (ages 5 and 11). The example, however, involves an interaction between the mother's sister, who was babysitting, and the three boys. During the observation period when the event occurred, the three brothers were being taken care of by their Aunt Ruth (age 23). The aunt suggested that they bring out the chemistry set, which she had given them for Christmas.

Chemistry set. The chemistry set used in this interaction is a product of Skilcraft and is recommended for ages 9 and older. Its contents are (a) a manual containing 250 experiments and their procedures, (b) five bottles of chemicals, (c) three test tubes and a rack to hold them, (d) a test tube clamp, (e) litmus paper sheets, (f) a chromatography booklet, (g) a metric chart, and (h) a table of elements. The back of the chemistry set container displays a periodic table of elements and a metric conversion table.

Each experiment has a set of procedures specified in the manual. In general, each experiment has the following set of phases: (a) a preparation phase, (b) an assembly phase, and (c) a completion phase. The manual is typically consulted in the preparation phase to select an experiment and specify the materials necessary to carry it out. Most of the specified equipment and materials are contained in the set, but on occasion it is necessary to use some item that is common to most households (e.g., pliers, sugar, scissors).

Once the necessary equipment and materials for a particular experiment are set up in the preparation phase, the different goals in the task serve as a checklist. The assembly phase is typically characterized by the selection and measurement of ingredients and the mixing of the items, using the necessary tools. The completion phase is where the desired end state of the experiment is accomplished, given that all went well. This phase typically ends with cleaning up the work area.

Sequence of the events. The time is about 6:30 P.M. Ruth, Tyrone, and David are watching television (while David simultaneously practices his balance on his bicycle equipped with training wheels). Elliot is in another room (out of everyone's view). During the commercial between television shows, Ruth makes a suggestion to Tyrone.

6:32 P.M.

RUTH: Why don't we play with the chemistry set I got you guys for Christmas?

TYRONE: O.K., I'll go get it (*Leaves the room*).

Suddenly, a crash is heard from the kitchen.

RUTH: Elliot, what are you doing!

ELLIOT: Nothing.

Ruth gets up, seeming a bit agitated, and walks to the kitchen. Elliot has broken a bowl. Ruth gives him a scolding and instructs him to clean up the mess he's made. Ruth supervises while David looks on.

PREPARATION PHASE

In the meantime, Tyrone has brought out the chemistry set and puts it on the dining room table. By 6:35 P.M., Tyrone has taken out the manual and is looking through it briefly.

RUTH: So, which experiment should we do?

TYRONE: Let's do [a particular experiment].

ELLIOT: (*Leaving the kitchen and entering the dining room*) No, I want to do [a different] experiment.

DAVID: No.

RUTH: Come on, you guys, can't we agree on just one?

The discussion about which experiment to do goes on for a while. Ruth tries, but fails, to get the boys to reach a consensus. After several attempts, Ruth selects a different experiment altogether. The boys accept her selection without contest.

ASSEMBLY PHASE

RUTH: (*Consulting the manual*) First we have to find the cobalt chloride. Elliot, why don't you get that for us?

Following his aunt's instructions, Elliot begins looking through the various chemical containers, apparently reading the labels.

RUTH: *(Still consulting the manual)* We're going to have to have some sugar and sulphur too. I'll get the sugar. Tyrone, you get the sulphur.

With that instruction, she goes to the kitchen. Tyrone picks up the manual and begins to read it.

ELLIOT: *(Still looking through the chemical containers)* Ty, is this sulphur?

TYRONE: *(Looks up from the manual and reads the label)* Yeh.

Tyrone takes the container and places it on the table. Then he goes back to reading the manual.

RUTH: *(Returns from the kitchen with a small container of sugar)* Elliot, you still looking for the cobalt chloride?

ELLIOT: Yeh. I can't find it.

RUTH: C-O-B-A-L-T C-H-L-O-R-I-D-E. I know you can find it. David, come measure this sugar for me.

ELLIOT: *(Again searches the chemical containers, picks one out)* Ty, is this cobalt chloride?

TYRONE: *(Puts down the manual and takes the container from his brother)* Yeh.

RUTH: We need four measures of sugar. This is how you make one measure. *(She demonstrates for David.)*

David continues the operation, making four measures of sugar.

RUTH: What's that you have there, Tyrone?

TYRONE: I've got cobalt chloride! *(He had actually started the measuring operation earlier, when first Elliot found it.)*

RUTH: We need a half measure of sulphur.

Elliot begins to measure the sulphur as Ruth observes him and the other boys.

6:57 P.M.

RUTH: Half a measure, Elliot. That's close enough.

Upon completion of his operation, Elliot turns his attention to his brother David. He tackles David and they begin to wrestle.

Tyrone watches as Ruth begins to assemble the ingredients the boys have measured.

RUTH: Got some thread, Tyrone?

TYRONE: Yea, just a minute.

COMPLETION PHASE

Ruth completes the experiment and puts the final results on the table. She calls the younger boys back to inspect their creation. Finally, it is time to clean things up. At this point, the boys run off and Ruth is left alone to take care of things.

In summary, it was demonstrated that across the three phases of the task, Ruth mediated each of the boys' contributions to the experiment. She selected an experiment in Phase I, selected ingredients for each participant, and ended up cleaning up the mess. She constrained each boy's contribution differently, providing as much help as she felt was necessary.

Protocol Analysis

The transcript of the discourse was recorded with paper and pencil by the ethnographer. It is very difficult to make straightforward claims about cognitive processes with this kind of data, but some interesting questions are brought to bear in a simple analysis. Out of 22 verbalizations recorded in the excerpt presented, 12 were generated by Ruth. All but the last related to the task of organizing the activities of the children. If these notes were to tell us anything about what anyone was thinking, wouldn't they tell us about what Ruth thought each child was capable of doing in this task? When Ruth spelled out the words C-O-B-A-L-T C-H-L-O-R-I-D-E, does it not say something about the nature of the task that she thought Elliot was up against? We must assume that she meant it to help him. What would she have to assume about how Elliot goes about finding the chemical, in order for her to believe that it would help?

She certainly does not assume that Elliot is a good reader, because if he was, there would be no reason to spell the words out. The sound of the words alone should be enough for a good reader. Consider that it would be insulting for her to do this for Tyrone, who is older and more experienced. On the other hand, she does not assume that Elliot cannot read at all, because if this were the case, he could make no use of the letters. She would not have spelled the words out for David; it surely would not help him.

What theory of Elliot's abilities and the task facing him could Ruth have had in mind? And was it a reasonable one? There are 14 letters in the words she spelled. Could Elliot be expected to remember those 14 letters while he made the search? If they did not have some internal structure for him, he obviously could not. A successful search for a label with 14 unrelated digits on it is a very difficult task. So either Ruth did not recognize any limits on short-term memory (a strong possibility) or she assumed that Elliot did recognize some structure in the sounds of the letters (a stronger possibility). Personally, I think it is an elegant example of a child being steered through his zone of proximal development. Finding the chemical unassisted may have been beyond him, but Ruth provided (a) encouragement to try, and (b) a strategy (i.e., actually spelling it out). In fact, it is my guess that Elliot could not hold all those letters in his head, but he probably could hold the first several of them, and that should have made his search a lot easier.

DYNAMIC TEACHING

Background Knowledge

The crux of the problem with specifying what teachers need to know about students' knowledge and learning lies in the conception of teaching and learning as two separate and measurable activities, assumed to be relatively stable across content domain, time, and setting. Previously, we reviewed a theoretical approach and an educational event that occurs at home, both suggesting that education is a dynamic social process. Specifically, teaching and learning are interdependent elements in a single unit of activity. The implication of such a view for teaching is to turn away from efforts to *control* for the influence of culture (i.e., background knowledge) in practical and cognitive activities and to turn toward dynamic teaching procedures (which involve the liberal use of probing) that capitalize on the content of the activity. Such procedures should involve the frequent use of probing. In this way the students' abilities, and background knowledge, can be assessed while they are acquiring *new* concepts and skills.

The goal of dynamic teaching is not only to see what students can do today, but to get an idea of how they are doing what they are doing and to estimate the potential paths of learning and development. These issues are important not just in the teaching of so-called basic skills but in any area where the desirable skills need to be flexibly applied in new situations.

Examples of Use in Special Education

The dynamic teaching approach can be found in the field of special education, where assessment of the specific nature of individual differences in learning and thinking is more important than comparisons with a normally distributed population. In special educational settings, dynamic assessment techniques have been used to distinguish between a lack of achievement due to the absence of previous experience and a lack of achievement due to some inherent or organic deficiency. In the former case, it would be inappropriate to use standardized tests, which assume equal access to developmental and educational opportunities. Dynamic assessment of individual strengths and weaknesses is frequently found in clinical evaluations. Brown and French (1979) provide an interesting review of Soviet work on the development of dynamic assessment in special education.

In the United States, Johnson and Myklebust (1967) call the use of dynamic assessment *clinical teaching* because the child is assessed while being taught new skills or concepts. Clinical teaching engages the individual being evaluated in a joint activity with a more competent other, the clinician. The clinician introduces a new concept or skill into the joint activity and watches the ways in which the person under evaluation makes use of the new skill or information in subsequent interactions. Initially, the clinician provides a great deal of support in the form of guidance, modeling, and prompting. The clinician provides the child with opportunities to participate in whatever way he or she is capable, making careful observations with regard to the type and amount of help that most facilitates the child's learning process.

A highly skilled clinician can also modify the tests or tasks used in more standard assessment. When a child fails to perform at age or grade level, the clinician can vary the parameters of the task systematically, changing the output requirements, the modality, and the materials used. For example, a child who reads slowly and with many errors may be read to and questioned about the story as a way of assessing comprehension skills. If the child were questioned about a story he or she read out loud, no useful assessment of comprehension or thinking skills could be made. Using these techniques, a skilled clinician can determine the nature of a child's specific learning disability as situated within the full system of the "child reading." Without such techniques, the specific learning disability may become as much a barrier for the assessment process as it is for the child.

Based on similar principles, the Learning Potential Assessment Device (LPAD) was designed by Feuerstein (1979) to aid in the development of specific psycho-educational programs for children in Israel from diverse cultural backgrounds. The device uses I.Q. test-like items in a test-train-test pattern to assess the child's degree of "modifiability." The underlying assumption is that some people, at some time and in some domains of their development, can, with guidance and training, perform beyond their independent level of functioning. For others, the level at which they can function alone is a valid measure of their potential of performance (see also Brown & Ferrara, 1985; Brown & French, 1979).

The Zone of Proximal Development in Teaching

What teachers need to know about their students' knowledge and learning requires either extensive observation and longitudinal analysis of student performance on any given lesson or a dynamic approach to teaching wherein the stimulation and probing of student responses is used extensively. The paths to facilitating cognitive change in others are numerous and varied, and it would be impossible to enumerate the skills required to teach effectively. However, based on Vygotskian theories and studies of teaching, we can extract some essential practices involved in effective teaching, especially regarding the effective teaching of ethnically and linguistically diverse students. Two key points stand out:

1. A teacher must have readily accessible a wide variety of teaching strategies and practices that she or he can draw upon according to the needs of students;

2. She or he must be able to apply these strategies effectively in order to create a zone of proximal development in which learning can take place.

The first point is well stated by Jordan (1980):

> What is being advocated here is that the selection of teaching practices be informed by knowledge of the children's cultural background. The process involved can be seen as selecting from a "library" of potentially available teaching strategies and practices, those which are best suited to a particular population of children. It is neither necessary nor desirable to "reinvent the wheel," or to ask teachers to do things which are so unfamiliar to them as to make it difficult for them to operate comfortably and effectively in their own classrooms. Rather, what is advocated is the consideration of the full range of good educational practice, and a selection from that range based partly on the fit of the selected practices with the cultural background of the children to be served. (p. 7)

Although Vygotsky's approach stresses the importance of culture in the intellectual development of students, teachers need not learn a specific curriculum or a teaching style for each cultural group they may encounter in the classroom. The task of creating such a curriculum would be as impossible as creating as many culture-specific assessment devices as there are culturally homogeneous groups in the United States. Rather, teacher training must inform potential teachers about the patterns of culture, including their own, that influence the teaching/learning process. Additionally, teacher training must prepare teachers to be open to experiencing and appreciating the history and cultures of their particular students, and to help students value their own histories.

The Role of the Teacher in Constructing a Zone of Proximal Development

The importance of the social organization of instruction lies in the fact that the establishment of a shared understanding allows for the interpsychological functioning integral to a zone of proximal development. This aspect of the Vygotskian theory of development has been elaborated by Rommetveit (1979) and Wertsch (1985). Wertsch states

Because an adult and a child operating in a zone of proximal development often bring divergent situation definitions to a task setting, they may be confronted with severe problems of establishing and maintaining intersubjectivity. The challenge to the adult is to find a way to communicate with the child such that the latter can participate at least in a minimal way in interpsychological functioning and can eventually come to define the task setting in a new, culturally appropriate way. (p. 161)

The establishment of shared situation definition is necessary for the child to understand the value of the "expert" or adult version of the skills that are a part of the instructional goals. Intersubjectivity is achieved through language and joint activity, which allow each participant to transcend what Rommetveit (1979) described as the participants' different "private worlds" to enter into a temporarily shared social world.

The study of this movement from interpsychological to intrapsychological functioning requires the development of a new methodology. In his article on alternative paradigms in evaluation research, Patton (1975) makes the case for the development of a methodology that is closely related to the phenomenon under investigation. "Different kinds of problems require different types of research methodology" (p. 13). In the study of any learning activity, the unit of analysis has to be the act or system of acts that constitutes the teaching/learning process (Leont'ev, 1973; Moll & Diaz, 1985; Talyzina, 1978). Any suggestions offered to teachers regarding what they need to know in order to be most effective cannot be simplified to focus on either the process of teaching alone or the product of the teaching activity. The suggestions must include both. This point is emphasized by Au and Kawakami (1984), who analyzed the dialogue engaged in by a highly experienced teacher in conducting a reading lesson and concluded that

Process-product distinctions become blurred. It is difficult, if not impossible, to distinguish teaching behaviors directed at developing comprehension skills from those aimed at assessing understanding of the text at hand or establishing propositions. . . . Instruction aimed at the overall development of reading comprehension skills must take place using some text as its raw material. Even though the text may be seen merely as a vehicle for comprehension instruction, and long-term retention of text information is not a goal, ideas in the text are still the topics of discussion. Thus, propositions established in lessons should not only be viewed as ends in themselves, but as indicators of successfully negotiated, and often academically productive, interchanges. (p. 220)

Many researchers have applied Vygotskian theories of learning and development to research on the educational process. A number of these studies have analyzed individual lessons to examine the interaction of the teacher and the students within a zone of proximal development. In many of these studies, the protocol of social interaction in the service of the teaching/learning process is used as data; the discussion is segmented into teacher-student interchanges as units of analysis.

Annmarie Palincsar, together with Ann Brown and others, developed a reciprocal questioning procedure in reading comprehension. In her paper on the role of dialogue in providing scaffolded instruction, Palincsar (1986) specifies many aspects of the role of the teacher in creating and maintaining a zone of proximal development for instructional purposes. Au and Kawakami (1984) also identify effective teaching behaviors related to interactive teaching. Their study involved a reciprocal questioning technique for teaching reading comprehension skills. The KEEP (Kamehameha Early Education Program) reading procedure has been demonstrated to be extremely effective in raising the reading comprehension achievement test scores of Native Hawaiian children (Calfee et al., 1981). Drawing from Palincsar, Au and Kawakami, and the work of members of the Laboratory of Comparative Human Cognition (1982) in applying Vygotsky's principles to teaching, the following knowledge and abilities are suggested as being essential for teachers in order to effectively create and maintain a productive zone of proximal development.

- Ability to create learning tasks that (a) combine several instructional objectives, and (b) place particular emphasis on the use of skills and concepts that are new to the students or just emerging in the repertoire of the students

- Ability to assess dynamically the initial "ability" of individuals and groups so that instruction may be aimed above (but not too far above) that level

- Ability to elicit and sustain student interest by tying activities to meaningful goals, in order to foster intrinsic rather than extrinsic motivation

- Ability to use modeling, questioning, and direct explanation in order to make the purpose of the task, as well as the execution of the task itself, clear to pupils

- Disposition to be tolerant of responses that are divergent from the teacher's point of view (though the teacher may need to reorganize the activity, or use prompts and questions to redirect the students' thinking when there is indication of little contact being made with students)

- Disposition to give specific praise, acknowledgment, and encouragement, and to restate correct responses in order to highlight the relevant information

- Ability and disposition to create and to bring students into classroom dialogue

- Ability to create and carry out tasks in which students become actively involved with teachers and other students

- Ability to adjust support based on evaluation of pupil performance

- Disposition to withdraw support so that students may gradually increase their independent control over the execution of the task.

Considering this entire list of essential teacher knowledge and abilities, the "ability and disposition to create and to bring students into classroom dialogue" is perhaps the most important. It is fundamental to what teachers need to know. Without it, the student is relegated to a passive role in the teaching/learning process. More important, when teachers do not create classroom dialogue, students are denied the opportunity of becoming *actively* involved in lessons in a manner that will allow them to use their previous experiences, interpretations, and knowledge.

In the final analysis, I would agree that although many factors influence the outcome of classroom lessons, the teacher plays a most powerful and influential role in constructing the educational context. In carrying out this role, teachers need to know and be sensitive to the patterns of social and intellectual activity with which students have had previous experience with in their homes and communities. It is only on this basis that teachers can successfully learn about the students' other relevant experiences, engage the students in meaningful dialogue, and, finally, create with the students a shared understanding of classroom lessons and their outcomes.

REFERENCES

Au, K. H. P., & Kawakami, A. J. (1984). Vygotskian perspectives on discussion processes in small-group reading-lessons. In P. Peterson, L. C. Wilkinson, & M. Hallinan (Eds.), *The social context of instruction: Group organization and group processes* (pp. 209-225). Orlando: Academic Press.

Brown, A. L., & Ferrara, R. A. (1985). Diagnosing zones of proximal development. In J. V. Wertsch (Ed.), *Culture, communication and cognition: Vygotskian perspectives* (pp. 273-305). New York: Cambridge University Press.

Brown, A. L., & French, L. A. (1979). The zone of potential development: Implications for intelligence testing in the year 2000. *Intelligence, 3,* 255-273.

Calfee, R. C., Cazden, C. B., Duran, R. P., Griffin, M. P., Martus, M., & Willis, H. D. (1981). *Designing reading instruction for cultural minorities: The case of the Kamehameha Early Education Program.* New York: Ford Foundation, Division of Education and Research.

Cole, M., & Griffin, P. (1987). *Contextual factors in education: Improving science and mathematics education for minorities and women.* Madison: University of Wisconsin, Wisconsin Center for Education Research.

Feuerstein, R. (1979). *The dynamic assessment of retarded performers: The learning potential assessment device, theory, instruments, and techniques.* Baltimore: University Park Press.

Johnson, D. J., & Myklebust, H. R. (1967). *Learning disabilities.* Orlando: Grune and Stratton.

Jordan, C. (1980). *The adaptation of educational practices to cultural differences: Configurations from the Hawaiian case.* Paper presented at the Conference on Culture and Education, Brigham Young University, Laie, HI.

Laboratory of Comparative Human Cognition. (1982). Culture and intelligence. In W. Sternberg (Ed.), *Handbook of human intelligence* (pp. 642-719). New York: Cambridge University Press.

Leont'ev, A. (1973). Some problems in learning Russian as a foreign language [Special issue]. *Soviet Psychology, 11*(4).

McNamee, G. D. (1987). The social origins of narrative skills. In M. Hickmann (Ed.), *Social and functional approaches to language and thought* (pp. 287-304). Orlando: Academic Press.

Moll, L. C., & Diaz, S. (1985). Ethnographic pedagogy: Promoting effective bilingual instruction. In E. Garcia & R. Padilla (Eds.), *Advances in bilingual education research* (pp. 127-149). Tucson: University of Arizona Press.

Palincsar, A. S. (1986). The role of dialogue in scaffolded instruction. *Educational Psychologist, 21,* 73-98.

Patton, M. Q. (1975). *Alternative evaluation research paradigms.* Grand Forks, ND: University of North Dakota Press, North Dakota Study Group on Evaluation.

Rommetveit, R. (1979). On the architecture of intersubjectivity. In R. Rommetveit & R. M. Blaker (Eds.), *Studies of language, thought and verbal communication* (pp.   ). London: Academic Press.

Talyzina, N. F. (1978). One of the paths of development of Soviet learning theory. *Soviet Education, 20*(11), 28-48.

Vygotsky, L. S. (1962). *Thought and language.* Cambridge, MA: MIT Press.

Vygotsky, L. S. (1978). *Mind and society.* Cambridge, MA: Harvard University Press.

Wertsch, J. V. (1985). *Vygotsky and the social formation of mind.* Cambridge, MA: Harvard University Press.

12

Teachers, Schemata, and Instruction

SIEGFRIED ENGELMANN

The question this chapter addresses is: What should teachers know about learning? I'll try to provide part of the answer in the first part of the chapter. The second part expands on some details and focuses on why I would not follow any of Floden's recommendations in Chapter 10.

Teachers should have a special kind of knowledge about teaching. That knowledge derives from the ability to execute the details of effective instruction. The teacher should know how to present tasks to students and should demonstrate appropriate pacing, appropriate inflections and stress, appropriate responses to students who perform well, and appropriate responses to students who make mistakes. The teacher should be able to correct mistakes in a way that is technically sound but that doesn't "punish" students. The teacher should be able to demonstrate a range of presentational skills that permit "whole-class" responses and skills in terms of managing students in a way that promotes hard work and positive work attitudes. The teacher, in summary, should be a technician.

In addition to these skills, the teacher should know how to diagnose problems quickly and provide timely remedies. These skills are quite different from the probing and remedies that Floden describes. Rather, the teacher should be able to get information from students at a high rate and know how to identify problems (based on student responses) and how to fix these problems quickly, not by stepping outside the instructional program, but by repeating parts of the program that present difficulties to students. Related to this diagnostic issue, the teacher should know how to achieve a high criterion of performance, moving fast on activities that students have already mastered and making sure that all new material is mastered. The teacher should be able to use students' performance to determine whether they are appropriately placed in an instructional sequence. The basic rule is that unless students are perfectly firm on at least 70% of the tasks or activities the teacher presents, they are in over their heads.

If students perform at much above 90% correct on "new material," they already know the material and should be placed in a higher level of the program.

KNOWLEDGE TEACHERS NEED

Teachers should have knowledge about the relationship between teaching and student performance. On a global level, they should know that all students in a regular classroom can learn the various skills that are supposed to be taught in arithmetic, science, language, reading, and other subjects. They should understand that the remedial students are a product of what had been unintentionally taught, that current poor performance in math and science represents a gigantic teaching failure—not a student failure—and that teaching is a precise, logical game. They should know that students' responses are mainly a function of teachers' behavior and that changes in teachers' behavior cause changes in the students' performance.

Teachers should understand why efficiency is important. The idea is to beat the clock to teach more in a specified amount of time so that the students learn relatively more during that time. Over a school year, the minutes saved each period, each day, create a substantial difference in how much can be learned by the end of the year. Teachers should also know what is not efficient—lectures during which students simply grow older, time-consuming demonstrations, poorly focused activities that are not targeted on identifiable instructional objectives, and tasks or activities that do not involve *all* the students and do not yield responses at a high rate. (When the responses are at a low rate, the potential for diagnosis is at a low rate, and it becomes difficult to determine who is learning what and who is completely lost.) Teachers should be able to discriminate between a "lumpy" teaching sequence and a good one. They should be able to identify the activities that involve untaught skills, and the tasks that are far too ambitious in what they attempt to teach.

PROBLEMS IN ESTABLISHING KNOWLEDGE

There are several problems with establishing this knowledge in teachers. The first is that it is impossible to induce this knowledge as knowledge (and not mere verbal tabloids) without a lot of direct experience. Furthermore, the experience must be with programs that have the *potential* to teach all students. Because most teachers are trained in traditional teacher-training institutions, they will probably never even observe *good* teaching. They may be fortunate enough to learn some good management skills, but the technology of good teaching goes far beyond these skills, and this technology simply cannot be taught if the instructional programs are poorly designed. The reason is that the instructional sequence is responsible for inducing the appropriate "schemata."

In a spiral sequence, like that of the typical math basal, students work on a particular topic, like fractions, for a while. Then they launch into a sequence of other topics before returning to fractions. The return may be 60 school days later. Furthermore, the activities are very poorly designed. The number of "taught" examples is inadequate, and the applications prompt students to figure out their own strategies for working the "practice exercises" that follow. If teachers try to teach this program well, the best they will create are students like Benny who have been "conditioned" not to attend to instructions, who make up strategies and interpretations that work for the various problem sets presented by the text but that are dead ends. These students also have incredible deficits in their knowledge (such as not knowing that $\frac{1}{2}$ and 1.2 do not express the same value). Benny is *not* an unusual case.

A teacher teaching this kind of program will not learn what good teaching is. If the teacher made sure that students were firm on every unit presented in the program, he or she would not cover very many units, and in the end, students would reveal problems. Similarly, the teacher teaching "fact versus opinion," as it is presented in reading basals, and teaching it well, would do students a great disservice because they would come away from the teaching with the misconception that there is some dichotomy between "fact" and "opinion." They would not understand that somebody could say, "I think the capital of California is Sacramento," and that the opinion could express a "truth." Similarly, every topic in science, math, and reading presented by the textbooks most widely used will induce misinformation or "distorted schemata" at a high rate.

Consider the treatment of fractions in a typical basal. The first three fractions presented are $\frac{1}{2}$, $\frac{1}{3}$, and $\frac{1}{4}$. These are studied ad nauseam, typically in the third grade. The strategy encouraged in worksheet problems is to count the pieces in the pie or the block. If there are 2 pieces, the fraction is $\frac{1}{2}$. Students usually perform well until they encounter a fraction that does not have 1 as the numerator.

Imagine the incredibly inappropriate schemata that are induced by this introduction. Students assume that all fractions are less than 1, that they represent a piece of something, and that the top number of the fraction is simply a showpiece that has no significance. Of course these students will have trouble later. But the cause of the problems they will experience is the instructional sequence. Before a teacher could get good information about what excellent teaching is, the teacher (or somebody) would first have to rewrite the entire instructional sequence, as well as the instructional sequences for the other topics presented in the program.

instructional sequence (Point 2), then it follows that the only legitimate solution would be an overhaul of the sequence.

Schemata

The first problem has to do with schemata and what they are. *Food*, according to Floden, is a schema within the constellation of other facts or relationships. We could therefore argue that any higher-order class name functions in the same way—vehicles, buildings, animals, plants, and so on. The problem is, where do higher-order nouns end and lower-order ones begin? Since these designations are a function of the particular context in which they are applied, virtually all nouns become potential schemata. *Ball* is a schema because in different situations different balls would be "appropriate." Possibly baseball is a schema, too.

In addition to these nouns are rules that may run counter to experience, like "the Earth is round." Is it possible that these are actually *superordinate* schemata of some sort? After all, we must distinguish between "Earth" in the context of the world, not something used for planting things and building dikes. And we certainly don't mean *round* like a disc. In addition to these contextually embedded words is the meaning of the rule itself. Whether or not we consider rules as superordinate schemata, they would be in the class of schemata. But what wouldn't be in that class? We would have to search very far if the apparent criterion for calling something a schema is that it can be manifested in a variety of contexts. Something as elementary as the color purple resides in the sky, in perfume bottles, and in images created by closing ones eyes and pressing against the lids (images that have no counterpart in the outside world). So whatever is not a schema must be rote labels of the highest order.

Possibly, it is not fair to try to categorize concepts and relationships as "schemata." Possibly, the valid test is simply whether students use past knowledge to interpret present learning experiences. If so, then schema theory is perfectly trivial with respect to instruction. We don't need a theory to tell us that we would have great difficulty teaching a student to add fractions with unlike denominators if the student had no arithmetic skills (couldn't count, couldn't identify numerals, and so forth). Furthermore, we would quickly discover why "prior knowledge" is prior in instructional sequences. If we attempted to teach our perfectly naive student how to add fractions with unlike denominators, we would need to teach the various skills that should have been introduced prior to the introduction of this operation (basic equivalence, counting, and so forth) before we could *communicate* efficiently with the student. If we started with the teaching of fractions with unlike denominators, our communication would come across to the student as one of the gibberish passages that Floden presents.

The central thrust of how Floden treats schemata seems to be to provide a framing that will mobilize the appropriate knowledge set and guarantee success.

It won't work. Here's why: In instruction, what counts as a schema depends on what has been taught and what is to be learned. Nobody has a completely articulated schema for "fractions." Some mathematicians might come close, but the properties of fractions are potentially too pandemic to assume a "limit" or a lid on knowledge. Similarly, students in the fifth grade don't have complete schemata for fractions. Either they have a schema that is appropriate for the applications that are to be presented next or they don't. If they don't, their "current knowledge" is either incomplete but not distorted, or distorted in some way with respect to what is to be taught next.

The three possibilities are that students have perfect background knowledge, incomplete background knowledge, or distorted background knowledge. Here's a diagram of the possibilities:

Perfect background knowledge	Incomplete background knowledge	Distorted background knowledge

Note that "perfect background" means simply that students have the prerequisite knowledge for what is to come next and that what will be presented will necessarily *modify the schema*. (If this weren't the case, we wouldn't have to teach anything because students would already know it.)

Since students with perfect backgrounds present the easiest case, let's start with them. At some point in the teaching, these "perfect" schemata will become either incomplete or possibly even distorted, even if the teaching sequence is well designed. But what does schema theory tell us to do about restoring undistorted schemata that incorporate new knowledge? I'm not sure. The summary of things that Floden suggests should happen is reasonable. But the concrete descriptions of what the teacher does are unreasonable. Certainly the new teaching should be linked to students' knowledge, and certainly the teaching should mobilize the appropriate framework (such as adding and subtracting fractions). Since the original schemata are now inappropriate, students should exchange inappropriate schemata for better ones. But they *don't have access to an alternative schema* because it hasn't been taught yet.

When we start teaching the new material, we are creating some form of conceptual change. So possibly we are supposed to engage in conceptual change teaching, with circuitous demonstrations to create dissatisfaction and questionable verbal explanations, such as "this will help you out later." We encounter a problem in applying conceptual change teaching because we are unable to help students draw on appropriate schemata. They don't have the appropriate schemata and won't have them until the successful teaching of the new operation has been completed.

The teaching will not necessarily be successful. There are three possibilities: the teaching could be incomplete; it could create great distortion; or it could be perfect. Whatever happens to the students, however, will occur as a function of the teaching, not of any "advance organizers," explanations, or obliquely related demonstration. The framing that is shown through the examples and the tasks that are presented "cause" the schemata that students come away with. The methods used to change them is what renders the instruction successful, partially successful, or a disaster.

Diagnosis and Remedies

Consider Benny, the fifth grader with great deficits in math knowledge. Through his responses, he indicates precisely what his conceptual problems are. Indeed his description of the causes is probably quite accurate. Benny has been reinforced for winging it, making it up as he went along, and trying to psych out the various worksheets. The problem was instructional because Benny was successful, which means that the worksheets actually reinforced Benny's psyching-out behavior. To fix up Benny, however, is quite another matter. We could make statements about what we would need to do: We need to modify his schemata. We need to show him the relationship between fractions and decimal values. We need to create a conflict, and we need to resolve it. And we need to do it efficiently.

Here's an effective way of doing it that does not involve any of the conceptual change steps that Floden suggests; however, it will do everything Floden would like to see done. Figure 12.1 introduces a problem set.

Fractions	Equivalent Fractions	Decimals
$\dfrac{1}{2}$	$\dfrac{}{100}$	●
$\dfrac{5}{4}$	$\dfrac{}{100}$	●
$\dfrac{3}{4}$	$\dfrac{}{100}$	●

FIGURE 12.1: **Exercise to teach conversion of fractions.**

For each row in Figure 12.1, Benny is to complete the fraction with the denominator of 100 that equals the first fraction in the row. Then Benny is to write the decimal notation. When we introduce the exercise, we may discover that Benny doesn't know how to convert the fractions in the first column into 100th fractions. So we'll teach him that. The conversion step is important because it shows Benny that the fractions *are equal*. They are equal because we multiply the fractions in the first column by a fraction *that equals 1* to get the equivalent fractions. Multiplying by 1 doesn't change the original value so the fractions must be equal. To convert the 100th fractions into decimals, Benny simply reads them: "fifty hundredths." That's exactly what he writes for the decimal number, .50.

As part of this exercise, we'll have Benny circle the smallest fraction and make a box around the largest *decimal* number. This part of the exercise will challenge Benny's notion that $\frac{1}{2}$ and 1.2 are equivalent. He'll see that the "mediator" is the 100th fractions. They provide the conversion and they show that $\frac{1}{2}$ can't equal 1.2 because $\frac{1}{2}$ is the smallest fraction, and 1.2 is the largest decimal number.

After Benny has successfully performed on some of these tables (for more than one lesson), we introduce a variation that presents *dollar amounts* in the last column. With this, we have given Benny a new slant on the entire operation. He now sees how decimals and percents interface and how their equivalence works ($\frac{1}{2}$ dollar is \$.50; $\frac{5}{4}$ dollar is \$1.25). Why not introduce the "dollar" link from the beginning, rather than having Benny work the problems "mathematically"? We want to discourage Benny from making any more homemade interpretations. We want to make sure that he processes the full range of fractions, including those like $\frac{9}{5}$. If we give Benny the green light to think of fractions in terms of dollars, he may come up with an inappropriate strategy for working the problems.

That's the solution—very simple, very quick, and guaranteed to work. Note that the "dissatisfaction" is short circuited. We simply work with what knowledge Benny has and show him the appropriate *relationships*. We point out the relationship between dollars and decimals, but, after the fact, not as a premise or rule for handling conversions, because we want to establish *the mathematical operation* as the primary one for driving this relationship. The remedy is provided with no windy explanations, no seductions, and no wasted time on activities like counting out money. Yet, when Benny completes the exercises and their extensions to word problems and so on, we will have greatly modified his schemata for "money" (because we will have enlarged what he already knows into a greater constellation of knowledge that includes equivalent fractions), his knowledge of fractions (because they will be more precisely related to decimal notations), and his understanding of equivalence. All these changes will come about as a function of what we do and how we do it through the details of instruction.

Furthermore, if Benny's instruction had included activities like the ones described above, Benny would not have either the knowledge deficiency of how fractions relate to decimals or the notion that the game is to psych out worksheets. The issue is one of instructional design. On issues of design, Floden says simply,

> Students will understand and remember better if they use the appropriate organizing principles they have already mastered to make sense of what they are learning. This requires subject matter knowledge of appropriate ways of organizing and interpreting content.

So what is left for schema theory, except to add "dissatisfaction" exercises that are unnecessary and inefficient demonstrations? Although Floden provides no suggestions for preparing Benny, Floden does address some "distorted schema" problems. For each of his problems, I'll provide a remedy that I guarantee will work. None of these remedies will resemble what Floden suggests, but I'll also guarantee that his remedies won't work.

The flat Earth: From student responses, we know what kind of instruction they received, mostly rote information. What must be implanted in their heads, however, is a "transformation," an understanding of how to relate phenomena they have viewed on the Earth to the "round Earth" phenomenon. Here's how we do it with *second graders*:

1. We teach major "continents" *using the globe.* As part of this teaching, we present the globe in different orientations so that students get used to identifying North America, for instance, when the globe is upside down. They also learn to identify where they are on the globe.
2. We present the relative notion of up and down on the globe by putting a "figure" on different parts of the globe and indicating *up and down* for that person. The rule we present is: "Down is always toward the center of the Earth. Up is always the opposite direction." (We show how a person looks when he or she "jumps" up from different parts of the globe.)
3. We follow with worksheets that show people on different parts of the globe. For some exercises, each person would be holding a ball. For some tasks, students would draw an arrow to show the direction the ball would move if the person dropped it. For other exercises, they would draw an arrow to show the direction of the ball if the person threw it straight up into the air.
4. Next, students would do tasks with the globe that involve going from "continent to continent" or to different places within a particular continent. They would move a figure on the globe, when the globe was

presented in different orientations. These exercises would illustrate that the orientation of the globe is irrelevant to whether the figure on the globe appears upside down or rightside up.

5. Extension activities involving the solar system, rotation of the Earth, and so on, follow.

Note that this sequence would not be presented in a "lesson." Rather, it would be an ongoing activity that spanned possibly 12 lessons but not requiring more than a few minutes during each lesson. In the end, students will have an understanding of "round Earth" that permits them to map what they know about flat Earth on the surface of the spherical Earth. Note that there would be no studies of Columbus, no looking up in the sky, nothing but a frontal attack on the various relationships (or schemata) that we wish to teach.

Photosynthesis: This example reveals the necessity of instructional design. It also illustrates how students could have a reasonably perfect schema for instruction that precedes "photosynthesis" but how inappropriate framing and poor instruction could cause incredible problems. Floden asserts that "plants, like animals, need food to provide energy for growth and the operation of the systems of the organism." He asserts that "starch stored in the roots or seeds . . . *is* food." Wrong on both counts. The starch is no more food than your muscles, fingernails, or fat is food. They may become "food" for other organisms, but certainly not for you.

Floden's experiment is a classic example of two things that should never be done: (a) present an experiment that doesn't prove anything; (b) present an experiment before the fact. We have done studies involving before-the-fact (or before-instruction) experiments. The bottom line is that even the relatively short ones are a waste of time. Students either don't remember what happened in an experiment or are unable to relate the experiment to what they learn later. After all, they do not have the schema necessary to provide a relevant relationship. So it is difficult for them to "store the information without distortion" before they can finally use it.

In any case, Floden's teacher grows the plant in darkness to show that a plant with plenty of water and soil will die and die soon, according to Floden. And this experiment is supposed to demonstrate that soil and water could not be "food." Obviously, the experiment doesn't show that at all. A knowledgeable student could raise havoc with this "demonstration." He or she could bring in three dead plants, saying, "I took the first one out of the soil and put it in distilled water, in sunlight. It died in a few hours. I used a hairdryer to dry out the soil in the second one. I put it in the sun. It died in a few hours. I took the third one, pulled it out of the soil, laid it on the dry ground, in sunlight. It died right away."

In the meantime, what is happening to the teacher's plant? It's growing like crazy in the darkness. The reason is that sunlight inhibits stalk growth. In darkness, the inhibition is removed, and the plant grows very rapidly. Does the plant die "soon"? Depending on the plant, and its dormancy responses, it may live for months. So the experiment basically compounds the infraction of trying to teach students something that is not true. The truth is shown largely by the four experiments (the teacher's *and* those performed by this student). Plants need sunlight and raw materials that are provided by water and soil. Plants (or green plants) also need regular air for carbon dioxide.

How would we do it the right way? We would do what Floden suggests won't work. We teach the students carefully and, of course, relate what is new to what they already know.

1. We begin with a reorganization of knowledge (or schemata). We indicate that all organisms need two primary things to grow and stay alive: raw materials and energy.

2. We teach students about energy. Specifically, we teach them the major forms: mechanical, radiant, electrical, chemical, and heat. We also teach the rule that energy in one form can be converted to energy in another form. We give them lots of exercises in which they identify the form of energy that is being shown, and we present conversions from one form to another.

3. We teach basic facts about chemical reactions, illustrating them with things like "burning." The test of a chemical reaction is that we end up with chemicals different from the ones we started with.

4. We apply the rule about what all living things need to grow and stay alive (raw materials and energy) to animals, showing students that all the "mechanical" things the organism does use energy (just like a car using up fuel) and that the source of raw materials and *energy* is food. The major raw material that is added to the animal's "food" is oxygen. The organism extracts energy from the food through chemical reactions. The basic reaction is a form of "burning." (We're warm because there's a kind of chemical burning going on inside of us.) "Burning" is a simple way of saying: the game organisms play is to go from higher-energy chemicals to lower-energy chemicals, which are the ones we end up with when something burns.

5. Finally, we apply the basic needs, energy and raw materials, to plants. The source of energy is the sun, not food. The raw materials come from soil, air, and water. Enter photosynthesis (which simply permits the plant to convert lower-energy chemicals into higher-energy chemicals).

Certainly the framing is important. But it is not possible to separate the framing from the instructional design. And the design must take into account where students are going from here. We always want to teach them in such a way that what they learn later can be easily related to what they already know so the new schemata do not contradict earlier-taught ones and do not stand as islands unrelated to what had been taught earlier. But ways of achieving these links *do not automatically spring from the diagnosis of the problem*. And the remedy is often complicated.

Remedies from Diagnostic Information

For all the examples that Floden presented, I gave instructional remedies that will work if they are developed appropriately. Would I expect a teacher to provide these or other workable remedies? No. Why not? Because I've worked with a lot of teachers, and I appreciate both their problems and their limitations. Teachers typically do not know how to *teach* "concepts," information presented by "rules," or transformations. Typically, the teacher talks *about the concept* or rule, but does not reduce it to the necessary exercises, tasks, and extensions that teach the concept or rule. Once, several colleagues and I presented more than 50 teachers with the assignment, "Teach your students the rule that liquids and gases move from a place of high pressure to a place of low pressure." The basic teaching would involve presenting the rule, having students say it, then applying the rule to a series of simple examples (diagrams that show the place of high pressure and the place of low pressure), and then having students draw an arrow showing the direction of movement. (Other examples show arrows indicating the direction of movement and require the students to label the high and the low.) Not one teacher did it or even came close. Most talked about the "water cycle" or did some whimsical experiments that did nothing but consume time. None taught.

We don't have to go beyond Floden's chapter, however, to discover that mere identification of the problem does not necessarily imply that a workable remedy will follow. Floden states the problems, but provides no remedy for Benny, none for flat Earth (except to warn the teacher that even after reading about Columbus, students may have failed to adopt the appropriate schema), and one for photosynthesis that will impart distorted schemata. So effective solutions are not glib and simple. And their complexity raises a serious question about whether teachers should spend time probing. Certainly they will discover problems, but if the identification of the problem does not guarantee an *effective* remedy, the probing may be a waste of time and cause the teacher to actually teach less.

Most of the instructional materials available to teachers are hopeless from the standpoint of instructional design. Checklists of "objectives" are a joke, representing things that are presented in a program, not things that are presented in a way that could lead to uniform mastery. It would be comforting to suppose that teachers could fix up the programs, but when and how is that going to happen? Will teachers stay up all night trying to reorganize the curriculum so they will have the potential to teach? And how are teachers going to learn how to do it the right way?

Teachers have neither the time nor the training to do it. They typically remain slaves to their instructional programs. In another study I was involved in, even teachers who reported that they deviated extensively from the specifications of their basal reading programs actually followed more than 95% of the program specifications (for the regular part of the lessons, not the "enrichment" activities). The relationship between teacher and instructional program is a lot like that of an automobile driver and car designer. To drive the car, we don't have to know how the carburetor works or the details of the turbulence inside the combustion chambers. Those are the designer's problems. The driver should have a machine that has the potential to perform well in various driving conditions. So it is with teaching. The program designer is supposed to create a "machine" that will work well, if used appropriately.

The programs that we developed have scripted presentations, a feature that strikes traditionalists as being stultifying to the teacher's creativity and ability to interact with students. These criticisms are based on distorted schemata of teachers, their creativity, and the importance of framing concepts in a way that has the potential for creating unambiguous communication with students. Anyone working with teachers on *effective* teaching would quickly learn about the advantages of scripted presentations and of the details of an effective sequence (such as not spending an entire "lesson" on a particular idea, since information about "learning" shows that students can't assimilate a great deal of information presented at one time and that they learn things faster when practice is "spaced" over a series of days).

Certainly by teaching these programs, the teacher will learn both about the content and about students. Warped or greatly distorted schemata will not occur in these programs, which is something the teacher may observe. And, we hope, there will be the transfer of skills to other situations. Meanwhile, the teacher is not burdened with "probes" because they are totally unnecessary. Student performance on the activities presented in a well-designed program provides the teacher with all the information that is necessary to determine whether there is a problem: If students do the exercises without making mistakes, there's no problem. If they make mistakes, there is a problem, but the remedy is straightforward. The teacher does not have to step outside the program, but merely repeats exercises or tasks that had been missed and brings students to a high level of mastery. If the program is poorly designed and actually teaches something as misleading as "plants make their own food," the teacher is out of luck. Unless the teacher reorganizes the entire "unit" and throws away the text, students will come away with varying degrees of distorted schemata.

Floden's remedies are based on the assumption that what students learn is influenced or "caused" by what the teacher does. (Otherwise, why provide the "dissatisfaction" activities, the explanations, etc.?) If this assumption is valid, then probing and after-the-fact remedies are not the primary solution. The primary solution would be to go back and fix up the programs so they didn't convey distorted schemata and so they effectively induced the relationships and facts that would permit students to learn in an orderly and efficient way. Floden's basic assumption is correct: Students are lawful. They learn exactly what the teacher teaches, although much of what is actually communicated to the students is unintentional. If a remedy is effective in correcting a misconception, it should be introduced before the fact as part of the initial teaching to buttress against the misconception.

Since the problem that schema theory is supposed to address is that of organizing content so it makes sense to pupils, and since the curriculum is what determines whether it will make sense or be gibberish, the primary solution must be one of instructional design, not probing; and it certainly should not be practices based on the assumption that the teacher who can't view instruction from the pupil's viewpoint will be able to organize the content so it makes sense to pupils.

In summary, teaching is an act that involves orchestrating many details. Some are details of content, and the content is conveyed primarily by the verbal and nonverbal applications of rules or principles, the juxtaposition of things that are done in the lesson, the amount and use of vocabulary and facts. Through these details an organization is conveyed. If the framework created by the activities is vague, abstract, or unclear, students will employ a variety of "sense-making" strategies, most of which will be inappropriate or distorted. If the design has the potential of conveying the appropriate relationships and discriminations, and if it is continuous with what students will learn later, it has the potential to make sense to any student who is adequately prepared for the program. These design issues are not effectively handled by teachers and do not derive automatically from a description of a "distorted-schema" problem.

Even if the program is well designed and has the potential of making sense to all the students, the design represents only a potential. This potential will be realized only if the teacher is proficient at conveying the information and executing the various behaviors that are needed to make the communication real. This reality occurs only if the students are taught to a high level of mastery (so they are relatively fluent or automatic in applying the facts and relationships), are motivated to learn, and understand that they are expected to learn. The skills that this teacher must have are far from trivial. Relatively few teachers possess them; however, these skills can be taught. And teachers who possess them have a great potential to induce content so it makes sense to pupils.

REFERENCES

National Council of Teachers of English, Commission on Reading. (1987, November). *Report card on basal readers*. Paper presented at the NCTE Invitational Conference on the Basal Reader, Los Angeles.

Students' Cultural Backgrounds

The United States differs from virtually every other nation in the diversity of students who may share a single classroom. Though many of our school systems sort students into ability tracks, they are less systematic in their efforts than schools in other countries often are. And although our cultural majorities and minorities still live in relatively separate neighborhoods, they are more integrated than majorities and minorities in many other countries. These facts create unique and uniquely difficult teaching situations, for teachers may find themselves facing students of varying ability, varying cultural backgrounds, varying languages. It seems reasonable to assume that teachers will be more successful if they understand something about these different students, but what is it they should know?

In the following two chapters, Carl Grant and G. W. McDiarmid address this question. Grant reviews the history of racial attitudes in this country, the many ways in which white perceptions of nonwhite cultures are communicated to both groups, and the untested assumptions that teachers, who themselves are predominantly white, may hold about students of color. He argues that offering teachers knowledge of different cultures may reinforce, rather than alter, their own attitudes, and that a better approach would be to help teachers understand not only this nation's history of race relations but also their own personal histories and how their own biographies influence their perceptions and understandings of different groups.

McDiarmid also questions the likely outcome of teaching teachers about the many cultures from which their students may derive. But instead of suggesting that teachers learn to examine the influence of their own biographies on their views, McDiarmid suggests that teachers need to construe their task as one of rendering academic subjects meaningful to diverse students. If this is the task, cultural backgrounds are relevant to teaching but are not reasons for excusing students from learning. Examining the role of culture in perceptions of academic subjects can help teachers find ways to portray their subjects honestly, even to diverse students.

13

Culture and Teaching: What Do Teachers Need to Know?

CARL A. GRANT

My area of teaching and research—race, class, and gender in school and classroom life, and multicultural education—often gives me the opportunity to meet and have discussions with both preservice and inservice teachers. Many of these teachers (and a growing number of policy makers) impatiently demand, "Tell me about the culture of these kids . . .," meaning students of color and poor students. "Give me some tips that will help me teach them." These teachers usually want a recipe for teaching students whom they believe to be culturally deprived or culturally different; or they want a list of "do's and don'ts" that will keep "these students," as they are often referred to, on task.

Such lists and recipes do exist as products of the deficit theory and can be found in the educational literature (see, for example, Cheyney, 1967; Kendall, 1983; Morine & Morine, 1970; Reissman, 1962, 1976; Trubowitz, 1968; Webster, 1966a, 1966b). Deficit theories became very popular, gained some academic respectability, and shared a prominent place in the educational debate in the 1960s and 1970s. Although they are not put forth in the literature as major reasons why students have difficulty learning, these ideas have not been completely dismissed by some educators (see, for example, Grant & Sleeter, 1986).

Deficit

Similarly, other teachers will say, "I have heard that these kids learn differently because they are 'culturally different' and/or 'linguistically different' and are socialized differently from my colleagues [white middle class] and me. What does research say about the way these students learn and are socialized? Will this information help me to do a better job teaching them? Where can I get this information?" Information on teaching the "culturally and/or linguistically different individual," which grew out of the cultural different hypotheses (see, for example, Baratz & Baratz, 1970), is available, along with applications for classroom use (see, for example, Hale, 1982; Stodolsky & Lessen, 1967).

The above questions are requests for a remedy to the educational problem of how to teach African-Amerian, Hispanic, Native American, and Asian-American students and students whose native language is not English. Many of the teachers asking these questions have very serious intentions and really want to see their students have successful academic learning experiences. How to answer these nagging questions that teachers are raising is the charge of this chapter.

Indeed, the guidelines for this chapter instructed me to address "what teachers need to know about how students' cultural backgrounds can influence learning," and I was to "assume that your teacher may be required to work in a variety of schools and must be prepared for a variety of curricula." Like many of the teachers, these guidelines implicitly ask for manageable answers that will help in working successfully with a rapidly growing population of students of color (Today's Numbers, 1986). These students, according to Orfield (1987), are being increasingly isolated, in the inner city ghettos and barrios, from any contact with mainstream American society in a nation that is rapidly moving toward two classes—the "haves" and the "have nots" (Harrington, 1984; Wacquant & Wilson, 1989). Besides the tall order stated in the guidelines, there is, from my perspective, a serious concern accompanying this request. This concern is how such narrow discussions and recipes for educational policy and practice are often used. Social scientists and educators (who are among the "haves") seek direction for social and educational policy and process that will directly affect people of color; these often lead to work that is seriously flawed and cause the victims—the "have nots," who tend to be people of color—to be incorrectly understood and portrayed or to be blamed. Ralph Ellison (1966), in a review of Gunnar Myrdal's *An American Dilemma*, spoke to this point:

> Myrdal sees Negro culture and personality simply as a product of a "social pathology." Thus, he assumes that "it is to the advantage of American Negroes as individuals and as a group to become assimilated into American culture to acquire the traits held in esteem by the dominant White Americans." This, he admits, contains the value premise that "here in America, American culture is 'highest' in the pragmatic sense. . . . Which, aside from implying that the Negro culture is not also American, assumes the Negro should desire nothing better than what Whites consider highest." (p. 301)

The testing movement started long ago by Yerkes, Goddard, Thorndike, and Termin is another example of the work of social scientists negatively affecting people of color. We will have more to say about the testing movement later. Similarly, scholars of color would argue that the Coleman Report (Coleman et al., 1966) is another example of social scientists, in their attempt to help resolve problems confronting people of color, causing as much harm as good (see, for example, Bowles & Levin, 1968; Grant, 1972; Guthrie, 1972; Mosteller & Moynihan 1972).

My purpose thus far has not been to avoid my task, but to point out that the topic, "What teachers need to know about how students' cultural backgrounds can influence learning," carries with it a great deal of historical and contemporary social and educational ferment. This ferment is, in part, conditioned by the different ideologies and points of view that give direction to policies and practices of schools. For the topic to receive the response it needs, it must be contextualized and examined from a point of view that is not alien or repressive to people of color. This context needs to include a history of schooling from the perspective of people of color, a discussion of the need for teachers to understand their own biography and enculturation, and an examination of what the literature says (or does not say) about the influence of culture on the teaching and learning of students of color.

PEOPLE OF COLOR:
INDIVIDUALISM, SCHOOLS, AND CULTURE

To understand the cultural background of students of color and to teach them successfully, it is important (and maybe even necessary) to understand how their culture has been and is accepted in school and society. Respect for the culture of people of color has not existed; in fact, cultural disrespect in the form of racism toward people of color began centuries ago and is deeply rooted in the political and social history of our country. Article 1 of the U.S. Constitution declared that representation in the House of Representatives should be based on a population count of the "whole number of free persons . . . excluding Indians" and "three-fifths of all other persons." Even the passage of the Fifteenth Amendment to the Constitution did very little to foster cultural respect for people of color. In fact, disrespect toward the culture of people of color in the form of racism has been an institution in this country.

Institutions, as understood from a sociological perspective, may be groups or social practices that tend to serve broad, as opposed to narrow, interests and do so in ways that are both accepted and enduring. Institutionalization is thus the process by which unstable or loosely patterned actions are socially integrated to form orderly stable social structures. Cultural superiority and elitism on the part of whites have become so thoroughly institutionalized into the country's social fabric that many people, including educators, fail to recognize some of the many guises it assumes. For example, opinion polls often show whites and people of color as having different opinions about whether African-Americans receive equal pay for equal work and about the treatment of African-Americans in the criminal justice system. A recent NAACP Legal Defense Fund and Education study (Johnson, 1989) conducted by Lou Harris, reported that 67% of whites agreed that equal pay generally prevailed and 66% of African-Americans disagreed. Similarly, 61% of whites rejected the idea that the criminal justice system treated African-Americans unequally, a statement that was supported by 80% of African-Americans. Further, a *Newsweek* poll ("Black and White," 1988) pointed out that there are significant differences between the ways African-Americans and whites view their relationships in society today, especially in comparison to each other (p. 23).

Formalization is another part of the institutionalization process. Our nation's founders, by putting into words the belief that slaves were not full persons, gave formal recognition and acceptance to the idea that some cultures were superior to others. Our nation's founders were among those who helped to institutionalize the white cultural superiority and elitism in American society and schools. As the social practice of promoting white cultural superiority and elitism became formalized, those who had an interest in its maintenance tended to take steps to conserve it. Laws, as a product of formalization, are not sufficient. To become institutionalized, social practice must be integrated into the personal value systems of those who will enforce and perpetuate it. Our public schools provide an excellent vehicle for this part of the institutionalization process.

The schools and teachers as chief instruments of this process became very important in the institutionalization of white cultural superiority. Schools took advantage of the opportunity provided by compulsory attendance statutes to instill in the minds of this country's young people that segregating people of color from white people was legally sanctioned and socially important. This segregation also permitted and encouraged the teaching of racist concepts necessary to espouse and maintain white cultural superiority. Some of this teaching was quite direct through the use of biased textbooks and the absence of teachers and administrators of color. Other parts of this process were less obvious, such as the misuse of testing instruments to inaccurately and unjustly label and negatively classify students of color. Let's review some aspects of the process.

Some of the most respected institutions in society give legal and social credence to the white cultural superiority and racism of these undertakings. For example, in 1896 the Supreme Court case *Plessy* vs. *Ferguson* established the "separate but equal" doctrine that gave direction to racial relationships in the schools and greatly influenced social behaviors throughout the country. This doctrine also said to students of color, in policy and practice, that their culture was not respected and therefore could not be beside (in persons or artifacts) the white culture in school. *Plessy* also institutionalized practices that were supported by the federal courts, permitting white students to be provided with school buildings, equipment, and personnel before African-American students were. As Ihle (1986), tells us,

> Three years after *Plessy*, Blacks in Richmond County in Georgia brought suit
> because the county, which operated a high school for White girls and another
> for White boys, closed the only Black high school in order to accommodate
> more Blacks in the elementary grades. The Supreme Court chose not to get
> involved; despite the clear violation of the "separate but equal" doctrine, the
> Court ruled in *Cumming* v. *Richmond County Board of Education* (1899) that
> federal law was not broken and the county could allocate its tax money as it saw
> fit. (p. 2)

The renunciation of *Plessy*, with the passage of *Brown* in 1954, laid the
legal foundations to mandate integration of public schools and civil rights
guarantees during the 1960s. These measures were supposed to give a positive
and sustaining direction to race relations in this country and allow the cultures
of *all* students to come together and have equity and equality in the classroom.
A recent report, however, by Orfield (1987), points out that this is not
happening. Orfield reported that there had been little overall change in the
segregation of African-American students since the early 1970s. He argued that
three of the four administrations since 1968 were openly hostile to urban
desegregation orders, and that the Carter Administration "took few initiatives in
the field" (p. 1). Hispanics, Orfield observed, were becoming more segregated
in virtually all parts of the country and in almost every period in the 16 years
in which national data have been collected.

Additionally, he argued that the most segregated states in 1984 were states
that previously fought for integration. The old hotbeds of abolitionism, Illinois
and Michigan, and a pioneer in modern civil rights law, New York, had a very
large number of African-American students but a smaller proportion of African-
Americans in their total enrollment than many southern states. Furthermore,
Orfield (1987) noted

> The States are primarily distinctive in terms of the scale of their segregated
> resident areas, the fragmentation of school districts within their large
> metropolises, and the lack of any city-suburban desegregation plans in any of
> their largest urban communities—New York City, Chicago, and Detroit. (p. 5)

Textbooks should provide the opportunity for all cultures to be seen as equal
and to be celebrated in the classroom, but this is not and has not been the case.
In the eighteenth and nineteenth centuries, textbooks promoted cultural
denigration and inferiority of people of color. Native Americans were depicted
as noble savages, fond of cruelty, and as having little regard for civilization.
African-Americans were characterized as "gay, thoughtless, unintelligent, and
subject to violent passion" (Ellison, 1966; Gould, 1978). Asian-Americans,
when they were included, were frequently presented in a manner that implied
they were socially inferior (see, for example, Committee on the Study of
Teaching Materials, 1949). The culture of all people of color was summarily
degraded.

The decades following the 1950s witnessed some positive change in the portrayal of the culture of people of color in textbooks, but by no means and in no way was their treatment equal to that of white people. A study of textbooks published by the Michigan Department of Public Instruction in 1963 concluded

> Minority children frequently grow up unaware of great portions of prideful heritage, partly because of omissions or distortions in school books. When this occurrence is coupled with other kinds of discrimination confronted in our society, they are left with the feeling of frustration, negative self-image, and distrust for education, and a cynicism regarding democracy. (p. 2)

In 1970, Michael Kane reported on a study of people of color in textbooks. He observed that there was some recent improvement in the way African-Americans were presented. The historical references to Native Americans had also improved, but their portrayal in contemporary society was weak or inaccurate. Kane also reported that there was little improvement in the treatment of Asian-Americans and little attention paid to Spanish-speaking Americans.

Other studies of textbooks (see, for example, Butterfield, Demos, Grant, Moy, & Perez, 1979; Costo & Henry, 1970; Dunfee, 1974) reported similar results. Women of color and Hispanic-Americans were underrepresented in text materials and were rarely shown in decision-making positions, and the culture of people of color in comparison to the white culture was not portrayed in an esteemed and celebrated manner. Recently, Sleeter and Grant (1991) analyzed 47 textbooks presently in use in grades K-9 for social studies, reading and language arts, science, and mathematics, with copyright dates between 1980 and 1987. They found that textbooks still show the white culture as superior to the culture of people of color. Whites receive by far the most attention, are presented in the greatest number of roles, and dominate the story line and list of accomplishments. Furthermore, the Sleeter and Grant study reveals that the cultures of different groups of color were rarely shown in relationship to one another, just in relationship to whites. For example, African-American cowboys of the West were not discussed interacting with Native Americans, Asian-Americans, or Mexican-Americans, who also lived at that time in that region of the country.

Teachers of color are important role models for *all students, especially students of color.*

> The race and background of their teachers tells them something about power and authority in contemporary America. . . . These messages influence children's attitudes toward school, their academic accomplishments, and their views of their own and others' intrinsic worth. The views they form in school about justice and fairness also influence their future citizenship. (Carnegie Forum, 1986, p. 79)

By their presence, teachers of color indicate to students of color that their cultural group is respected and academically capable. For example, interviews conducted with students of color have shown that many of them are particularly pleased and gratified when they have a teacher of their own background, especially when they are in a school where there are few teachers of color on the staff (Grant & Sleeter, 1986). Similarly, Bandura and Walters (1963), G. Grant (1978), and others have pointed out the importance of role models in conveying positive messages. Teachers are important role models to the students in their classes, and, although successful teaching is not determined by a person's color, many educators are arguing that the growing shortage of teachers of color will have a negative impact on all students, especially students of color. (I would encourage departments of teacher education to have their students see *Stand and Deliver*. This film will provide an excellent opportunity to discuss teaching, culture, and the desire and dedication of teachers.)

For example, Gordon (1988) and other scholars of color have argued that one of the major educational battles in the twenty-first century will be for the hearts and minds of people of color. She pointed out that "people of color are having a difficult time realizing the American dream because they are not only battling against racism, but an evolved culture that combines racism with elitism, an inherited empirically founded Spencerian rationale, and capitalism" (p. 156). Gordon's observation does not bode well for how the culture of students of color is received in school. In fact, she argued that "African-American parents and educators must supplement school learning with after-school or weekend programs focused on their *specific needs and cultural idiosyncracies*" (italics added, p. 157).

As the 1980s began, the shortage of teachers of color was emerging at an alarming rate. In public schools, 91.5% of the teachers were white, 7.8% were African-American, and 0.7% were classified as other. By 1986, 89.6% were white, 7.0% were African-American, and 3.4% were classified as other (Harris & Harris, 1988). As we move into the 1990s, there are few indicators that the shortage of teachers of color, particularly African-American teachers, will get better. The dismal figures and the forecast of the number of educators of color working in public schools suggest that the culture of people of color is, and probably will remain, just as proportionally underrepresented as it has been.

School tests are one of the most devious and vocal forms of communications to students of color about their culture. Educators have used tests to sort, select, and keep students whose culture was different from their own in "their place" for decades. Spring (1972) argues that the testing movement was started by social scientists to identify the low-culture immigrating "ignorant hordes" at the turn of the twentieth century. The schools were to stamp out the evil of ignorance by educating immigrants, especially those who were not from northern Europe and not endowed with Anglo-Saxon cultural traditions and language. The I.Q. test, especially, has provided a means for educators to attack and castigate the culture of students of color. Test developer Lewis Terman's (1916) words are still too often the policy and practice heard in school today.

> Their dullness seems to be racial, or at least inherent in the family stocks from which they come. The fact that one meets this type with such extraordinary frequency among Indians, Mexicans, and Negroes suggests quite forcibly that the whole question of racial differences in mental traits will have to be taken up anew. . . . There will be discovered enormously significant racial differences . . . which cannot be wiped out by any schemes of mental culture. Children of this group should be segregated in special classes . . . they cannot master abstractions, but they can often be made efficient workers. (pp. 27-28)

An example of why Terman's words are not outdated today is that the 1960 version of Terman's Stanford-Binet intelligence test, which was still being used in the 1980s, asked students to determine "Which is prettier?" and counterposed portraits of nonwhite people against those of white Anglo-Saxon individuals. The correct choice, according to Terman, is the Anglo-Saxon representative.

Tracking in schools is another way the culture of students of color is undermined in schools. For example, in a California court in 1972, plaintiffs in *Larry* vs. *Riles* challenged the validity of two intelligence tests to measure accurately the intelligence of African-American children because, as a result of these tests, a much higher percentage of African-American than white children was being tracked to special education classes. Although African-Americans represented only 28% of all children attending school in California, they constituted 66% of the children in special education programs. Psychologists brought in to testify for the prosecution demonstrated that the I.Q. tests were unreliable instruments for judging the ability of African-American students to learn, because the tests assumed that children were familiar with the customs and language of white middle-class Americans.

More recently, Oakes (1985) argued that tracking based on bias can influence the self-concept of students of color. She pointed out that students, even in the early grades, know who is in the top group, average group, and low group, and why. Oakes (1985) explained it as follows:

> Rather than help students to feel more comfortable about themselves, the tracking process seems to foster lowered self-esteem among these teenagers. Further exacerbating these native self-perceptions are the attitudes of many teachers and other students toward those in the lower tracks. Once placed in low classes, students are usually seen by others in the school as dumb. . . . Closely related to students' self-evaluations are their aspirations for the future and the educational plans they make. Students in low track classes have been found to have lower aspirations and more often to have their plans for the future frustrated. (p. 8)

My purpose thus far has been to remind you that, in policy and practice, historically and presently, schools undermine and marginalize the culture of students of color. Thus, policy and practices designed to provide teachers with information about the culture of students of color must also provide them with a knowledge and understanding of the history discussed above, to avoid putting students of color in academic and social harm's way.

TEACHERS AND CULTURE

For teachers to use effectively any information that they receive about the culture of their students, they must understand their own biographies and enculturation and how these give direction to their thoughts and actions regarding the educational information they receive. The psychological literature is replete with accounts of peoples' actions being directed by their past behavior (see, for example, Adler, 1963; Bandura, 1971; Bronfenbrenner, 1979; Erikson, 1963; Gould, 1978; Okun, 1984). The nightly news, talk shows, and the popular press regularly provide accounts of the influence of past behavior on current actions. For example, we often hear or read about how a person who was abused as a child becomes an abuser of his or her children. Similarly, the rejection of Robert Bork's nomination to the Supreme Court was based on his past actions toward civil rights and the beliefs by his opponents that his past actions were indicative of his potential future dealings with civil rights litigation.

Our concerns about the enculturation of teachers should be just as energized as were the concerns over Bork, for Bork had an opportunity to face and respond to those who questioned his background and past actions. Most students of color are not provided such an opportunity. Many teachers do not have substantive conversations with students about their life experiences and ambitions. Nor do they inquire into students' cultural knowledge about the academic and social aspects of schooling (see, for example, Grant & Sleeter, 1986; Sleeter & Grant, 1991). Teachers often label students of color as academic and social misfits and place or leave them on a track that will lead to a culture of poverty and a life of despair.

What do we know about the biography of the teachers to whom we want to give this cultural information? Will the information be used to provide important and useful insights into learning styles of students of color? Will this information be used to perpetuate ideas from the cultural deficit hypothesis and encourage teachers to believe that these students have deficits and negative differences and are therefore not as academically capable of learning as white students? These are important and timely questions, given the dropout rates and poor achievement scores in many schools that students of color attend. Also, anyone who has done an in-depth study of urban schooling, or of a school where there is a significant enrollment of students of color, is aware of how these students often do not receive the best teaching and social and academic challenges because of their cultural background (see, for example, Gouldner, 1978; Grant & Sleeter, 1986; Payne, 1984).

Recently, educators have begun to pursue the area of biography and autobiography to better understand teachers and their teachings. Educators are using "life history" methodologies to understand teacher socialization and its implication for the classroom. Zeichner and Gore (1990) saw promise for these methodologies in helping to explain why teachers teach as they do. Zeichner and Gore argued that "these interpretations and critical studies have begun to provide us with rich information about the ways in which teachers' perspectives are rooted in the variety of personal, financial, religious, political, and cultural experience they bring to teaching" (p. 21).

Many of these teachers' perspectives are shaped by their enculturation in society. What has society been "saying" to its citizens about people of color that could influence a teacher's biography? Let's see. There have been positive gains in civil rights and race relations that could positively influence the biography of teachers toward students of color, but there has also been and continues to be too much negative influence regarding people of color. Society, while using equal opportunity rhetoric and demonstrating some evidence of color blindness and fairness, is still very racist and promotes white cultural superiority. Cobbs (1988), an African-American psychiatrist, informed us about how we, as a society and individually, deal with racism:

> Individually and collectively, Americans continue to be passive in acquiring any knowledge about the psychology of race. We underestimate its implications for how and with whom we conduct our lives. Most of us, when confronted with racial attitudes in any form, fall back on a comfortable intellectual laziness which elevates stereotypes to facts, and converts individual behavior to group characteristics. This, I believe, is normal human behavior. (p. 64)

Let's examine some of society's institutions with which teachers interact, to see how people of color are perceived and treated. In journalism—the Fourth Estate—the American Society of Newspaper Editors reports that only 7.02% of journalists at daily newspapers are Asian-American, American Indian, Hispanic, or African-American. More devastating is that 55% of the daily newspapers employ no journalists of color. Furthermore, in broadcasting, 15% of news jobs were held by African-Americans in 1979; in 1986, that figure was down to 13%, and those in the business fear the decline is continuing, especially among African-American males ("Why Economists," 1988).

In politics, although people of color are more active and play a broader role in local and state politics in some regions of the country, the national level shows they have very little political muscle and are severely underrepresented in the power structure. Among the U.S. senators currently in office, two are Asian-Pacific Islander; no present senator is Native American, Hispanic, or

African-American. The House of Representatives includes 26 African-Americans (5.9% of the total membership), 12 Hispanics (2.75% of the total membership), 5 Asian-American's or Pacific Islanders (1% of the total membership), and 1 Native American (.002%).

In education and income in 1980, African-American adults in the United States had completed an average of 12 years of schooling, just one-half year less than the average number of years completed by white adults, but the average African-American family earned only 59% as much as the average white family. Moreover, the income gap between African-Americans and whites had diminished by only 1% between 1967 and 1979 (U.S. Department of Commerce, 1981). More recently, according to the Center for Budget and Policy Priorities, the median family income of African-Americans declined in the last decade from 59% of that of whites to 56% ("Why Economists," 1988). Furthermore, the unemployment rate for African-Americans was more than twice that for whites, a situation that has remained unchanged for two decades (U. S. Department of Commerce, 1979).

In housing, there have been numerous articles describing the poor conditions for people of color, especially the poor among them. Some articles argue that new housing construction for the poor has come to a virtual halt ("Decent Affordable Housing," 1988). Other articles describe housing where poor people of color have to live as "hell" ("What It's Like," 1987). And still other articles point out that, in the housing market, racial steering is still evident in some areas ("Steering Blacks," 1987). How do teachers receive this information? Do they believe that the reason people of color live in racially segregated, inferior housing is because they don't want to work and have a better life? Do they believe that living in poverty is linked to culture? Many of the white teachers at both the preservice and inservice levels find a good deal of credibility in the victim-blaming hypothesis. This occurs, in part, because the history of oppression toward people of color has been omitted or conveyed to them in a desensitized manner.

The education profession in general is similar to society in institutionalizing racism. There is a long history, as noted earlier, of how people of color have been marginalized or kept out of the social, political, and economic system. Therefore, it is necessary for teachers to analyze their biographies in order to determine how the enculturation process influenced them about race, class, and gender issues in regard to other cultures. For example, numerous narratives written by white teachers explain how their own life experiences were often a barrier to the schooling of students of color.

Decker (1969), a beginning teacher, described how an urban school presented a world completely new to her and students whom she didn't understand. The noise level at the school and being immersed in an African-American world were all new to her. She said, "I was struck . . . by the blackness. Being immersed in a Negro world was new to me, and in the dim, artificial light of the corridors, faces seemed to disappear. It struck me funny. I laughed for days" (p. 37). She further observed that it was difficult to understand what the students were saying, that there was a language barrier between the students and her. She explained, "It was Christmas before I could understand them without watching mouths." Decker's background and life experience were very different from those of the students she worked with. Speaking about the teachers who taught her, she said

> "Teachers were such gray people—gray suits, gray skin, gray personalities. They taught from yellowed notes they'd made up thirty years ago, *and hated all the Negroes and Jews that were moving to the Philadelphia Main Line* [italics added]. Things just weren't what they used to be, what with the "new element" and all. (p. 22)

On entering the profession, many new teachers have backgrounds and life experiences that are more similar to Decker's than, they argue, to those of the students they will teach. According to a recent AACTE report, approximately 80% of the new teaching force grew up in suburban and rural settings and are strongly desirous of teaching only in that kind of environment (American Association of Colleges for Teacher Education, 1987). The differences in life experiences between students and teachers causes teachers to experience culture shock.

Parkay (1983), a neophyte white teacher, described in her narrative the culture shock and fears she experienced working with African-American students:

> During my first year at DuSable [a high school on Chicago's southside] I was frequently very anxious and frightened. On occasion, I even had nightmares about the place. I despaired of ever understanding or accepting the students' behavior and attitudes that were so strange and threatening to me. I experienced what anthropologists and sociologists have termed "culture shock." (p. 18)

Parkay (1983) listed several other fears about the school that she said contributed to her culture shock—fear of being manipulated; fear of aggressive, intrusive behavior; fear of encirclement and loss of autonomy; and fear of violent primitive behavior. In very explicit words, she illuminated my concerns about a teacher's biography and the need for teachers to understand themselves in relationship to the culture of people of color. She said, "If the lower class school to which a teacher is assigned contains a significant percentage of Black students, most middle class teachers are apt to experience anxiety related to their students' race" (p. 52).

Canfield (1970) provided a similar experience of how biography influences a teacher's classroom behavior. Being temporarily assigned to work in a

Chicago inner-city school, Canfield described the desire to teach and the frustrations of teaching that were present, in part, because of his acculturation:

> Every minute I taught in the classrooms, and as I walked through the halls and met kids on the street, I wondered if I were being accepted, if they thought I was real. . . . I was . . . driven to be accepted by what Black militants would term my own mad fancies and guilt feelings as a White liberal. (p. 37)

Canfield (1970) also acknowledged, like Parkay (1983), the difference in the biographies of the teachers and the students they teach. He observed

> Most, yet not all, of the teachers in the school were irrelevant to the lives of the students whom they taught. A student would quickly identify the teacher with his or her subject and block them both out of his mind. (p. 38)

Longstreet (1978) also provided an insightful account of how her lack of understanding of the culture of students she was teaching turned them off and annoyed her:

> Many teachers at Harlem school confessed to a feeling of "strangeness" at the school. . . . These theoretical concerns are sometimes not seemingly as important as the more overt and direct effects on teachers of being in the new cultural setting. Virtually no permanent friendships existed between Black and White teachers, and even the informal lunchroom talk fests revealed White and Black teachers to be aloof from one another. Some White teachers attributed the lack of response in the children as based in anti-White feelings. And some of the Black teachers concluded that the failure of children to learn was grounded in anti-Black feelings among White teachers. These feelings were a microcosmic reflection of the larger societal macrocosm where similar reactions are engendered. (p. 11)

Other nonbiographical studies of classroom life have also pointed out how teachers' biographies influence their actions. For example, based on a three-year ethnographers' study of junior high school, Grant and Sleeter (1986) argued that one of the major barriers to students of color receiving a quality education was the teachers' biographies, their lack of understanding—of race, class, gender, and disability issues—and their teacher preparation experience (both preservice and inservice).

The above narratives allow us to use the teachers' own words to point out the importance of acculturation and biography for influencing teacher behavior. It is too academic and socially costly to students of color to be taught by teachers who do not know who they are and what they are about. It is also unprofessional, improper, and inappropriate for educational decision makers to allow unprepared teachers to attempt to help others when these teachers must first help themselves.

UNCERTAINTY AND CONTRADICTION
IN THE LITERATURE

Thus far, I have argued that giving teachers cultural information about students is premature and problematic, because teachers need to have an understanding of their own biographies and how past life experiences regarding race, class, and gender influence present action. I have also argued that teachers need to have an understanding of how the school (the educational system) has a history of degrading the culture of students of color. There is a third reason why giving teachers information about the culture of students of color is problematic. That is because there is a great deal of debate and uncertainty in the educational literature regarding culture, ethnicity, and learning. This debate and uncertainty make it difficult to decide and raise additional questions regarding what we should tell teachers about culture and learning. For example, some educators argue that students' cultural background influences learning, and others argue that cultural information about students can lead to stereotyping. Of these perspectives and others, which ones should we stress? Should we provide the teachers with all the perspectives and then have them form their own opinion? Or, has a larger question surfaced out of this debate? For now, let's briefly discuss some of the perspectives.

Some educators (Boykin, 1986; Carbo & Hodges, 1988; Erickson, 1987; Gibson, 1987; Kendall, 1983; McDermott, 1987; Trueba, 1988) argue that a student's cultural background influences learning. However, some of these educators, for example, Kendall (1983), argue that

> there is indeed a fine line between awareness of potential effects of ethnicity on learning styles and expecting a child of a particular ethnic group to behave in a particular way. Ideally, the teacher does not view any child as a cultural or ethnic representative but responds to each one as an individual for whom culture or ethnicity is merely one aspect of her or his personality. . . . It is essential that teachers not make assumptions about a child's learning style solely on the basis of the child's cultural heritage. (pp. 13-15)

Ward (1973) argues that culture and language program the mind. Trueba (1988), in a recent criticism of cultural ecologists—especially Ogbu and his classification of minority groups as "autonomous," "immigrant," or "castelike"—argues that there is a very close relationship between language, culture, and cognition; therefore, a theory is needed to integrate conceptually the explanation of successful learning activities, especially for children who find themselves in cultural transition. However, Ogbu (1987) counters that language and cultural differences do not influence groups unless they are stratified. He also points out that failure to recognize the differences between primary and secondary cultural differences often results in global and stereotyped descriptions of minority-group cultures. Lundsteen (1978) points out that achievement motivation is different from culture to culture.

Other educators claim that cultural explanations of differential achievement can provide a basis for stereotypes. For example, Weisner, Gallimore, and Jordan (1988) indicate that cultural differences often result in global and stereotypical descriptions of minority-group cultures. Some educators, for example, Romero, Mercado & Vasquez-Faría (1987), state that individuals may not always be shaped by culture but may simply represent idiosyncratic behavior particular to an individual or a family. Brunner (1973) also states that culture does not produce completely divergent, unrelated modes of thinking.

Still other educators (Gordon, 1979; Morris, 1978; Stodolsky & Lessen, 1967) argue that ethnicity is a factor that can determine cognitive style. However, Spangler also points out that acculturation may be a factor in determining cognitive style, and there is a great deal of variation between groups. Some educators point out that social class is an important determinant. Gordon (1979) and Shade (1981, 1982) claim that a student's social class can confound the impact of ethnicity. Hale (1982), drawing on some of the work of Havinghurst (1976), argues that within a complex society social class and ethnicity interact in the shaping of human behavior, but the interaction is a complex process. Rossi (1961) earlier made a similar observation: "While . . . studies . . . unfortunately find socio-economic status playing a role in achievement, it is not entirely clear how it does so" (p. 269). It could be interpreted that these educators were arguing, in principle, not only that it is valuable to explain to teachers the importance of cultural influences on students of color, but also that culture must be understood in relationship to socioeconomic status.

Finally, there are some educators who question the existence of ethnic styles. Weinberg (1977), in his analysis of ethnicity and learning, argues that the existence of ethnic learning styles is problematic. Similarly, Anderson (1977) and Henderson (1980) point out that cognitive style studies are contradictory. Anderson shows that cognition is due to the situation, and that school, teacher, and student traits, not cognitive preference, are the cause of a lack of school services. Banks (1976) also indicates that there are numerous reasons affecting students of color: "Findings are as diverse as are the theoretical and methodological approaches that generate them" (p. 6).

Should some or all of this information be provided to teachers—or should it be left up to them to make their own determination? I am not advocating the de-skilling of teachers as far as cultural information about students of color is concerned, but one should point out the problematic nature of the information and the varying points of view. I would argue that teachers need to be provided with all of this information, and they also need to be provided with the time and resources to gain an understanding of what it means to their teaching.

Given this time for analysis, they may question "the question" and ask, Is this debate so static that it can be answered from a singular perspective? They may argue that some real questions aren't being examined, for example, Why should teachers be given a recipe for working with students' culture, when students' ascribed characteristics are so diverse and they represent so many groups within groups? Students are Asian-Americans, African-Americans, Hispanic-Americans, Native Americans, and white Americans; they are males and females from different socioeconomic classes; and they represent a wide range of cultural diversity. Teachers may ask, Why aren't students considered as individuals, who have been influenced by their particular background and circumstances and, therefore, need to be taught with this consideration in mind? These and many other questions that teachers would raise move us closer to the heart of this dilemma. The major point is not to give teachers a cultural recipe for working with students of color, but to get them to realize that to work successfully with any students, especially students whose race and socioeconomic status are different than their own, they will need to raise many questions, starting with questions about themselves. Recipes for teaching students of color can become a means of transmitting racist discourse and practice.

Finally, it is important for educators to realize that the educational problems experienced by students of color cannot be resolved by being interpreted as the main cause for students' lack of educational success. Educators must understand that *they* (and the overall structures of school and society) play a major role in the lack of academic success of students of color. Until that is understood educational success will escape all involved.

REFERENCES

Adler, A. (1963). *The practice and theory of individual psychology.* Paterson, NJ: Littlefield Adams.

American Association of Colleges for Teacher Education. (1987) *Teaching teachers: Facts and figures.* Washington, DC: Author.

Anderson, K. (1977). *Cognitive style and school failure.* South West Anthropological Association.

Bandura, A. (1971). *Psychological modeling: Conflicting theories.* Chicago: Aldin-Atherton.

Bandura, A., & Walters, R. (1963). *Social learning and personality development.* New York: Holt, Rinehart and Winston.

Banks, C. (1976). *Achievement motivation and Black children* (IRCD Bulletin). New York: Yeshiva University.

Black and white in America. (1988, March 7). *Newsweek.* pp. 18-23.

Baratz, S., & Baratz, J. (1970). Early childhood intervention: The social science base of institutional racism. *Harvard Educational Review, 40,* 29-50.

Bowles, S., & Levin, H. (1968). The determinants of scholastic achievement: An appraisal of some recent evidence. *Journal of Human Resources, 3,* 3-34.

Boykin, A. W. (1986). The triple quandary and the schooling of Afro-American children. In U. Wesser (Ed.), *The school achievement of minority children: New perspectives* (pp. 57-92). Hillsdale, NJ: Erlbaum.

Bronfenbrenner, U. (1979). *The ecology of human development.* Cambridge, MA: Harvard University Press.

Brunner, J. (1973). *Beyond the information given; studies in the psychology of knowing.* New York: Norton.

Butterfield, R. A., Demos, E. S., Grant, G. W., Moy, P. S., & Perez, A. L. (1979). A multicultural analysis of the popular basal reading series in the International Year of the Child. *Journal of Negro Education, 57,* 382-389.

Canfield, J. (1970). White teacher, black school. In Kevin Ryan (Ed.), *Don't smile until Christmas.* Chicago: University of Chicago Press.

Carbo, M., & Hodges, H. (1988). Learning styles strategies can help students at risk. *Teaching Exceptional Children, 20*(4), 55-58.

Carnegie Forum on Education and the Economy. (1986). *A nation prepared: Teachers for the 21st century* (Report of the Task Force on Teaching as a Profession). New York: Author.

Cheyney, A. (1967). *Teaching culturally disadvantaged in the elementary school.* Columbus, OH: Merrill.

Cobbs, P. (1988). Critical perspectives on the psychology of race. In T. Dewart (Ed.), *The state of black America 1988* (pp. 61-70). New York: National Urban League.

Coleman, J. S., Campbell, E. G., Hobson, C. J., McPartland, J., Mood, A. M., Weinfield, E. B., & York, R. L. (1966). *Equality of educational opportunity.* Washington, DC: U.S. Department of Health, Education and Welfare.

Committee on the Study of Teaching Materials in Intergroup Relations. (1949). *Intergroup relations in teaching materials.* Washington, DC: American Council of Education.

Costo, R., & Henry, J. (1970). *Textbooks and the American Indian.* San Francisco: Indian Historical Press.

Decent affordable housing for all. (1988, January 25). New York Times, p. Y23.

Decker, S. (1969). *An empty spoon.* New York: Scholastic Book Services.

Dunfee, M. (1974). *Eliminating ethnic bias.* Alexandria, VA: Association for Supervision and Curriculum Development.

Ellison, R. (1966). *Shadow and act.* New York: Signet.

Erickson, F. (1987). Transformation and school success: The politics and culture of educational achievement. *Anthropology and Education Quarterly, 18,* 335-356.

Erikson, E. (1963). *Childhood and society* (2nd ed.). New York: Norton.

Gibson, M. (1987). The school performance of immigrant minorities: A comparative view. *Anthropology and Education Quarterly, 18,* 262-275.

Gordon, B. (1988). Implicit assumptions of the Holmes and Carnegie reports: A view from an African-American perspective. *Journal of Negro Education, 57,* 141-158.

Gordon, E. (1979). Human diversity, pedagogy and educational equity. *American Psychologist, 34,* 1030-1036.

Gould, R. (1978). *Transformations.* New York: Simon and Schuster.

Gouldner, H. (1978). *Teachers' pets, troublemakers, and nobodies*. Westport, CT: Greenwood.

Grant, C., & Sleeter, C. (1986). *After the school bell rings*. Philadelphia: Falmer.

Grant, G. (1972). On equality of educational opportunity. *Harvard Educational Review, 42*, 109-125.

Grant, G. (1978). Values/diversity in education: A progress report. *Educational Leadership, 35*, 6, 443-448.

Guthrie, J. W. (1972, July 22). What the Coleman reanalysis didn't tell us. *Saturday Review/Education*, pp. 30, 45.

Hale, J. (1982). *Black children: Their roots, culture, and learning styles*. Provo, UT: Brigham Young University Press.

Harris, S., & Harris, L. (1988). *The teacher's almanac*. New York: Hudson Group.

Harrington, M. (1984). *The new American poverty*. New York: Holt, Rinehart and Winston.

Havinghurst, R. (1976). The relative importance of social class and ethnicity in human development. *Human Development, 19*, 56-64.

Henderson, R. (1980). Social and emotional needs of culturally diverse children. *Exceptional Children, 46*, 598-605.

Ihle, E. L. (1986). *Black girls and women in elementary education: History of black women's education in the south, 1865-present* (Instructional Modules for Educators, Module I). Washington, DC: U.S. Department of Education, Women's Educational Equity Act Program.

Johnson, T. (1989). *Poll finds blacks and whites worlds apart*. New York: NAACP Legal Defense Fund.

Kane, M. B. (1970). *Minorities in textbooks: A study of their treatment in social studies texts*. Chicago: Quadrangle.

Kendall, F. E. (1983). *Diversity in the classroom: A multicultural approach to the education of young children*. New York: Teachers College Press.

Longstreet, W. (1978). *Aspects of ethnicity: Understanding differences in pluralistic classrooms*. New York: Teachers College Press.

Lundsteen, S. (1978). *Cultural factor in learning and instruction*. New York: Columbia University (ERIC Document Reproduction Service ED 162 012).

McDermott, R. (1987). The explanation of minority school failure, again. *Anthropology and Education Quarterly, 18*, 361-392.

Michigan Department of Public Instruction. (1963). *The treatment of minority groups in textbooks*. Lansing: Author.

Morine, H., & Morine, G. (1970). *A primer for the inner-city school*. New York: McGraw-Hill.

Morris, L. (1978). *Extracting learning styles from social and cultural diversity: A study of American minorities*. Washington, DC: Department of Health, Education and Welfare.

Mosteller, F., & Moynihan, D. (1972). *On equality of educational opportunity*. New York: Random House.

Oakes, J. (1985). *Keeping track*. Binghamton, NY: Vail-Ballou.

Ogbu, J. U. (1987). Variability in minority school performance: A problem in search of an explanation. *Anthropology and Education Quarterly, 18*, 312-334.

Okun, B. (1984). *Working with adults: Individual, family and career development.* Monterey, CA: Brooks/Cole.

Orfield, G. (1987). School desegregation needed now. *Focus, 15*(7), 5-7.

Parkay, F. (1983). *White teacher, black school.* New York: Praeger.

Payne, C. (1984). *Getting what we ask for: The ambiguity of success and failure in urban education.* Westport, CT: Greenwood.

Reissman, F. (1962). *The culturally deprived child.* New York: Harper & Row.

Reissman, F. (1976). *The inner-city child.* New York: Harper & Row.

Romero, M., Mercado, C., & Vázquez-Faría, J. (1987). Students of limited English proficiency. In V. Richardson-Koehler (Ed.), *Educators' handbook: A research perspective* (pp. 348-389). New York: Longman.

Rossi, P. (1961). Social factors in academic achievement: A brief review. In A. H. Halsey, J. Flond, & C. Anderson (Eds.), *Education, economy and society* (pp. 269-272). New York: Free Press.

Shade, B. (1981). *Afro-American cognitive style: A variable in school success?* Madison: University of Wisconsin, Madison Research and Development Center for Individual Schooling.

Shade, B. (1982). *Afro-American patterns of cognition.* Madison: University of Wisconsin, Wisconsin Center for Education Research.

Sleeter, C., & Grant, C. (1989). Student cultural knowledge versus classroom knowledge. In C. Sleeter (Ed.), *Empowerment through multicultural education.* Buffalo: SUNY Press.

Sleeter, C., & Grant, C. (1991). *Race, class, gender, and disability in current textbooks.* New York: Routledge and Chapman.

Spangler, K. (1982). *Cognitive styles and the Mexican-American child: A review of literature.* Unpublished manuscript, University of Alaska, Anchorage. (ERIC Document Reproduction Service No. ED 221 285)

Spring, J. (1972). *Education and the rise of the corporate state.* Boston: Beacon.

Steering blacks around islands of whites. (1987, December 15). *New York Times,* p. Y16.

Stodolsky, S., & Lessen, G. (1967). Learning patterns in the disadvantaged. *Harvard Educational Review, 37,* 546-593.

Terman, L. (1916). *The measurement of intelligence.* Boston: Houghton Mifflin.

Today's numbers, tomorrow's nation. (1986, May 14). *Education Week,* p. 14.

Trubowitz, S. (1968). *A handbook for teaching in the ghetto school.* Chicago: Quadrangle.

Trueba, H. (1988). Culturally based explanations of minority students' academic achievement. *Anthropology and Education Quarterly, 19,* 270-287.

U.S. Department of Commerce, Bureau of the Census. (1981). *Statistical abstract of the United States.* Washington, DC: U.S. Government Printing Office.

U.S. Department of Commerce, Bureau of Statistics. (1979). *The social and economic status of the black population in the United States: An historical view, 1890-1978.* Washington, DC: U.S. Government Printing Office.

Wacquant, L., & Wilson, W. (1989). The cost of racial and class exclusion in the inner city. *Annals, AAPSS, 501,* 8-25.

Ward, T. (1973). Cognitive processes and learning: Reflections on a comparative study of cognitive style in fourteen African societies, *Comparative Education Review, 17,* 1-10.

Webster, S. (1966a). *Educating the disadvantaged learner.* San Francisco: Chandler.

Webster, S. (1966b). *Knowing the disadvantaged.* San Francisco: Chandler.

Weinberg, M. (1977). *Minority students: A research appraisal.* Washington, DC: National Institutes of Health.

Weisner, T., Gallimore, R., & Jordan, C. (1988). Unpackaging cultural effects on classroom learning: Native Hawaiian peer assistance and child-generated activity. *Anthropology and Education Quarterly, 19,* 327-353.

What it's like to be in Hell. (1987, December 4). *New York Times,* p. Y16.

Why economists can't say why the poor get poorer. (1988, January 18). *New York Times,* p. E5.

Zeichner, K., & Gore, J. (1990). Teacher socialization. In W. R. Houston (Ed.), *Handbook of research on teacher education.* New York: Macmillan.

14

What Teachers Need to Know About Cultural Diversity: Restoring Subject Matter to the Picture

G. WILLIAMSON McDIARMID

Most discussions of what teachers need to know about cultural diversity focus on what teachers need to know about learners—their interactional or learning styles, their social norms and cultural values, their relations to social and political structures. Grant moves considerably beyond these formulations with his discussion of teachers' biographies and of the relationship between teacher and learner. Absent from his and other discussions of culture, though, has been a consideration of the relationship between the learner and *the subject matter*. I propose to restore subject matter to considerations of what teachers need to know about students from diverse cultural backgrounds. What teachers most need to know about diverse learners concerns their relationship to knowledge, the meaning and value they have constructed from their experiences outside school, and their encounters with subject matter inside school.

Yet, even as I argue for such knowledge and understanding, I am aware that many of the issues that teachers face in teaching culturally diverse learners are genuine dilemmas. For example, I remember holding a spirited discussion with a group of fourth-grade Yup'ik Eskimo students about a walk-in cooler that had broken down in a school. As we worked to fix the cooler, we talked about freon gas and gases in general, and I had them speculate about what the compressor did to the gas. After a lengthy analysis of the cooling system and how it worked (and how it didn't work), I asked, "So, why did the walk-in break down?" One of the students who had been most involved in the conversation replied, "Ghosts."

She was not joking. Spirits are part of the life of the Yup'ik Eskimo people. So how was I, as their teacher, supposed to handle this? Did I gently point out that there may be physical causes? Did I laugh it off? Did I ignore it? What role did these beliefs play in my students' thinking about other subjects? Did I need to address the issue once and for all, knowing that it was part of their framework for understanding whatever they encountered in school? What kind of trouble would this get me into with the students, with the community, with my fellow teachers who were also Yup'ik?

Such dilemmas are commonplace in the experience of teachers who work with culturally diverse students. Even a deep understanding of both subject matter and students does not resolve for us the dilemmas of teaching such children. Nor does it solve the dilemma that the children who most need the knowledge, understandings, and skills that teachers could provide are the same children who are least likely to *value* school knowledge. Yet, without the knowledge and understandings for which I am arguing, teachers are woefully ill equipped to struggle with these dilemmas. Rather than seeing such knowledge as a solution to the dilemmas of teaching culturally diverse learners, I see it as a bare necessity.

In thinking about this issue, I have drawn on several sources of data. The first is the 1989 Teacher Education and Learning to Teach (TELT) study of the National Center for Research on Teacher Education. By surveying, interviewing, and observing prospective teachers, we have been trying to see what teachers and prospective teachers know and what they learn from teacher education programs about teaching mathematics and writing to diverse learners. A second source is my experience as a classroom teacher at the secondary, middle school, and elementary levels in a variety of cultures—Greek, African, Alaskan Native, European, and the rural American South. Finally, as a teacher educator, I have tried to understand how my mostly white, mostly middle-class students think about teaching students with whom they share few values, few expectations, and few common experiences, either in or out of school.

David Hawkins (1974) has argued that what distinguishes the teacher-learner relationship from other adult-child relationships is the participants' mutual involvement with something outside themselves. Hawkins writes, "Adults and children, like adults with each other, can associate well only in worthy interests and pursuits, only through a community of subject matter and engagement which extends *beyond* the circle of intimacy" (p. 49). To represent this relationship, Hawkins proposes what he calls the I-Thou-It triangle, in which I (the teacher), Thou (the learner), and It (the subject matter) constitute the three corners.

This representation seems apt because it not only keeps subject matter in the picture but places it on an equal basis with the teacher and the learner. Rather than being taken for granted or an afterthought, subject matter is in the triangle, to be considered in any discussion of teaching and learning. What changes, what varies from one discussion to the next, one context to the next, one classroom to the next, and, indeed, one subject matter to the next are the particular factors that condition each pair of relationships in the triangle: the relationship between learners and subject matter, between teacher and subject matter, and between teacher and learners. Moreover, teachers not only must understand these relationships but must understand them well enough to generate some good ideas about how to improve all of them. As Hawkins (1974) notes, the quality of the adult-child relationship hinges on the participants' mutual engagement "in worthy interests and pursuits." Teachers are responsible for representing the subject matter as "worthy interests and pursuits,"(p. 49) especially to learners whose experience both inside and outside school may lead them to believe that subject matter knowledge is worthless.

In what follows, I will argue that teachers need to know about and address the values and understandings their learners bring with them; that this knowledge is as critical to their capacity to represent content meaningfully to diverse learners as is knowledge of the subject matter; and that teachers also need to know how arrangements such as ability grouping and tracking can create differences in what different students learn and in how they understand subject matter content.

LEARNERS' RELATIONSHIPS TO THE SUBJECT MATTER

Many students think school knowledge has little to do with them, their friends, and family. They don't know where the information and ideas in their textbooks and about which their teachers talk come from, why they need to learn these things, and what such things have to do with them and the world in which they live. For some students, the disembodied and alien nature of what they are expected to learn is less problematic than it is for others. Yet, despite this apparent lack of meaning, some students grow up believing, as an article of faith, that school knowledge is important and that doing well in school will be rewarded. They see examples of people who have gone to school, continued on to college and, in some cases, professional school, and developed financially and socially rewarding careers. And their peers, like-minded students, tend to reinforce the importance of learning what is taught in schools. These students rarely question the ultimate value of the knowledge they encounter in schools; they take it as it comes, try to remember what their teachers and the textbooks say, and on various assessments reproduce as best they can what they've learned.

Other students, particularly poor children and those of color, may see little evidence of the value of school knowledge. They may know few people who have done well in school and continued their education. If they know such people, they are likely to consider them anomalies, weirdos, and "dweebs" who cravenly conform to the expectations of the teachers and administration. In their study of an all-black high school in Washington, DC, Signithia Fordham and John Ogbu found that "peer group pressures against academic striving take many forms, including labeling (e.g., 'brainiac' for students who receive good grades in their courses), exclusion from peer activities or ostracism, and physical assault" (cited in Ravitch, 1989). Grant and Sleeter (1988), discussing the views of 24 youths from a multi-ethnic neighborhood whom they followed from middle school to high school graduation, explain as follows:

> Students' everyday experience with school taught them that it was boring and that the content was irrelevant to daily life. It may be important for attaining a career goal, but if the medicine was bitter, why ask for more than the doctor prescribes? So the students accepted minimal homework and a low involvement with class work, and developed other interests and behavior patterns, centering largely around sports, that filled their time and probably would have caused them to resist a sudden increase in school work (a "what if" they never faced). (p. 36)

For these students, then, schooling and school knowledge are, at best, to be endured.

Notice that these students may be no different from successful students in their perception of the lack of relevance of school knowledge. Neither group sees a relationship between themselves and what they are expected to learn. The difference is that this second group fails to see any justification for learning school knowledge. Having witnessed few who follow the schooling route to financial and social success, these learners can't imagine themselves doing so. When I interviewed the mother of several teenagers as part of a study of why so few Alaska Natives pursue careers in the health professions, she told me: "One reason we don't get into some fields is because we don't know what's available—nobody around here is into it." She was not referring to the lack of information as much as to the lack of personal relationships with people who are health professionals. Alaska Native students literally could not imagine themselves as health professionals.

Not only do poor and nonwhite learners have little direct contact with those who have benefited from schooling, but their own daily confrontation with schooling underlines the senselessness of most of what goes on in school. Robert Everhart (1983), in his study of students in a working-class junior high school, offers numerous examples of students' encounters with unconnected knowledge that they were required to learn for its own sake. For instance, Everhart records an exchange in Mrs. Marcy's English class over vocabulary words. Everhart notes that in this class students were "expected to memorize definitions rather than to understand what a word and its relations to other words meant."

"To look over carefully or examine in detail is what, class? Roger?"
"I don't know."
"Dale?"
"Canvass."
"Right. Mike, to make or utter a chuckling sound?"
"Uh, ch-, chat, chatal or something like that."
"Close, who can help him? All right, Tina?"
"Chortle."
"Good, 'Alice chortled when she saw his clothes that day.' How about the word for modern or not long past? Yes, Philip?"
"Recent."
"Yes. Tina, you have a question?"
"Yeah, how are we going to have these words on the test tomorrow; I mean will you give us the definition and we'll have to fill in the word?"
"Yes, that's the way we've always done it and I don't see any reason to change now. Okay, how about the word for concise or pithy?"
Linda immediately raised her hand and volunteered the word *terse*.
"Good, Linda." Linda turned to Tina next to her, smiled triumphantly, and said, "I'll always remember that one because she uses the word 'pithy'." (p. 58)

A comparison of how vocabulary is learned inside and outside schools points up not merely the artificial and disembodied nature of activities such as Everhart describes but their ineffectiveness as well (Miller & Gildea, 1987). Not only is the meaning of a word dependent on its context, but the learners' understanding of that meaning is similarly dependent on their prior experience and knowledge as well as the classroom context in which the word is used (Brown, Collins, & Duguid, 1989). Confronted by a succession of similar encounters with disembodied information that they are expected to remember and reproduce, unengaged learners confirm over and over again their view that school knowledge is an end in itself, unconnected to the world outside school.

Given their experience with school subject matter, many students develop views of various subjects as disconnected bodies of facts, rules, and procedures, so that subsequent encounters with the subjects are conditioned by this view. They learn to expect subject matter knowledge to be boring, disconnected, and meaningless. This point is particularly salient for teachers who would like to help students understand subject matter knowledge as meaningful, historically and socially constructed, and traceable to our efforts to understand the social and natural world. Even though many students find their encounters with subject matter knowledge boring and mechanical, they come to regard the school's definition of knowledge in certain areas as the only one, in the absence of competing ideas. Consequently, teachers who choose to depart from such a conception of knowledge and skills may meet with resistance from learners and their parents.

TEACHERS' RELATIONSHIP TO THE SUBJECT MATTER

Teachers portray subject matter to students through the topics, questions, and ideas they present to students; the sequence in which they present these substantive matters; the kinds of discourse they encourage in the classroom and the kinds of activities they organize; the examples, illustrations, analogies, metaphors, and so on that they employ to represent concepts to students; the textbooks and other materials that they and the students use; and what they choose to evaluate and how they do it.

A critical issue is how teachers go about deciding which representations they will use. Teachers must evaluate various representations not only for how well they portray the concepts being taught but also for the opportunities they offer students to understand the ideas. Consequently, representations depend both on teachers' understanding of subject matter and on their understanding of the learners they teach.

Teachers are themselves, however, products of schools that are probably similar to those in which they teach, at least in the ways knowledge is defined and taught. Evidence that teaching practices have been pretty stable throughout this century seems fairly persuasive (Cuban, 1984). Despite the dizzying rate at which information is expanding, the view that the knowledge pupils should learn in schools is fixed, agreed upon, and reproducible on various assessments pervades not merely schools but our society as a whole (Cohen, 1989). And the knowledge presented at colleges and universities does not differ greatly from that presented in K-12 school settings (Bennett, 1984; Boyer, 1987; McDiarmid, 1990). Most disciplines are presented as bodies of facts, procedures, theories, and ideas that need to be memorized with no apparent purpose. So, after receiving a college degree, teachers have subject matter knowledge that may differ from that of their students in the sheer number of facts and ideas they can recall, but their understanding of the underlying concepts in a field may be scarcely greater than that of their students. They may still see few or no connections among ideas and information within a field or between disciplines; may still not understand the nature of knowledge in the field or how new knowledge is generated and tested or who helped generate this knowledge; and may still hold their own grade-school notions of how the subject matter is taught and learned (Ball & McDiarmid, 1990).

Teachers, then, may perceive subject matter knowledge just as learners do—as a given, a part of the landscape that is school, as only tenuously and vaguely related to the world beyond the school walls. When prospective teachers were asked what they would say to students who complained about having to learn regrouping in addition since they had calculators, few could come up with reasons likely to convince unengaged students (Neufeld, 1988). One prospective teacher suggested, lamely,

> Sometimes your calculator's batteries run out. And you need to balance your checkbook. . . . I'd say, "You're not always going to have your calculator with you." (p. 10)

Another, reflecting the somewhat circular logic that what is taught in school is important because schools teach and test it, offered the following rejoinder:

> When you're taking different tests, you're not allowed to have a calculator. So what are you going to do then? (p. 11)

Teachers' understanding of the origins of subject matter, of who has contributed to the development of ideas in the field, and of the connections to the broader world determines in large part their own relationship to the subject matter as well as their view of their students' relation to it. Teachers who see themselves and their students as capable of generating as well as consuming knowledge represent the subject matter in fundamentally different ways than do teachers who see knowledge as received and themselves and their students as consumers. Teachers and students who debate whether zero is odd or even, and what it means to divide 3 by 16, or who undertake to write a history of the buildings in their neighborhood or of the local transportation system develop together conceptions of mathematics and history in which they are included and in which they come to view themselves as capable of doing what experts in the field do.

Teachers' capacity to evaluate the appropriateness of the representations they make of their subject matter depends, then, on their view of learners as well as on their understanding of the learners' relationship to the subject matter. Representations need to take into account what learners are already likely to know and understand about the subject matter as well as the experiences and knowledge they bring with them from their environment. Representations may be appropriate either because they draw on learners' initial understandings or—if these initial understandings of the subject contravene those of most people in the field—because they force learners to confront their taken-for-granted understandings (Floden, Buchmann, & Schwille, 1987).

As this discussion demonstrates, teachers' subject matter knowledge for teaching involves their understandings of the relationship of the learners to the subject matter. Representations, however faithful they may be to the subject matter, are useful and appropriate only insofar as they address the understandings and experience of the learners for whom they are intended. As classrooms contain learners who may differ dramatically in their past experiences with the subject matter, in their initial understandings, in the value they place on the subject matter, in their view of themselves as doers of the subject matter, and in their understanding of the relationship between the subject matter and the world outside school, teachers must be able to generate a variety of representations for any given idea. The differences the teacher needs to be concerned about are the differences in students' relationships to the subject matter. These are the differences often neglected in teacher preparation programs.

THE RELATIONSHIP BETWEEN TEACHER AND LEARNER

The third side of Hawkins' triangle represents the relationship of the teacher and the learner. Much of the literature on cultural diversity has focused on this relationship, in particular on the interactions between culturally different teachers and learners, interactions that the various actors interpret according to their experiences, beliefs, and values. I would like to take a different tack, premised on Hawkins' contention that it is the mutual concern with subject matter that distinguishes the teacher-learner relationship from other adult-child relationships. Consequently, I focus on aspects of the teacher-learner relationship that are likely to influence the shared interest in subject matter. As in all relationships, perceptions and beliefs travel in two directions.

In discussing teachers' beliefs, I will be relying heavily on data from the Teacher Education and Learning to Teach Study (1989) of the National Center for Research on Teacher Education. While most of the data comes from preservice teacher education programs, our early analyses indicate that on many dimensions, most teachers' beliefs and views do not change dramatically in response to their teacher education program. I will focus, in keeping with Hawkins' notion of the I-Thou-It triangle, on teachers' views and beliefs of learners as learners of subject matter.

The first thing to note about prospective teachers' views of learners is that most, like most practicing teachers we interviewed, reject stereotyping of students even when the stereotypes are not derogatory. Teachers are quick to point out that each child is different, each is unique. Indeed, this belief is so widely held and proclaimed as to constitute a dogma. When we asked them what kinds of differences among learners are important to consider in teaching, prospective teachers spurned ethnicity, gender, and social class, asserting that all students should be treated the same. Differences that were important to them involved personality and behavior—that is, whether children were shy, disruptive, motivated, and so on (Paine, 1988).

For prospective teachers we interviewed, what follows from the dogma of the uniqueness of each child is a concomitant belief that each child has individual needs that the teacher is responsible to address. The best way of addressing these needs is by individualizing classroom tasks—indeed, prospective teachers in our sample thought teachers ought to tailor instruction to individual differences (Paine, 1988). However, these are the same people who unequivocally and consistently asserted the imperative to treat all children the same regardless of their ethnic or social class background. This is an important point, for the perceived importance of individualizing can yield discriminatory behaviors. For instance, we gave teacher candidates in the TELT study a description of a classroom in which the teacher was individualizing instruction and asked them to judge this teacher's strategies for individualizing. In fact, the teacher in this scenario gives a student from a low socioeconomic background a mindless task and gives a student from a higher socioeconomic background a more meaningful task. When presented with this scenario, only about 10% of our sample disapproved of the individualized academic tasks, even though the tasks represented the subject in radically different ways and offered clearly different knowledge and skills to the students.

What is going on here? On the one hand, these prospective teachers are proclaiming their commitment to equal treatment for all, and on the other hand, they approve of unequal opportunities to learn subject matter. Are they merely confused or frankly prejudiced? Are they unwitting ciphers in a society that reproduces itself over and over again by ensuring that students from different social classes learn their place in the economic order?

What these teachers believe is, in fact, consistent with the way in which society has dealt with differences among students throughout this century (Cohen, 1984). Even as schools were opening their doors to an increasingly diverse student population, they were differentiating among these students. As the number of immigrant children attending U. S. schools progressed geometrically during the first two decades of this century, tracking and ability grouping became part of the warp and woof of life and organization in schools (Cohen, 1984). The desegregation of schools in the South and in northern cities coincided, in the 1960s and early 1970s, with the advent of Title I and special education programs, further differentiating children. In the 1970s, various schemes for individualized education represented—for reformers, administrators, and teachers alike—the latest remedy for whatever ailed American schools.

So the idea of treating all groups the same by treating all students differently is not a paradox for which prospective teachers can claim authorship. Sanctioned by its embodiment in school policy and organization and, more recently, in instruction, this paradoxical view of treating differences among learners conditions how teachers view learners. If all learners are different, what are the sources of these differences, according to prospective teachers? As noted earlier, teachers are quick to deny that ethnicity and social class per se are differences to which teachers need attend in teaching. Instead, they talk about either personality factors—for example, shyness—or motivation. Motivation is a key concept in prospective teachers' views of differences among students. Some trace motivation back to the learners' families, as in the following:

Higher SES kids usually come from more motivated backgrounds, education-wise. You would have to know that if you got an entire class of low-SES kids, you are going to have to work on motivation much more than if you are working with upper middle-class kids. (Paine, 1988, p. 9)

Others, more than 40%, seem to think that students are responsible for their own lack of motivation; that is, they have a bad attitude. One prospective teacher, in reaction to one of the teaching scenarios in our interview, justified a teacher's isolating a student who is described in the scenario as being "so active he sometimes disrupts others," as follows:

> He's, you know, he's, he's grown up with this attitude and you know he's not going to get rid of it in one year. She can help, ya know, and she can possibly get him going along with the class and not disrupting the class and making progress, but she's not going to solve the problem by herself. (Teacher Education and Learning to Teach Study, 1989)

By defining the problem as one of motivation, prospective teachers have also suggested the remedy: The teacher must motivate students to learn. How do prospective teachers believe students can be motivated to learn? They indicated either by praise, or what they call "positive reinforcement," or by getting the students to view the subject matter of school as "fun" (Teacher Education and Learning to Teach Study, 1989; McDiarmid & Price, 1990).

The importance of praising students and positively reinforcing appropriate behaviors, like the notion that every child is unique, approaches the category of dogma among teachers. In the scenario mentioned above, prospective teachers rarely commented on the tasks the children were assigned or their backgrounds; rather, they were most likely to focus on the teachers' use of praise. As one prospective teacher explained about the teachers' decision to individualize,

> [The teacher] knows what students are capable of doing what tasks. And those that are below average and having a hard time, she's giving a lot of comfort to [Vicki]. . . . She's letting James know that he is doing a good job even though he is not capable of keeping up with the rest of the students. (Teacher Education and Learning to Teach Study, 1989)

What is troubling about these prospective teachers' views is their lack of attention to students as learners of subject matter. More teachers and prospective teachers believe that deficiencies in the learners—lack of a good home life, ability, or enthusiasm—account for school failures than believe that poor teaching is responsible. Most seem to believe that the differences that matter in school are individual differences of personality and attitude and that the way to address these is by individualizing—that is, differentiating the tasks that students do.

At the same time, there seems to be little awareness that differentiating tasks and assigning them on the basis of students' perceived ability may result in unequal opportunities to learn the subject matter. Teachers, particularly elementary teachers, may not think of themselves as representatives of their subject matter, but that is what they are for their students.

CONCLUSION

So what is it that teachers need to know about cultural diversity? Using Hawkins' representation of teaching as a three-cornered relationship among teachers, learners, and subject matter, I argue that teachers need to understand all three pairs of relationships in the triangle, how those relationships have been formed, and how they can be improved.

Student-Subject Matter Relationships

1. Teachers need to know how school knowledge is perceived in their learners' cultures—their peer, family, and community cultures. Resistance to school authority and knowledge among poor, working-class, and minority youngsters is well documented. '

2. Teachers need to know what kind of knowledge, skills, and commitments are valued in the learners' cultures. Such knowledge is critical to developing representations of subject matter that either bridge or confront the knowledge and understandings that learners bring with them.

3. Teachers need to know about students' prior knowledge of and experience with the subject matter. The frameworks of understanding, based on prior experience, that learners use to make sense out of new ideas and information are also critical if teachers are to represent their subject matter in ways that help students understand.

I can't leave these ideas without addressing the issue of where teachers learn these things. If teachers are to discover what their learners understand, value, and are curious about, the teachers must create opportunities for learners to talk about these things in the context of the subject matter. Creating opportunities to talk and listening to what learners say also convey to students respect for them as people whose ideas may be of value to others and who are capable of understanding new ideas.

Teacher-Subject Matter Relationship

1. Teachers' ideas about how a given subject matter is taught and learned
    determine, in part, the kinds of opportunities they create for learners to
    understand.

2. Because of differences in learners' prior experience and understandings,
    teachers need a repertoire of different representations for a given idea,
    concept, or procedure. Teachers' ability to generate or adapt representations
    and their capacity to judge the appropriateness of representations for
    different learners depend, probably equally, on their understanding of their
    subject matter and their knowledge of their learners.

3. Teachers' understanding of the relationship of their subject matter to the
    world enables them to help students understand these connections. Such
    connections are critical to learners' need to see the relationship between
    what they are studying in school and the world in which they live. Such
    connections are critical if teachers are to help disadvantaged learners
    increase their control over and within their environment.

Teacher-Student Relationship

1. Teachers need to understand the role that they and schools play in limiting
    access to vital subject matter knowledge by addressing what they define as
    individual differences through organizational arrangements such as
    individualization, tracking, and ability grouping.

2. Teachers also need to know that, for learners, they are representatives of
    their subject matter. If they represent mathematics as repetitious drill and
    practice, and if they express negative attitudes toward mathematics, their
    learners are likely to develop similar beliefs and attitudes.

3. Teachers need to consider their role in the classroom and how that role
    shapes the roles students assume. If students are to explore problems and
    ideas with classmates, teachers need to consider how their behavior
    facilitates or inhibits such collaboration.

In sum, teachers can be exquisitely sensitive to differences among their
students and be knowledgeable about various cultural groups from which their
students come; yet, if they lack a conceptual understanding of the subject matter,
they may be unable to help their students develop meaningful understandings of
school subjects. Alternatively, teachers may be formidably knowledgeable about
the subject matter, yet be unable to render the subject meaningful to students and

unable to help students learn it. Knowledge of subject matter, of students, and of the relationship between the two are all necessary to teaching.

REFERENCES

Ball, D. L., & McDiarmid, G. W. (1990). The subject matter preparation of teachers. In W. R. Houston (Ed.), *Handbook of research on teacher education*. New York: Macmillan.

Bennett, W. (1984). *To reclaim a legacy: A report on the humanities in higher education.* Washington, DC: National Endowment for the Humanities.

Boyer, E. (1987). *College: The undergraduate experience in America.* New York: Harper & Row.

Brown, J. S., Collins, A., & Duguid, P. (1989). Situated cognition and the culture of learning. *Educational Researcher, 18*(1), 32-42.

Cohen, D. K. (1984). The American common school: A divided vision. *Education and Urban Society, 16,* 253-261.

Cohen, D. K. (1989). Teaching practice: Plus ça change . . . (Issue Paper 88-3). East Lansing: Michigan State University, National Center for Research on Teacher Education.

Cuban, L. (1984). *How teachers taught: Constancy and change in American classrooms, 1890-1980.* New York: Longman.

Everhart, R. B. (1983). *Reading, writing and resistance: Adolescence and labor in a junior high school.* Boston: Routledge & Kegan Paul.

Floden, R., Buchmann, M., & Schwille, J. (1987). Breaking with everyday experience. *Teachers College Record, 88,* 485-506.

Grant, C., & Sleeter, C. E. (1988). Race, class, and gender and abandoned dreams. *Teachers College Record, 90,* 19-40.

Hawkins, D. (1974). I-thou-it. In *The informed vision: Essays on learning and human nature* (pp. 48-62). New York: Agathon Press.

McDiarmid, G. W. (1990). The liberal arts: Will more result in better prepared teachers? *Theory Into Practice, 29,* 21-29.

McDiarmid, G. W., & Price, J. (1990). Prospective teachers' views of diverse learners. A study of participants in the ABCD project. East Lansing: Michigan State University National Center for Research on Teacher Education.

Miller, G. A., & Gildea, P. M. (1987). How children learn words. *Scientific American, 257*(3), 94-99.

Neufeld, B. (1988, April). *Why do I have to learn that? Prospective teachers' ideas about the importance of the subjects they will teach.* Paper presented at the annual meeting of the American Educational Research Association, New Orleans.

Paine, L. (1988, April). *Orientations towards diversity: What do prospective teachers bring?* Paper presented at the annual meeting of the American Educational Research Association, New Orleans.

Ravitch, D. (1989, March 6). Back to basics. *The New Republic,* pp. 13-15.

Teacher Education and Learning to Teach Study (1989). Unpublished raw data. East Lansing: Michigan State University, National Center for Research on Teacher Education.

Part III

CONCLUSION

15

Merging Subjects and Students into Teaching Knowledge

MARY M. KENNEDY

The viewpoints offered in these chapters present a dilemma: They are quite diverse, yet each by itself is credible. Since each is credible alone, it would be foolish to select one from each group and reject the others. Moreover, within every group, we learn something from the *juxtaposition* of these perspectives that adds to what we learn from the individual chapters. The differences between C. Anderson and Lawson in science, between Banks and Wilson in history, and between Romano and Hillocks in writing help us better understand these academic subjects. In most cases, these authors are not describing different phenomena, but rather different perspectives on the same phenomenon. For instance, Lawson describes science as a process of discovery of the nature of things via the creative generation of alternative hypotheses and their testing, whereas Anderson describes science as a process of *collective* sense making. Neither definition is contrary to the other; they merely emphasize different aspects of science. Similarly, Floden, Engelmann, and A. Anderson are not talking about different phenomena. All of them are talking about how students learn. Viewing these phenomena from multiple vantage points allows us to understand them far better than we could from only one vantage point.

Few outsiders of a discipline have such opportunities. And few teachers have such opportunities. If teachers had the kind of multifaceted, deep understanding of academic subject and of diverse learners that these authors describe, if they viewed their academic subject and their diverse learners from the multiple perspectives described here, we would not be worrying about education as we continually do in this country. Indeed, very few teachers hold the kind of knowledge that these authors described individually, let alone the ability to view either their subject or their learners from more than one perspective.

This is not to say that teachers have not taken courses in academic subjects or courses in learning or child development, but rather that they have not obtained through these courses the kind of knowledge that the authors of this volume describe. The term *liberal education* is often used to mean that students are exposed to multiple perspectives on various phenomena—that their education has broadened their perspective. But instead of the integrated knowledge and deep understanding that our authors advocate, college often simply helps students accumulate discrete pieces of subject matter knowledge. It is not only possible but likely that students will finish college with the impression that each subject consists of an agglomeration of numerous pieces of knowledge and that they will be unsure whether or how the pieces are related.

This disparity in outcomes between a liberal education and a college education occurs with respect to dispositions as well. Many of the authors of this volume described attitudes toward subject matter knowledge or toward learning that should arise from a liberal education but that do not necessarily obtain from a college education or from majoring in a particular subject. Clemens lists numerous attitudes he wants in a mathematics teacher: He wants a teacher to be humble, unafraid, reverent, opportunistic, and versatile, for instance. Indeed, Clemens defines his topic not as what teachers should *know*, but rather as what they should *be*.

The problem is multiplied for those college graduates who plan to teach, for they must not only integrate content within and across academic subjects, but must also integrate their knowledge of academic subjects with knowledge of diverse learners. If each teacher must have the full depth and breadth of understanding suggested here, and must have this quality of knowledge both about the academic subject and about diverse learners, and if, furthermore, these two aspects of their knowledge must be integrated into a body of knowledge about *teaching* academic subjects to diverse learners, then we have a serious problem: We are unlikely to educate more than a handful of teachers to have the full range of knowledge described here, let alone produce an entire teaching population that meets this standard.

The most prevalent solution to this problem is to reduce the knowledge burden of teaching by creating specialist positions. Secondary schools, and even many elementary schools, recognize academic subject specialties, and elementary schools often also recognize specialization according to the type of child the teacher works with. Thus we have remedial teachers, bilingual teachers, and special education teachers, as well as teachers of music, mathematics, or language arts. Sometimes teachers are specialists in both a type of child and a subject, so that, for instance, we could have a remedial reading teacher or a vocational special education teacher.

But specialization alone does not reduce the knowledge burden enough to make it manageable either for teachers or for teacher educators. The optimal package of knowledge and understanding, even within a given academic subject, is still tremendous. The ideal specialist in teaching writing, for instance, is someone who is a writer, as Romano suggests; who knows the research on teaching writing, as Hillocks suggests; and who is familiar enough with the different schools of thought in writing that she or he can develop a coherent and defensible approach to writing instruction, as Gage suggests. In addition this person also understands diverse learners and how diverse learners learn to write, and can examine his or her diverse learners through the eyes of Floden, Engelmann, A. Anderson, Grant, and McDiarmid. And the social studies, as Wilson points out, themselves comprise numerous disciplines. Her suggestion is that teachers specialize in one of these subjects, but that they be required to know at least something about the *nature* of the other social studies subjects—about how economics differs from political science, for instance, and how history differs from anthropology. Such knowledge would, contends Wilson, at least enable teachers to learn more about these various areas of study. In the absence of such understanding, teachers may hold misconceptions that prevent them from learning.

Another approach to reducing the knowledge burden of teaching consists of partitioning the task of teaching in some way that emulates the partitioning that occurs in other professions: Physicians, lawyers, and architects, for instance, rely not only on specialists but also on a variety of assistants. Though physicians make most of the important decisions about patient treatments, many of the diagnostic tests and actual treatments are provided by nurses, nurses' assistants, and lab technicians. But teachers often do not want to delegate tasks, for even apparently mundane tasks can provide opportunities for teachers to learn more about their students. Moreover, teaching is a highly personal activity, and teachers often feel that their relationship with their students might be jeopardized if an assistant took over some of the teachers' responsibilities. Because of these special characteristics of teaching, it has proved difficult to find satisfactory ways of partitioning the work.

Finally, an often-advocated solution to teachers' knowledge burden is simply to declare that only one of these bodies of knowledge really requires formal education and that the other can be picked up on the job. Some people argue, for instance, that teachers need mainly to know their academic subject, and can learn about learners in the process of teaching them. Equally popular is the view that it is more important for teachers to know about diverse learners, either because they can rely on textbooks to take care of the subject matter or because they will actually come to understand the subject better through the process of teaching it.

But teachers do not teach academic subjects in the absence of diverse learners, nor do they teach diverse learners in the absence of academic subjects. The interdependence between these two objects of teaching is apparent in the chapters in this volume, for even though each author was asked to write about *either* an academic subject *or* an aspect of diverse learners, most actually wrote about *both* academic subjects *and* diverse learners. It proved hard to discuss one without considering the other; academic subjects and diverse learners are the yin and yang of teaching—opposing and yet complementary forces. Teachers must respond to the demands of each, yet must do so within the constraints imposed by the other: An erudite portrayal of an important concept has no value if students can't understand it, but neither does an engaging portrayal that is inaccurate.

MODELS OF TEACHING AND LEARNING

Many of the differences we observed among our authors derive from different assumptions about what teaching consists of, and these various models represent valid and probably enduring differences of view about the nature and purpose of teaching. The arguments are so prevalent, and have persisted for so long, that they warrant further examination. Below, I review some of the more prominent models of teaching and learning, and try to demonstrate that, regardless of the model one subscribes to, teachers still must know not only about subject matter, and not only about students, but also about the relationship between the two. The models of teaching that I describe do not differ in terms of whether teachers need most to know yin or yang; instead they differ in how these two objects of teaching are assumed to constrain and define one another.

The Additive Model

Probably the most popular model of teaching is the *additive* model. In this model, the main task of the teacher is to cover content—to give students as much specific content as possible. This view of teaching academic subjects to diverse learners is most apparent in Engelmann's chapter. By *content* I mean the facts, concepts, principles, or laws that have been gathered through decades or centuries of inquiry into a subject. Academic subjects are usually presumed both to increase the volume of their content and to change the character of their content over time. Historical content, as Wilson points out, evolves with the discovery of new details about events and with the development of new interpretations of events; science content grows and changes with new research findings as well as new theoretical developments; and literary content expands with new pieces of literature and changes with new interpretations of existing pieces.

Just as an academic subject can be defined by the content it contains, learners can be defined by the content they contain. Indeed, under this model, the most critical dimension of learner diversity has to do with the content learners know and do not know. Moreover, the *difference* between what learners know, on the one hand, and what is available to be known in the subject, on the other, defines the teacher's task: The teacher tries to reduce the gap between what students know about a subject and what they *could* know.

From a conceptual standpoint, this is probably the simplest model of the teaching process. In it, both academic subjects and diverse learners are defined by the specific pieces of content that can be known or that are known by a particular learner. Yet even in this relatively straightforward, additive model of teaching, subject matter and learner are yin and yang to each other. What makes subject matter content relevant is determined not by the subject alone, but rather by what learners do not yet know. University literature teachers, for instance, rarely consider elementary grammar as part of their content, nor do college calculus teachers include long division in their definitions of mathematics. These aspects of their respective subjects are not relevant because, presumably, their students already have learned them. Similarly, the most relevant aspect of learners is inherent not in the learners themselves, but rather in what they do and do not know about the subject. Neither subject nor learner has teaching significance alone, but each gains significance when juxtaposed with the other.

The Process Model

An alternative to the additive model is the *process* model. Under this model, the main task of teaching is to help learners develop skill in the processes and methods of inquiry that enable people to function within a given academic subject. This view of teaching academic subjects to diverse learners is most apparent in Lawson's chapter on science and in Romano's chapter on writing. By *process*, I mean methods of operating, strategies, rules of evidence, and forms of argument that are or can be employed by those who contribute to the development of the academic subject. Some of these processes are tacit—a novelist may engage in a number of writing processes, such as brainstorming, drafting, revising, and so forth, and may "use" rules of sentence structure or story structure routinely, yet not be able to describe these processes and rules to someone else. Others are explicit—the historian who challenges another's findings must be able to articulate her rules of evidence. Whether tacit or explicit, though, these processes provide practitioners with the means of contributing to their field: to evaluate new ideas, challenge or defend them, interact with one another and with the subject—in general, to function within their field.

Students, too, favor certain processes and methods of inquiry, reject others, and may be unaware of still others. To the extent that diverse learners use processes that differ from those considered fruitful within a particular academic subject, the teachers' task is to reduce the discrepancy between these two sets of processes.

Though this second model of teaching places a different demand on the teacher than the first, and introduces a different form of relationship between subject matter and learner, it does not alter the essential interdependence between subject matter and learner. For the significance of a subject's particular processes derives not from the academic subject alone, but instead from the processes used by the learners; and the significance of the learners' processes is determined not by the learners alone, but instead by the difference between the learners' processes and those deemed appropriate to the subject.

The Conceptual Change Model

A third model of teaching is the *conceptual change* model. In this model, the main task of the teacher is to help students form concepts that are like the concepts formed by experts in a field. This model is particularly apparent in both chapters on science and in Floden's chapter on student learning. By *concepts*, I mean the models, hypotheses, impressions, and other mental images of phenomena, all of which constitute an important part of academic subjects. Academic subjects do not, after all, come to us prefabricated, but are instead formed by human beings. Growth in a field comes not only from the accumulation of more content, but by reformulating our understanding of the content we already have.

Students, too, form such images, but because they are novices in these fields, their images often differ from those of experts in the fields. When this occurs, the teacher's task is not to add more content to the learners, but instead to alter the concepts and images students have already formed in their attempt to make sense of the content they have encountered.

This model of teaching offers a substantially different challenge to the teacher than either the additive model or the process model presents, in that the first two models both suggest that teachers add to students' store of knowledge, whereas the third model suggests that the teacher alters the student's store. Notice too that this model increases the difficulty of many ordinary teacher tasks, such as the evaluation of student progress. Under the earlier models, teachers can evaluate by asking students to recite back the information they have acquired or to demonstrate the skills they have learned. Under the conceptual change model, teachers must somehow learn how students think about a phenomenon, perhaps through interviewing the students or examining student sketches. If students are not particularly articulate, it may be difficult for teachers to see students' thoughts well enough to know how they compare with the prevailing ideas in the field.

But although the third model introduces a different relationship between subject matter and learner, it does not eliminate the interdependency between them. Both academic subjects and diverse learners are still defined in relationship to one another. The most significant aspects of the subject are those concepts that are not understood or that are misunderstood by learners. And, conversely, the most significant aspect of the learner is the particular concept or image he or she has generated instead.

The Learning Community Model

Yet another model of teaching emphasizes the formation of a *learning community* in the classroom. This model of teaching academic subjects to diverse learners is most apparent in C. Anderson's chapter on science, Ball's chapter on mathematics, and A. Anderson's chapter on student learning. By learning community, I refer to such norms as the kind of scholarship that is valued or shunned, the kinds of findings that are considered important as opposed to routine, the kinds of issues that are considered worth pursuing, and how members of the group are expected to interact with one another. Such norms, which are often tacit, can nevertheless influence learners' perception of, and interest in, particular academic subjects. When James Watson (1968) tells the story of discovering DNA, he describes, among other things, the competitiveness he felt toward other biologists and reveals some disparaging views of women colleagues. Without realizing it, he gives us an insider's view of a highly competitive, male-dominated social norm in biology. C. Anderson argues that the European male social origins of science may alienate some students from this area of study.

Teachers may not want to enculturate their learners into this particular learning community, and may choose instead to form a learning community of their own that is less competitive and more pluralistic, while at the same time encouraging a respect for argument and for empirical evidence. In that event, the teacher's task becomes one of simultaneously using learners' norms to improve on the norms of the scholarly community, and using the norms of the scholarly community to improve on the norms of diverse learners. Thus, C. Anderson suggests that teachers have an obligation to nurture scientific values and habits of thought among all groups of students, even those for whom these values and habits of thought are more alien. Similarly, Banks argues that a major goal for social studies teachers is to help students become reflective decision makers and civic actors. These authors want students not only to learn the subject matter, but to become members of a community of individuals who draw on substantive ideas and use them to influence social and scientific progress.

This model of teaching introduces yet another form of relationship between subject matter and learner, one that may require teachers to alter not just the students, but the subject as well, in their effort to reduce the differences between students and subject matter. Teachers may choose to blend the two sets of norms, creating a new norm that respects both subject matter and student. Under this model of teaching, what is relevant about academic subjects are those norms that deviate most strongly from student norms, and what is relevant about student norms are those that deviate most strongly from subject matter norms.

The Transformational Model

A fifth model of teaching is the *transformational* model. It suggests that the teacher's task is to render academic content relevant and meaningful to diverse learners. It recognizes that students' relations with subject matter are not only substantive, but social and emotional as well. This model of teaching is suggested in both chapters on social studies, Gage's chapter on writing, Grant's chapter on diverse learners' cultural backgrounds, and McDiarmid's chapter on the relationship between students and subject matter.

Academic subjects are pursued because they are thought to be relevant and meaningful to a variety of human endeavors, yet the relevance and meaningfulness of a subject may not be apparent to students. Or different aspects of different subjects may seem valuable to different students. Or students may misunderstand the relevance of different subjects. If students do not perceive particular content, processes, or concepts to be relevant or meaningful to their own lives, they are not likely to strive to understand that material, let alone to master it.

One conclusion that can be drawn from this is that the teacher's task is to render the content, processes, or concepts meaningful by choosing analogies or metaphors that are understandable to the student and enable the student to better grasp these ideas. The teacher who can draw an analogy between the dilemma Brutus faces in *Julius Caesar* and dilemmas that students face (Wilson, Shulman, & Richert, 1987), who can illustrate the principles of electricity in relationship to the relative risk of carrying a battery-operated radio versus an outlet-powered radio into the shower, or who can use mathematical probabilities to interpret a weather forecast, is rendering academic subjects relevant by drawing analogies between the subject and the problems and issues diverse learners face in their daily lives.

The transformational model assumes that teachers must attend not only to students' cognitive relationships with academic content, but to their social and emotional relationships as well. In his review of Vygotskian theory, A. Anderson suggests that new psychological functions appear twice, once on a social plane and later, within the individual child, as a cognitive process. And Clemens emphasizes repeatedly the importance of students' emotional relationship with mathematics. Moreover, academic subject helps us understand or resolve certain personal and social problems, each also contributes to or even creates other such problems. This aspect of the relevance of academic subjects is highlighted by Banks when he points out that history tends to be about white European males, whereas anthropology tends to be about third world and minority cultures. And just as learners can be taught how·white historians have examined and portrayed the history of white settlers and Native Americans, so can they be taught how biological knowledge not only has led to improved medical care but has also introduced a host of new ethical issues in medicine.

In this model of teaching, subject matter and learners are still dependent on one another, but they hold yet another form of relationship with one another. According to this model, what is relevant about diverse learners is not only what they perceive to be relevant about a subject but also what they fail to perceive as relevant. And what is relevant about a subject is not merely what diverse learners perceive as relevant but also what diverse learners fail to perceive as relevant. Moreover, the transformational task itself is bi-directional. On one side, the teacher must transform academic content into something that is meaningful and relevant to diverse learners; but the teacher's success in this can be measured by the extent to which students are transformed into people with an active interest in these academic subjects, people who seek out further knowledge in this area and who draw on this knowledge as they interpret events around them.

How the Models Differ

Each of these models of teaching requires teachers to reduce the difference between subject and learner, but each does so in a different way. In the *additive* model, the teacher reduces the discrepancy by adding content to the learner. In the *process* model, the teacher reduces the discrepancy by helping learners add new processes and methods of inquiry to their repertoire, processes that more closely approximate the way experts in the field conduct their work. In the *conceptual change* model, the teacher reduces the difference by provoking learners to revise their models, hypotheses, or images of fundamental ideas in the subject. In the *learning community* model, the teacher reduces the discrepancy by creating in the classroom a learning community that draws on the norms of scholarship from the academic subject and on the norms of collegiality and equal participation that learners tend to prefer. Finally, in the *transformational* model, the discrepancy is reduced by rendering subject matter more relevant and meaningful to students, and by transforming students' cognitive, personal, and social relationships with academic content.

The differences among these models are especially apparent in the illustrations offered by chapter authors. In these chapters, for instance, four authors use photosynthesis to illustrate their points. The first author, C. Anderson, describes Ms. Copeland's teaching of photosynthesis. His description is illustrative of the *learning community* model of teaching and learning: Anderson claims, on the one hand, that Ms. Copeland's job was to "transform the children, to make them somehow more like scientists than they were before they came to her." But to do that, he continues, Ms. Copeland first had to transform science, to "create a body of scientific knowledge and a version of the scientific subculture that were accessible to her students." He further argues that the interactions we observed in her classroom were not unique to this topic, but instead reflected a *pattern of practice* that the teacher and students had developed together over time, one that enabled students to engage in a process of collective sense making. Copeland's students, then, were members of a learning community. One could argue that Copeland taught more about scientific processes and argumentation than about photosynthesis per se, but Anderson also argues that, for students to understand photosynthesis, they must go through a rather involved process of restructuring and integrating their personal knowledge of food.

Lawson recommends a *process* model to teach photosysthesis. He suggests that Ms. Copeland should have first asked students to generate hypotheses about the sources of food for plants and should have then helped them test those hypotheses with a series of formal experiments. If they contrast plants living in the sunlight with those living in the dark, for instance, they will discover that sunlight is important to plant life. Similar contrasts, comparing the presence and absence of water and the presence and absence of soil, will enable students to determine which of these various conditions is necessary for plant survival. Such experiments enable students to determine which environmental conditions are necessary and which sufficient for plant life, but do not necessarily lead to the conclusion that plants actually make their own food. Lawson suggests that Ms. Copeland could introduce the idea of photosynthesis after students have done some of these experiments, and then help them test the photosynthesis hypothesis by testing for starch in the leaves of plants living in different environmental conditions. In Lawson's model, students learn both about the natural phenomenon and about the processes of generating and testing hypotheses.

Floden, on the other hand, uses photosynthesis to illustrate a *conceptual change* model of teaching and learning. He points out that if students believe water and soil provide food and that plants obtain food by absorbing it from the soil, they will miss the significance of the fact that plants actually *make* food from the materials they absorb. For Floden, the teacher's role is one of pointing out to students that their conceptions about the source of nourishment for plants cannot account for plant growth. If students believe plants absorb food from the soil, for instance, the teacher might consider doing an experiment in which plants are placed in the dark. The point of this experiment would be to raise questions about why plants need sun if it is possible for them to obtain food directly from the soil. Once students realize that their theories are inadequate, the teacher can introduce photosynthesis as an alternative hypothesis and can present arguments for why this is a better theory of accounting for plant food. Floden's method of teaching is more directive than Anderson's, and less procedural than Lawson's, and focuses more tightly on the goal of altering students' conceptions of food and its origins.

Finally, Engelmann uses photosynthesis to illustrate an *additive* model of teaching and learning. His ideal teacher presents the subject matter in a logical, rather than a psychological, sequence. He begins by pointing out that all organisms need both raw materials and energy. He then teaches the major forms of energy, and that energy from one form can be converted to another form. He gives students practice identifying forms of energy and conversions from one form to another. Then he introduces the rule that raw materials enable organisms to convert energy from one form to another. Animals use oxygen, a raw material, to convert higher-energy chemicals to lower-energy chemicals. "The game organisms play is to go from higher-energy chemicals to lower-energy chemicals, which are the ones we end up with when something burns." Finally, he tells them that plants obtain energy from the sun, not from food, and that they convert their raw materials, soil and water, from lower-energy chemicals to higher-energy chemicals.

These models differ in several ways. One difference, for instance, lies in what students actually learn. Through the additive model, students appear to learn more specific content than they do through the conceptual change or learning community models, but they do not learn the processes of science as they do in the process model or the process model or the learning community model, and they may not appreciate the significance of what plants do, as in the conceptual change model. And none of these models of teaching and learning attends much to the significance of photosynthesis to human beings, as a transformational model would. None examines the ecological relationship between animals and plants in the production and consumption of food, nor prompts students to consider where they would get food if plants ceased to make it.

Taken together, these five models of teaching demonstrate five forms of interdependency between subject matter and learner and constitute five reasons why we cannot reduce the knowledge burden of teaching by declaring that teachers can get by without knowledge of one or the other side of the interdependency—why neither knowledge of academic subjects alone, nor knowledge of diverse learners alone, will do teachers much good.

Indeed, this is *the* enduring dilemma of education. We know that good teaching requires highly sophisticated, multifaceted understandings not just of subject matter, not just of students, not even of both, but of the relationships between the two as well. We know that few teachers have, or have access to, such knowledge. And we know that the work cannot readily be partitioned in a way that genuinely reduces the knowledge burden.

One way out of this box is to revise our goals as teacher educators and policy makers, so that we define our task not as *solving a particular problem* of teacher knowledge, but rather as *managing a particular dilemma* (Lampert, 1985). We do the best we can, knowing that we will never attain the ideal we seek. If we view teacher knowledge as a problem to be solved, we seek—vainly,

I would argue—handy solutions that will ensure that teachers learn all the things defined in these pages. If, instead, we view teacher knowledge as a dilemma that must be managed, we do not pretend that there are handy solutions, but instead use these pages as a guide for thinking about this enduring dilemma of learning to teach. Indeed, their greatest value may be in helping us do as little *harm* as possible when we design teacher preparation programs, teacher assessment devices, and school regulations.

Another way out of this box is to alter our model of *learning to teach*, so that teacher learning is not assumed to be finished when students graduate from college, but instead is considered to evolve continually throughout a teacher's career. We might envision teachers gradually expanding their repertoire of teaching techniques, so that they become more adept and more sophisticated over time. Several of these authors suggested that this was a more appropriate view of learning to teach. This solution to our dilemma allows us more leeway in thinking about how to help teachers gain the kind of knowledge they need. Rather than pretending that teachers really do not need to know about learners or really do not need to know about subject matter, and rather than trying to design preservice teacher education that will provide the full range of knowledge and skills described in these chapters, we can search for ways to facilitate continuing development, for school structures that enable teachers to learn more from their peers, for incentive systems that encourage teachers to experiment in their own classrooms as they continue to develop their teaching repertoires, and for extended in-service programs that stretch teachers upward and that help them practice new and more demanding techniques.

REFERENCES

Lampert, M. (1985). How do teachers manage to teach? Perspectives on the problem of practice. *Harvard Educational Review, 55,* 178-194.

Watson, J. D. (1968). *The double helix.* New York: Penguin.

Wilson, S., Shulman, L. S., & Richert, A. E. (1987). "150 different ways" of knowing: Representations of knowledge in teaching. In J. Calderhead (Ed.), *Exploring teacher thinking* (pp. 104-124). London: Cassell.

About the Contributors

ALONZO B. ANDERSON is Executive Director of Learning Support Services and an adjunct professor of education at the University of Southern California, Los Angeles. His research interests include literacy development and teacher and learner interactions.

CHARLES W. ANDERSON is an associate professor of education at Michigan State University and a senior researcher with the Institute for Research on Teaching. His research interests focus on classroom science teaching and science teacher education.

DEBORAH LOEWENBERG BALL is an assistant professor of teacher education at Michigan State University, a senior researcher with the National Center for Research on Teacher Education, and a teacher of third-grade mathematics. Ball's work focuses on mathematics teaching and learning and on the role of subject matter knowledge in helping students learn mathematics.

JAMES A. BANKS is a professor of education at the University of Washington, Seattle, and past president of the National Council for the Social Studies. Banks is especially interested in social studies education and multicultural education.

HERBERT CLEMENS is a professor of mathematics at the University of Utah, Salt Lake City. The focus of his research is algebraic geometry. His interest in elementary education began when he spent seven years associated with a parent cooperative elementary school that his children attended.

SIEGFRIED ENGELMANN is a professor of special education at the University of Oregon. He supervises practicum students, trains other supervisors, and promotes the implementation of the University of Oregon Follow Through Program in participating school districts.

ROBERT E. FLODEN is a professor of teacher education and educational psychology at Michigan State University and Associate Director of the National Center for Research on Teacher Education. His interests lie in philosophical studies of teacher education and in educational research.

JOHN T. GAGE is an associate professor of English and director of composition at the University of Oregon. He is interested in the history of rhetoric, high school as well as college composition, and the preparation of high school composition teachers.

CARL A. GRANT is a professor in the Department of Curriculum and Instruction at the University of Wisconsin-Madison and Chair of the Department of Afro-American Studies. His interests include multicultural education; race, social class, and gender in school life; and preservice and inservice teacher education.

GEORGE HILLOCKS, JR., is a professor in the Departments of Education and of English Language and Literature at the University of Chicago. His interests include theories of composing and response to literature and their contributions to the analysis of teaching and curriculum in writing and literature.

MARY M. KENNEDY is a professor of teacher education at Michigan State University and Director of the National Center for Research on Teacher Education. Her research interests include research methods and policy as well as the issues addressed in this book.

ANTON E. LAWSON is a professor in the Department of Zoology, Arizona State University, Tempe. He is interested in science education, cognitive science, developmental psychology, learning theory, and how science instruction is influenced by and can influence the development of higher-order thinking skills and the acquisition of science concepts.

G. WILLIAMSON MCDIARMID is an assistant professor of teacher education at Michigan State University and Associate Director of the National Center for Research on Teacher Education. His research interests include the development of subject matter knowledge for teaching (particularly history) and how teachers' subject matter representations are shaped by their knowledge of their learners.

TOM ROMANO has taught high school students for 17 years, most of that time at Edgewood High School in Trenton, Ohio. He is currently a graduate student at the University of New Hampshire, completing work for a Ph.D. in reading and writing instruction. His research interest is the use of imagination and creativity in all genres of writing.

SUZANNE M. WILSON is an assistant professor of teacher education and a senior researcher with the National Center for Research on Teacher Education. Her research interests include the subject matter knowledge of teachers, particularly in history, and alternative forms of teacher assessment.

Index